# BLE OF TUC

| | | | | | | | | |
|---|---|---|---|---|---|---|---|---|
| — | — | — | — | — | — | — | — | **S** Salt 'N' Shake |
| — | — | — | **Tg** Twiglets | **Ni** Nik-Naks | **Mo** Monster Munch | **Si** Wotsits | **V** Quavers | **Sc** Square Crisps |
| — | — | — | **Cg** Sweet Cigarettes | **F** French Fries | **Cs** Chipsticks | **Rn** Ringos | **Hs** Hula Hoops | **He** Hedgehog Crisps |
| **Fe** Centres | **Wp** Walnut Whip | **Ti** Turkish Delight | **Pm** Parma Violets | **Lv** Love Hearts | **Ho** Horror Bags | **Gd** Griddles | **Ra** Rancheros | **Sd** Sky Divers |
| **Bd** andit | **Wl** Wagon Wheel | **Tf** Toffo | **Ch** Chewits | **Rf** Refreshers | **Fn** Sherbet Fountain | **Al** All Stars | **Zr** Zodiacs | **Fb** Football Crazy |
| **Ce** me Egg | **Pm** Pyramint | **Po** Polo | **Pa** Pacers | **Os** Opal Fruits | **Wa** Wham | **Sp** Space Dust | **Ou** Outer Spacers | **Sm** Scampi Fries |
| **Juh** rollers | **Uuq** Revels | **Gl** Fox's Glacier Mints | **My** Murray Mints | **We** Werther's Originals | **Ps** Fruity Pops | **Ag** Double Agents | **Sg** Spangles | **Dd** "Big D" Peanuts |
| **Mg** k Gums | **Mx** Dolly Mixtures | **Mi** Midget Gems | **Yb** Jelly Beans | **Pd** Pear Drops | **Lm** Sherbet Lemons | **Rh** Rhubarb & Custard | **Pi** Pineapple Chunks | **K** Kola Kubes |
| **Fr** resta | **U** Um Bongo | **Ka** Kia Ora | **Vo** Vimto | **Pp** Dr Pepper | **Rw** R. Whites Lemonade | **Ut** Quatro | **Lt** Lilt | **C** Coca-Cola |

# The Great British Tuck Shop

Steve Berry & Phil Norman

**Credits**
Confectionery collections: Lucy Bernstein, John Estlea (http://bit.ly/lyonsmaid), Dan Goodsell, Darren Wallington (http://bit.ly/70sCrispPackets).

Comic pages: Combom, Steve Hearn, Alistair McGown.

Badges: Frank Setchfield (http://www.badgecollectorscircle.co.uk).

**Acknowledgements**
Louis Barfe, Andy Blackford, Norton Canes, Paul Dennis, Sarah-Louise Heslop, Rob McKoen, Roger McKechnie, James Nichols, Jon Peake, Nicholas Pegg, Whitby Specialist Vehicles Limited.

**Thanks**
Rachel Faulkner, Corinna Harrod, Scott Pack, Liam Relph.

First published in Great Britain in 2012 by
The Friday Project
An imprint of HarperCollins*Publishers*
77–85 Fulham Palace Road
London W6 8JB
www.harpercollins.co.uk



1

The right of Steve Berry and Phil Norman to be identified as the authors of this work has been asserted by them in accordance with the Copyright, Designs and Patents Act 1988

A catalogue record for this book is available from the British Library

ISBN 9781906321451



Designed and typeset by Concrete Armchair
Illustrations by Jumping Bean Bag Ltd

Printed and bound in China

# THE KIDS IN YOUR SHOP ARE GOING TO BE ASKING FOR IT.

Manufactured by:
A. McCowan & Sons Ltd.,
Stenhousemuir,
Stirlingshire.

They've heard all about Wham on the radio, it's being backed by our biggest ever promotional spend.

The fruity, chewy, space age bar that sizzles with sherbet and only costs 10p.

And when they find out they can get a free space poster with Wham Bars there'll be no holding them back.

So order your supplies at your usual wholesalers or cash and carry now – **and get 20 pence off your first outer with the coupon below.**

And let them have it.

A wholesaler's handling fee of 1p per coupon will be paid.

20p 20p

This Voucher is worth 20p off your first WHAM outer. Present it at your Cash and Carry or Wholesaler.

Name/Company ........................

Address ..............................

..............................

20p **A. McCowan & Sons Ltd., Stenhousemuir, Stirlingshire.** 20p

For Suzy, Joanna
& Joanne

Swizzels Regd
BIG '77 OFFER
1p FRUIT FIZZERS
* THE ORIGINAL FIZZY SWEETS!
* EXTRA PROFITS FOR YOU!
* BIG VALUE!
* BIG SELLER
FRUIT FIZZERS
1p EACH 120 COUNT
PLUS
15p OFF
2 x 120 ROLLS
FROM YOUR CASH & CARRY
BUY NOW!
SUPERB
FREE TIGHTS
WORTH UP TO 30P WITH EACH OUTER OF 2 x 120 ROLLS
FROM YOUR WHOLESALER
SWIZZELS MATLOW LIMITED · NEW MILLS · STOCKPORT · CHESHIRE SK12 3HA
LOCAL AGENT: LOUIS SHERRY 'MORAY BANK' HERIOT ROAD, LENZIE

**CONTENTS**

Cadbury's
Welcome
Milk chocolate with fudge
and hazelnut centre

## FOREWORD

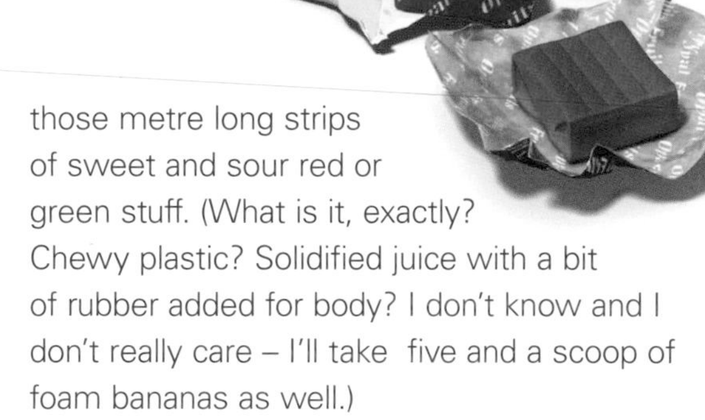


I am writing this while on a diet – the curse, of course, of being middle-aged and greedy. But one of the glorious things about this book is how it manages to sweep you up and back to a time when, not only did you not have to worry or even care how many calories were in, for example, an Aztec Bar or a packet of Spanish Gold, but it wouldn't have mattered if you did know! Because not only were the sweets so much better when we were young, so were our metabolisms. I could drink as many cans of Cresta as I liked then wolf down my own body weight in Space Dust and still, it seemed, not gain an ounce. Heaven.

I still love sweets, despite the disastrous effect they have on my physique. Who doesn't? Well, I know there are some out there who claim not to, but I am highly suspicious of anyone who doesn't occasionally pig out on large volumes of them. In particular those pinched, unhappy-looking weirdos who have trained themselves to eat healthily and enjoy it! The kind who you see eating apples, or snacking from ziplock bags of baby carrots or sliced peppers at theme parks and the movies when they could be eating popcorn and Twizzlers and Maltesers. Or Milk Duds, or Fruit Pastilles, or those metre long strips of sweet and sour red or green stuff. (What is it, exactly? Chewy plastic? Solidified juice with a bit of rubber added for body? I don't know and I don't really care – I'll take five and a scoop of foam bananas as well.)

So, as a lover and consumer and admirer of sweeties both new and old I not only welcome this book, I demand it! I have been waiting for such an exhaustive and mouthwatering catalogue of sugary nostalgia ever since they stopped making Spangles (which, legend has it, were the first thing Nelson Mandela requested after being freed for whatever it was he was supposed to have done but didn't. It was the thought of Spangles that kept him going! That's what I heard, anyway. Or Acid Drops).

In *Remembrance of Things Past* (or 'Recherchez de la Chose qui J'adore, comme licorice et photographs du jeunes femmes dans stockings etc' to give it its full fancy French title) Proust banged on about the smells, cakes and whatnots of his youth and how they became the most powerful and immediate triggers for his boyhood memories. This is what someone told me after they spoke to someone else who had a friend who read it. (Feel free to quote me on that.) And guess what? He's right. The smell of cheap tobacco on a cold morning as my fellow thirteen year-olds grabbed a last drag before slouching into school, the taste of that pink flat chewing gum that came as a freebie with most picture cards, or the confectionery cigarettes that less bold teens like me would eat then puff out on our breath on a chilly morning in the hope a passing girl would think we were actually smoking – those are probably the keenest and fondest recollections from about eight otherwise wasted years of my life.

So, to have the chance to wallow, unashamedly, in memories of the taste sensations that exploded daily on my tongue – to bathe in the litres of now sadly discontinued fizzy drinks that we gargled by the gallon, to rub my nose against the perfect photographic reproductions of the crude but powerfully effective packaging that parted me, and millions of other gluttons in the making, from our not-so-hard-earned pocket money – this book is about as close to time travel as you can get. See you in the 1970s... and I'll have a quarter of cola cubes.

**– Jonathan Ross, 2012**

Dear
AGONY
AGONY
column,
Last Friday
at
I was
woken up by a
. I crept
armed with a
,
only to catch my husband
,
eating the
and
!
Dear
GRIPPING
,
Forgive him it was only the
start of the
Week End
Week·End

# 1

# INTRODUCTION

**Opposite:** Domestic violence averted the Mackintosh's Week-End way.

**It was in *Tom Brown's Schooldays*, Thomas Hughes's atmospheric rites of passage novel, that the words 'tuck shop' first appeared in print. The likes of Billy Bunter, Roland Browning and Dudley Dursley might have carried the torch for other generations of roving, grazing gluttons, but the institutionalised indulgence of Hughes's Rugby school story was the first literary work to cement conspicuous consumption and childhood together.**

Ever since, the tastes, smells, sights and sounds of the tuck shop have inspired nostalgia: the electric crackle of the sherbet fountain; the chemical medley of pear drops and sugar mice; the anticipatory rat-a-tat-tat of chocolate limes hitting the scale pan; or the weird brown dust in a packet of Fish 'n' Chips sticking to your fingers. The right trigger can drill directly down to the most primitive parts of the brain, setting off hidden time-bombs of happiness. For anyone of a certain age, memories of childhood are irretrievably connected to the stomach.

The tuck shop was a great leveller. Everyone ate there, from the Walter Softies to the Bully Beefs (although the bullies would probably steal the softies' sweets too); Milky Bar kids, Flake girls and Fry's Five Boys; Monster Munchers, Fab-suckers and lemonade drinkers both secret and out of the closet. Forrest Gump almost got it right. Life isn't like a box of chocolates, but people are. In your allotted three score and ten, you will undoubtedly come across a soft one, a hard one, a nutty one, and one full of marzipan that nobody can stand. It literally takes allsorts.

There are two acknowledged golden ages of British tuck. The first came in the 1920s and 1930s when, despite the Depression, the big names of sweets and snacks consolidated their brands and expanded nationwide. The second came in the 1970s and 1980s when, despite the Depression, the big names of sweets and snacks put their accounts departments on indefinite leave and let their product

**Opposite:** Oh, pish, tush and a cheap laugh during a slow edition of *QI*! It's Fry's Five Boys (1902).

**Below:** Not in the Screwfix catalogue: Trebor Chocolate Toolbox circa 1981.

development departments go (fruit and) nuts, shunting out celebrity-endorsed chocolate bars, whimsically shaped corn snacks, cartoon-wrapped nougat delights and plutonium-hued sparkling sodas on a weekly basis.

Manufacturing moved into Technicolor, all the better to catch the wavering eye and stick in the mind for years to come. Sweet shops, until then like antique shops – arthritic, grey and fusty, trapping sunbeams in dust and quietly ossifying – were transformed into glittering Aladdin's caves, crammed to the rafters with individually wrapped sugared and savoury treasures. Somewhere between decimalisation and globalisation, creative confectionery enjoyed its most fertile period – an auspicious era that began with the last manned moon mission and ended as the first Sky channels beamed into unsuspecting British homes.

If that seems vague, it is deliberately so. For historians, specific dates are vital but, for the retronaut, experience trumps exactitude every time. In all honesty, which had more impact on the average schoolgoer, the communist revolution or the Cadbury takeover? The ephemera of confectionery are more transient than those of archaeology, which is why you will still find more excitement around the unearthing of a shop selling a Rowntree's Texan than of a museum showing a Roundhead's helmet. Even Churchill understood the importance of sweets, defeating Hitler with a stiff upper lip and a pocketful of jujubes – and what is it they say an army marches on, again? History is written by the victuallers.

That journey to the corner shop took on the nature of a pilgrimage for many a child, with a salivating smile and a skipping heartbeat. Exiting front door or school gate, you'd proceed with ever-increasing speed to the shop, maybe taking the long way round to pass the house where the future recipient of your last Rolo lived. Leaving your bike outside in a casual heap, you entered the subdued, welcoming, blue-and-white-vinyl-floor-tiled, no-cheques-cashed-thank-you interior. Inside, a fantastic cornucopia of riches. Some items had a past longer than the shopkeeper himself, while others would go on to outlive him. Many, with hindsight, would never see the year out.

None of this mattered to your prospective sweet purchaser, gloriously transfixed as they were in the moment, surveying the ranks of stock. Iconic

Mars bars sat next to the doomed likes of the Cadbury's Alamo. The Fruit Salad chew, old as the book of Genesis, shared shelf space with Trebor Fings, Rowntree's Junglies and other sugary mayflies. For every can of the Real Thing there were a dozen returnable bottles of ersatz pop from the factory up the road. In the disinterested eyes of the proprietor, all products, as long as someone bought them, were equal. No preferential treatment here.

You had to choose wisely, as funds were limited. Governmental sweet rationing may have ended in 1953, but the economic and parental varieties still held sway. The adult population's inflationary woes trickled down to the kids via swingeing confectionery cutbacks. Like 'snout' in prison, the rarity value of a decent bag of sweets gave its owner a certain social status along with the toothache. Every spare penny was spent on high-fat, salt and sugar products that we knew were probably bad for our hearts, but nevertheless good for our souls.

Plenty of books on sweets and snacks already exist, but they tend to come from the producer's side – weighty tomes of corporate history, trade routes and sales areas. There's nothing wrong with that, but where's the book written from the consumer's point of view? The two are often wildly divergent. To coin a phrase, Chocolate Oranges are not the only fruit. (Terry's also made a lemon, but it didn't do the business.) Many products came and went – mere footnotes in their manufacturers' inventories – but that doesn't mean they weren't coveted, adored, consumed with a passion and, just like old friends, noisily revisited a few hours later on the waste ground behind the prefabs.

Fortunately a lot of them tasted the same coming up as going down. They also tasted pretty much the same as each other. There is, after all – Marianne Faithfull aside – only so much you can do with a slab of milk chocolate, a cheesy corn puff or a lump of frozen water on a stick. The marketing men inevitably loom large in this tale, coupling childlike imagination with ruthless raiding of money boxes to create a world of hedonistic abandon, populated by models, mascots and maniacal showbiz personalities all merrily hooked on the product – whatever it may

**Opposite:** The high water mark of high concept sweet branding: Trebor Fings (1981).

**Below:** Dare you half-inch a Bobby Lolly? Circa 1977.

be – and keen to let the whole world know. Often in full song. For better or worse, their efforts made a generation what it is, and what follows is, as much as anything else, an account of how they focus-grouped our Funny Feet.

Millions of products were mocked up, marched out and formally trialled in regional tests, often several months before a national launch, and – if found lacking – put out of their misery entirely. But occasionally a lucky few went on to bigger and better things. This is why Mackems will swear blind that you could buy peanut M&Ms in 1985, and yet it is also why incredulous Cockneys will fight to the death to prove them wrong. Reliable brand 'birthdays' are hard to nail down, especially as the majority of British manufacturers have been absorbed into a succession of international confectionery, food and beverage corporations who have scant interest in lineage or continuity. That kind of stock can't be monetised on Wall Street, apparently.

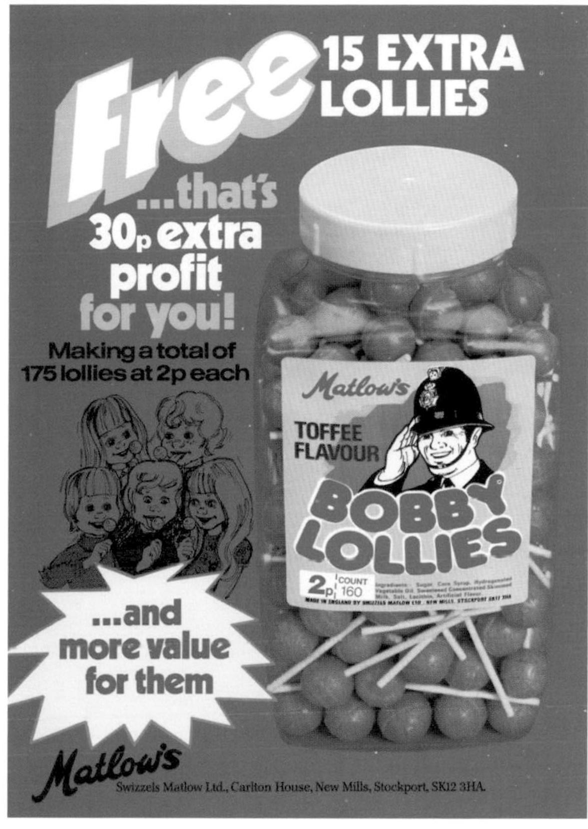


However, those big companies can't help but tinker and toy with their winning brands, all in the name of progress. Recipes are changed, formulas are tweaked, and – most heinously of all – the packaging is modernised. Do not despair. Despite the disappearance of some cherished childhood chocolate bars (ah, Mars Applause, you barely registered a ripple on the sentimental Richter scale), many sweets, crisps, snacks and pop are still available if you look hard enough. Only the artificial colours and preservatives have been jettisoned, in favour of 'all natural' ingredients. Don't believe those people who wax lyrical about the good old days of gobstoppers the size of your head, either. No, those Creme Eggs and Wagon Wheels haven't got smaller. Your hands have got bigger. In fact, with very few exceptions, the tuck shop fare of youth is served in heftier portions than ever before, as the waddling, wobbling outlines of twenty-first century obesity crises serve to illustrate.

So here it is, then, your very own unnatural preservative of the best of the Great British Tuck Shop, from the lowly cardboard box of cheap crisps, to the lofty glass jar of cola cubes. Go ahead, dive in – but don't spoil your tea, now.

Cadbury's
Buttons
Dairy Milk Chocolate
Children love
Cadbury's Dairy Milk Chocolate Buttons.

# CHOCOLATE

**Opposite:** Swing when you're winning. Cadbury's Dairy Milk Chocolate Buttons' "chocolate for beginners" campaign, circa 1975.

**Below:** Badge manners? Rolo (1937), Aztec (1967) and Curly Wurly (1970) lapel decoration opportunities for chocoholic kids.

**Opposite:** 'We can take on any old line. Anywhere, anytime.' Tim, Graeme and Bill lend a helping hand to 1977's Cadbury campaign. Kitten Kong not pictured.

**Modern chocolate has a truly global heritage. The ancient Mayans were the first to tap into its unique charms. They harvested cocoa beans as currency, bartered them with the Aztecs for jewellery and – who knows? – probably ripped off their own grannies down the Yucatan branch of Cash4Cocoa. More importantly, they also roasted it for a spicy, astringent drink called xocolatl, but the secret was soon stolen. The victorious Spanish conquistadors left Mexico with galleons-full, which made them very popular back home. Europe's well-to-do queued up for their morning draft of 'good hot jocolatte', adding milk, cinnamon, nutmeg and sugar – anything to embellish the rich, unctuous taste. It wasn't until the development of the cocoa press (by Dutchman Casparus Van Houten – no relation to Denise), which separated the fatty cocoa butter from the dark chocolate powder, that anyone thought to start moulding it into solids.**

Confectionery, not necessity, was the mother of invention. Technological breakthroughs followed accordingly: Menier's chocolate factory (1829); Nestlé's milk powder formula (1867); Sechaud's chocolate-filling machine (1913). Each brought affordable, tangible chocolate morsels closer to the (cocoa) masses. Never mind 1066 and all that: as industry laureate elect Roald Dahl zealously declared, 'These dates are milestones in history and should be seared into the memory of every child.' Knowing old Roald, he probably meant that literally. Still, it's no less gruesome a fate than drowning in a river of chocolate, Augustus Gloop-style.

Factories and familiar names sprang up across Britain – Fry, Cadbury, Rowntree – in the most part run by teetotal, pacifist men of faith who believed in the beneficial properties of their product. Little by little, chocolate revealed its versatility: as a gift for a loved one; a reward for an obedient child; or an amuse-bouche at the ambassador's receptions. Our appetite for the brown stuff continued to develop down the years, particularly around Christmas time. Even after roast turkey with all the trimmings, there always seemed to be room for a little segment of Terry's tap-it-and-unwrap-it Chocolate Orange.

The passing of time has brought with it more heinous crimes and unearthed the sinful side of the cocoa bean. In recent years, chocolate has been used and abused, whether as a shower-clogging syrup substitute for blood in Hitchcock's *Psycho*, or a saucy, valance-staining body paint for bawdy bedroom shenanigans. And what is the point of those edible toolkits? They're about as much use as a chocolate chastity belt. (Although the spanner might be quite handy for wrenching one open.)

Elvis Presley loved it. Saddam Hussein lived on it. From fountains and fondues to Scottish deep-fat fryers, chocolate gets everywhere. Especially over kids' faces. Before you know it, we'll be using it as currency. Chocolate coins, eh? Whatever next?

ADVERTISEMENT
SEND FOR THE GOODIES
WE'RE FREE WE'RE FREE
COME OFF IT EVEN TIM'S OLDER THAN THAT
GOODIES
TO GET A FREE GOODIES FUN BOOK FULL OF FAMOUS CARTOON CHARACTERS, CRAZY GAMES, TRICKS & STORIES SAVE ONLY 10 WRAPPERS FROM ANY OF THESE YUMMY BARS.
SMALL Crunchie
THE WOMBLES
Freddo
Fudge
SMALL Flake
Buttons
Furry Friends
Paddington Bear
curlywurly
THEN FILL IN THE COUPON AND SEND THEM OFF TO US.
PLEASE NOTE IF YOU REQUIRE MORE THAN ONE BOOK, YOU MUST SEND 10 WRAPPERS AND A 5p PIECE TOWARDS POSTAGE FOR EACH BOOK.
PLEASE ALLOW 28 DAYS FOR DELIVERY.
THIS OFFER IS AVAILABLE IN THE UK ONLY. (WHILST STOCKS LAST.)
ALL APPLICATIONS MUST BE RECEIVED BY 31st AUGUST, 1977.
SEND YOUR COMPLETED COUPON, POSTAGE CONTRIBUTION AND WRAPPERS TO:
CADBURY'S GOODIES BOOK OFFER
P.O. BOX 6, KETTERING, NORTHANTS
GOODIES FUN BOOK
for 5 to 8 years
GOODIES FUN BOOK
for 9 to 13 years
WE DO ANYTHING ANY FOR A LAUGH!
Please tick which book you require in first column also indicate number of books you require in second column.
TICK
NUMBER REQUIRED
1. The Goodies Fun Book (for ages 5-8 years.)
2. The Goodies Fun Book (for ages 9-13 years.)
NAME
ADDRESS
Cadbury
AD2

## ONE CHUNK LEADS TO ANOTHER

The first solid block of edible chocolate appeared in this country in 1847, courtesy the Fry brothers of Bristol. Although 'edible' in this case is a loose definition: even by the standards of today's pure cocoa brands, this one was a bitter tooth-breaker. It was only after Swiss chocolatier Daniel Peter unveiled the Gala Peter in 1886, the first soft milk chocolate bar, that bars of chocolate looked like they might be a good sister product for the already popular drinking variety.

There were scores of technical problems to overcome first, mainly to do with milk's tendency to go off at the drop of a hat. By 1902 Fry's had perfected their weirdly named Five Boys, and Rowntree punted out an Alpine Milk bar. This name was a bit of a giveaway that, as far as the public was concerned, in chocolate terms it was Swiss or nothing, a state of affairs underlined two years later when Nestlé imported the esteemed Kohler and Cailler recipe to their UK factory.

In the end, slow and steady George Cadbury won the race. Eight years in development, his Highland Milk bar tasted good enough to beat the Swiss. It was renamed Dairy Maid, and shortly after renamed again to Dairy Milk, on the advice of a Plymouth shopkeeper. Boasting '1½ glasses in every ½lb', it was

**Opposite:** Class and a half. Cadbury's Dairy Milk (1905), Sultana (1982), Whole Nut (1933) and Fruit & Nut (1928) offer scoffable sharing for all.

**Below:** Chock-A-Block. Astronomer's favourite, Mars Galaxy (1960) and the less-than-stellar Cadbury's Big One (1971).

launched in 1905 to great success. A year later, the plain Bournville appeared, followed by Fruit and Nut in 1928, Whole Nut two years after that, and a slew of tasty fillings from Caramello to the raisin and biscuit Tiffin from 1934 onwards. It wasn't Cadbury's game entirely – Nestlé added Rice Krispies to make their Dairy Crunch in 1938 – but a reputation was being forged. Even Hitler couldn't stop its advance: one press ad in the bleak days of 1939 advised: 'The habit of taking a block of Cadbury's Dairy Milk per day has been medically recommended as a sensible personal precaution for this autumn and winter.' If, of course, you could get hold of any.

After the war, diversification was the thing. Dairy Milk blocks added filling upon filling. By 1960, the usual suspects lined up alongside pineapple, peppermint, coffee, marzipan, strawberry and the intriguingly vague 'mild dessert'. A modern marketing man would express concern about 'dilution of the core product', and rightly, as this was the year of an unwelcome intruder. Already the leader in filled bars by a mile, Mars moved into chocolate blocks that autumn with Galaxy: quality chocolate in bigger sizes than Cadbury's, plugged with a massive ad campaign. Designed as a pre-emptive attack based on rumours Cadbury were working on a Mars bar rival, it did more damage to Cadbury than their Aztec would do to Mars's crown.

Cadbury fought back by dropping their prices and defending the brand with some rearguard campaigning. The late 1960s was full of entreaties for Britons to 'award yourself the CDM'. A nice idea, but a bit staid for such a forward-looking time, and in the early '70s it became more wistful still, asking punters if, in this modern, synthetic, concrete world, wasn't it good to know that 'there's always Cadbury's Dairy Milk'? Then in 1976 Rowntree launched their Yorkie, and such statements suddenly looked very optimistic. Hit even harder, Cadbury returned to the 'glass and a half' tagline they'd abandoned in the mid-'60s, and fought the lorry drivers of York with Cilla Black putting a chunk in her cheek on the top deck of a Blackpool tram. Meanwhile Frank Muir twisted his tongue round tales of bucolic Fruit

and Nut mania to the strains of Tchaikovsky, and a scarily omnipotent calypso band informed unwitting citizens of the world that, regarding nuts (whole hazelnuts), Cadbury take them and they cover them in chocolate. To seal this fightback, the bars themselves also became thicker (and pricier) once more.

The ever-changing sizes were in part due to the rocketing price of cocoa, which increased tenfold between 1973 and 1977. It made sense to shift the focus away from the actual chocolate, of which there was inevitably going to be a lot less, and onto the exotic innards.

And innards didn't come more exotic than 1970s innards, with Cadbury leading the way. Things started off simply with the self-explanatory Oranges and Lemons ('a happy new taste in filled blocks!'). Chips of various types were added: Crunchie pieces in Golden Crisp, mint shards in the well-loved Ice Breaker. A spate of Wild West branding came along (as it did to most snack foods at the time, for some reason). The gingham-clad raisin and biscuit slab Country Style was promoted with a sharpshooting variation on Spot the Ball, and Gold Mine – a Golden Crisp but with slightly smaller Crunchie chunks – carried on the frontier theme. They got more geographically adventurous with the Cadbury Classic range, featuring the tangy Ginger bar, the orange- and curaçao-steeped Grand Seville, and the papaya-stuffed Tropical Fruit. The other houses followed suit. In all, over forty-four new chocolate bars were introduced during the decade. Thirty were swiftly withdrawn, but that's still not a bad hit rate.

Terry's upmarket range was called Royal Gold. Coffee, lime, Turkish delight and marzipan temptingly resided within the shiniest of wrappers. They even broke up a bar, wrapping each tablet

**Opposite:** Short and sweet. Cadbury's Ice Breaker, circa 1973, and Gold Mine (1975) shared a brittle heart and an all-too brief shelf life.

**Below:** Terry's, employing neon-handwriting style logos to full effect in the futuristic '80s with Bitz (1983) and Dark circa 1982.

individually, packaging the lot back together again in slab form and calling it, for reasons obscure, the Oliver Twist. Nestlé, meanwhile, artfully dodged controversy by producing the reliably posh Superfine and Coffee Cream, with an occasional luxury item flourish, such as the muesli-adorned Alpine bar. Rowntree, by comparison, kept oddly quiet – Yorkie aside – during this product deluge. They scored an early winner with Mint Cracknel, a bar whose intriguing spun sugar centre was made in roughly the same way as nylon thread – as indeed was the facial hair of its on-screen representative, Noel Edmonds.

If diversity was the watchword in the 1970s, the following decade was all about consolidation. Cadbury rebuilt their own image behind Dairy Milk (which, from 1985, went king size, along with everything else). They reintroduced dormant varieties like roast almond and sultana, and added the odd new bar like 'when milk and plain collide' peculiarity Gambit, but the main draw was increasingly Cadbury themselves, embracing the '80s corporate brand mania like an old hand. Terry's, meanwhile, embraced the decade's other nascent trend, graphic design, to jazz up the wrappers of their crispy chip Bitz range. As with nearly all design of this vintage, what started off looking like something from a millionaire's pleasure palace in the Caribbean soon acquired the air of a Dunstable nightclub's ladies night flyer. More sure-footed was Logger, a standard segmented bar cunningly disguised as a tree, and advertised with a shameless Monty Python lumberjack sketch homage. Such visual depreciation was common by now, and everyone soon learned that strong, traditional lines suited them best. Combine this with a fashion for corporate takeovers within the industry, and the seemingly endless variety of the 1970s chocolate market seemed to thin out drastically after 1990. Rowntree were subsumed by Nestlé, Terry's by Kraft. Cadbury circled their wagons ever tighter, badging everything under the Dairy Milk label, while Mars continued to parry them with Galaxy. The shelves that had once heaved with wrappers of all hues and designs now bore endless ranks of relentlessly focus-grouped purple and brown. No more would entire lines be rebranded on the whim of a shop girl from Plymouth. This made sound business sense, but some of the fun had been let out, children of the future denied the Dickensian pleasure of bursting into a sweet shop and asking for 'an Oliver Twist, two Tiffins and a Big Wig, please!'.

**Opposite and below:** Opposite and below: Come up to the lab and see what's in the slab. Cadbury's Gambit (1967), Nestle's Feast circa 1974, Dairy Crunch (1965), Hazel Nut circa 1975, and Fizz Bang (1980); Cadbury-Fry's Tiffin (1967).

> 'Shelves that once heaved with wrappers of all hues and designs now bore endless ranks of relentlessly focus-grouped purple and brown.'

## * CARAMAC

Named after Halifax-based toffee tycoon John Mackintosh rather than the American beat poet author of *On the Road*, Kerouac – no, hang on – Caramac nonetheless seems to have had most in common with the iconoclast, hippie, jazz musings of the latter. First, for an entire decade or more, it defied all marketing logic by continuing to sell without a single commercial spot to its name. (Then

**Opposite:** The Eat Generation. Alternative caramel confectionery in the form of Caramac (1959).

**Below:** Hey, have you heard the one about your statutory rights? Rowntree Mackintosh aims for the funny bone in a 1982 comic ad.

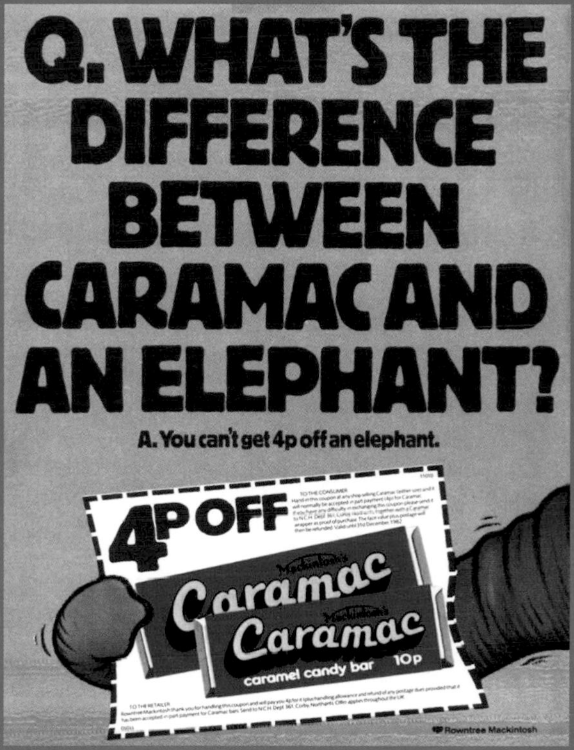

1991 saw a TV relaunch of the 'I was here all along' ilk, backed by a pointed, almost sardonic, version of the Tremeloes' 'Silence Is Golden'.)

Second, there was something so gritty in the texture, a viscous fudginess in that original recipe which was so very redolent of melting, syrupy brown nuggets of street heroin. Caramac felt like the detritus, sweepings from the post-war factory floor of Rowntree's production line, scooped up, tipped into a vat and boiled down into something altogether more… well, moreish. But, of course, it wasn't. Far from a happy accident, it was a careful concoction of sweetened condensed milk, butter, treacle and so on, intended to replicate as closely as possible the experience of chomping through its cocoa-based cousins.

In fact, like the best British home cooking, its appeal was driven by economics, austerity and nostalgia. Caramac was a stodgy Sunday sticky toffee pudding turned into a thin, anaemic bar. A bar that, for all the love and attention lavished on its preparation, could never call itself chocolate. Neither fish nor fowl, Caramac sought mainstream acceptance by arranged marriages to other, more established brands. Hence Carawheat, a Jacob's biscuit covered in a golden Caramac layer, and a later Breakaway version. Though what really took the biscuit was the cheeky twenty-first-century hook-up with a certain four-fingered wafer snack (presumably because of the pleasing, nursery rhyme result). Altogether now: Kit Kat Caramac, give the dog a bone…

**'Like the detritus, sweepings from the factory floor of Rowntree's production line, scooped up, tipped into a vat and boiled down.'**

## ✻ YORKIE

There comes a time in every sweet-toothed boy's life when he takes a look at the contents of the paper bag he's just blown his hard-pestered 50p on, and finds it lacking... something. Maybe it's the colour (all those pink shrimps), maybe it's the texture (soft, as a rule), but something about the whole affair suddenly seems a bit, well, wet. There are, of course, sweets to help you look a bit 'hard'.

**Opposite:** If you don't like trucking, tough luck! Plenty of choice for the school hard-case courtesy of Yorkie (1976).

**Below:** Wagon wheels! A Yorkie easter egg, circa 1982.

You could stock up on the bracing Army & Navy Mints – if you don't mind pulling faces all afternoon. You could pretend to tug on a chocolate Woodbine or ponce about with a liquorice pipe like a Fisher-Price Tony Benn, but not even the junior kids are fooled by that kind of carry-on. No, there's only one truly manly item of confectionery on the sweet shop shelves – the Yorkie bar.

This was a bit of marketing genius on the part of Rowntree employee (and later CEO of EMI), Eric Nicoli. Cadbury had let their main asset, the Dairy Milk, fall into a state of disrepair in the '70s. Rowntree saw their moment, and dived in with a bar of such unprecedented solidity that the word 'chunky' just wouldn't do it justice. The Yorkie mythology was stoked by an ad campaign harking back to their ancient Motoring Chocolate brand, wherein a Kwik Save Johnny Cash sang a driving country paean to the macho sweetmeat: 'Good, rich and thick/A milk chocolate brick.' On the screen a hard-bitten long-distance lorry driver hauled his Scammel across rugged terrain with only his trusty Yorkie bar for company (a pretty sad state of affairs in retrospect, but for a pre-pubescent boy a man at the wheel of anything bigger than a Datsun Cherry is little short of a god).

Most important of all, the Yorkie was the centre of possibly the only male initiation rite to involve emulsified cocoa butter. The ability to take a Yorkie straight from the fridge and bite off a chunk with a satisfying snap, and without leaving any fragments of teeth in the remaining bar, was as sure a sign of maturity as the ability to do press-ups or claim you'd copped off with Nadine Jones without inviting a dozen spontaneous impressions of Jimmy Hill. If you can eat a Yorkie without wincing, you'll be a man, my son.

**'For a pre-pubescent boy a man at the wheel of anything bigger than a Datsun Cherry is little short of a god.'**

## * AERO

For all the Wonka-esque mystique affected by chocolate makers, most confectionery innovations amount to 'let's bung this on top of this, stick some chocolate on it'. The invention of the Aero, however, really did involve science. Rowntree's technicians frothed up some liquid chocolate with a whisk, poured it into moulds and then – the clever bit – reduced the surrounding air pressure drastically so the tiny bubbles of

**Opposite:** 'Unforgettabubble, that's what you are. Unforgettabubble, milk chocolate bar.' A line of old King Cole for Rowntree's Aero (1935).

froth swelled up to a decent size. Then it was a matter of passing the moulds through ice-cold water to set, covering the result with a layer of solid chocolate, and the job was done.

It caused a sensation when it came out, albeit one helpfully whipped up by Rowntree themselves. The exciting new texture, they claimed, 'stimulates the enzyme glands' – a bit of shameless quackery they were soon forced to take back. Initially great sales began to tail off, in part due to an assortment of rivals appearing on the scene with undue haste, in particular Fry's two tryouts, the Ripple and the All-Chocolate Crunchie. Add to that a disputed patent, and things got panicky at Rowntree headquarters. Fruit and nut and whole nut variants were hurriedly bunged out to support the ailing novelty. Sales levelled off after a while, and the Aero, while no longer a craze, remained steady-as-she-goes.

They couldn't resist mucking about, though. An Aero Wafer introduced in 1950 didn't hang about too long, but in '59 the bright idea of changing the aerated centre from chocolate to peppermint gave the bar a new lease of life, and with orange and coffee centres arriving over the next couple of years, a nice little family was built up that would tick over happily for decades, with just a new campaign based around the word 'bubbles' knocked out every few years. Oh, and a short-lived lime variant in 1971.

Then, cometh the '80s, cometh the Cadbury's Wispa. Big trouble in Rowntreeland as the potential Aero spoiler was worriedly picked over. Luckily the two-year gestation period Cadbury took to get the Wispa going nationwide allowed Rowntree to remake the Aero in its image. By September of 1982, gone was the six-segmented flat format, a bumpy chocolate version of the traffic-calming measures in a well-to-do Cotswold village. In came the handy ingot size. In the process, something – no one was quite sure what – changed. The chocolate had become softer. No, the bubbles were bigger. No, it's the taste... It scarcely mattered, as the new bar more than held its own against the Bournville parvenu. But even today, plenty of former stalwart Aerovians feel slighted by the changes, their enzyme glands no longer stimulated in quite the same way.

**'Aero caused a sensation when it came out, albeit one helpfully whipped up by Rowntree themselves.'**

## * MILKY BAR

Though pre-dating Alan Parker's much admired all-juvenile *Bugsy Malone* casting policy by some two decades, the Milky Bar ads were surely made by marketing men both short on imagination and long on memory. A few short scenes were recycled and remade every few years for a new generation of chocoholic tots. To the tune of a honky-tonk saloon bar piano, and the repetitive mantra

**Opposite:** Milky Bars (1937) featuring the whip-crackaway whippersnapper himself. No sign of Big Chief Milky Bar, introduced in 1977 'for ethnic balance.'

**Below:** The return of the space cowboy. The Milky Bar Kid faces the final frontier, and unconvincing aliens, in a television advert circa 1982.

of the titular song's rhyming couplets, the 'strong and tough' Milky Bar kid would save faux Frontiersmen from some minor inconvenience or other before declaring, 'The Milky Bars are on me,' at which point a cheering crowd of sugar-crazed urchins would surge forward to grab the proffered treats.

That said, this was not chocolate as any British child had experienced it before, largely comprising cocoa butter (without the requisite powder), milk solids and vanilla, stretched out into a waxy, sugary tablet. Whiffing faintly of distant Common Market subsidies, it could appeal only to the most immature of tastes; the creamiest milk, maybe, but the Plasticiniest bar by far. Inevitably, the Milky Bar kid himself was as puny and pallid as the product he was paid to endorse, all alabaster skin and wire-rimmed specs, though eternally youthful thanks to a sequence of lead actor changes that would put *Doctor Who* to shame. The fortunes of each much heralded gunslinger would wane as the voice broke, the freckles faded and puberty inflicted an inescapable and implacable grip on his hormonal system. Cue the difficult transition back to normal life and a future career in loft conversion, panel beating or haulage, alongside the perennial tabloid 'off the rails' headlines. For the most unfortunate, that early, illusive taste of fame was as much a curse as a blessing.

Meanwhile, the campaign rolled on with such bandwagon-jumping anachronisms as 'the Milky Bar kid out in space' (defeating evil green overlord Zartan with a laser-deflecting silver platter) and 1987's circus-themed Buttons launch, though quite what recondite career path led the Milky Bar kid from cowboy to big top ringmaster went unremarked upon.

**'Inevitably, the Milky Bar kid himself was as puny and pallid as the product he was paid to endorse.'**

## BRANDED FOR LIFE

Wonderful as chocolate is, there's a limit to what you can do with a bar of it. Bung in a fruity filling here, sling some hazelnuts at it from over there, wrap it round a bit of frothy nougat... there are other options, but most of those risk a custodial sentence. As the big chocolate companies of the land expanded and consolidated, they found these tired old tricks, most of them dating from before the war, weren't giving them the brand range their national status required. So, if you can't jigger up the contents, why not play about with the shape? This had been going on since the start of the century, with the likes of Fry's Five Boys, a weird little bar decorated with the gurning expressions of one Lindsay Poulton, supposedly to demonstrate the tortuous emotional states gone through by the average small boy awaiting his cocoa fix.

Such high-concept wrapper action had no place in the modern chocolate era, though. Three simple pack-festooning candidates ruled the shelves: wacky cartoon animals, famous folk from the cinema and telly, and famous wacky cartoon animals from the cinema and telly. In 1970 Nestlé launched the *Winnie the Pooh* chocolate bar: bog-standard milk chocolate, but with a variety of characters from Disney's recent A.A. Milne revamp on the labels. The sheer cross-media crowd-pleasing of this sort of thing was too good to do just the once, so over the next couple of years they pulled the same trick with *The Aristocats*, *Robin Hood* and the ever-collectable *Doctor Who*.

**Opposite:** Chasing the pink pound – Nestlé's Pink Panther (1972). Everyone knows his name – Rupert, Rupert the bar (1971).

**Below:** TV hits! *Doctor Who* (1971/3), *Mr Men* circa 1977, and *The Wombles* circa 1976, sell out in the name of cocoa.

When the chocolate ran out, the endorsements didn't. The Pink Panther bar, a slab of strawberry-flavoured... stuff decorated with everyone's favourite slightly camp gentleman, scholar and acrobat, was the first and most memorable of these (even if some of those memories come with a slightly suspicious aftertaste). Others included a cream-flavour *Star Trek* bar ('She cannae taste any blander, Cap'n!') and various *Tom and Jerry* concoctions, including a banana variant.

BBC children's programmes, as a rule, weren't up for this sort of treatment, though since many were produced by third parties who kept merchandising rights close to their chests, there wasn't a lot the Beeb could do if, say, FilmFair decided to let Chocolat Tobler launch a range of bars named after (but, crucially, not flavoured with) *The Herbs*. And if they then went off to Nestlé and got them to make Paddington Bear and Wombles chocolate, well, there wasn't much Chocolat Tobler could do about that, either. Canny do-it-yourself cartoon maker Bob Godfrey similarly played the percentages, licensing *Roobarb* chocolate to Cadbury and the later Noah and Nelly bar franchise to Nestlé.

It was every furry stop-motion animal for himself. Oliver Postgate, needless to say, kept well away from this sort of thing.

Of course, not all hot intellectual property owners are up for handing out merchandising rights to the first sweet maker who gets them on the blower. Whether Barker and Dobson, otherwise highly esteemed manufacturers of Everton mints and the like, ever got in touch with ABC Television in 1978 to enquire about the spin-off state of affairs of the top-rating *Happy Days* is unknown, but their Fonz Rock Bar was a masterclass in endorsement-free cashing in, with its '50s jukebox stylings and cunning lack of any identifiable Henry Winkler presence on the wrapper at all. If you wanted official endorsement, perhaps it was best to aim low, as Austro-Welsh confectioners Caxton's did in 1972 when they rolled out their Doris Archer Fudge, with full consent from the fictional Radio 4 soap matriarch.

**'The marketing department took one look at the mousse-filled chocolate slab in their charge and thought, "Mousse? Moose!"'**

If all else failed, you could make up your own characters from scratch. The uber-cute critters that simpered from Nestlé's mighty, ever-expanding zoological Animal Bar range were

**Opposite:** Feeding time at the zoo, with Nestle's milk chocolate menagerie, Animal Bar (1963), and Fry's Super Mousse (1970).

**Below and overleaf:** Film fare. More cartoonish cash-ins from Galaxy and the adventures of *Noddy* (1970), Nestle's *Larry the Lamb* (1970), Cadbury's Soccerbar (1973), Monster Bar (1973) and *Roobarb* (1974).

a palpable hit with no telly counterpart needed, and their white chocolate Polar Joe bear bar didn't do too badly either. The same couldn't perhaps be said quite so emphatically of Fry's Super Mousse, where the marketing department took one look at the mousse-filled chocolate slab in their charge and thought, 'Mousse? Moose!' So was born the Bullwinkle-esque superhero star of the wrappers, hailed by Fry's as a 'mythological personality' who was sure to capture the hearts and minds of the nation's children overnight. He didn't. Neither did the cartoon band on the wrappers of Needler's Pop Chocs range: Slicer Orange, Miss Krispie and Big Drummer Cocoa bore no resemblance to any genuine band, even in 1974, and their pop chocs remained unpicked. And who can forget Trebor's Konks and

**Opposite:** 35% cocoa solids, 65% Beatrix Potter. Cadbury's Furry Friends promise further animal adventures, circa 1974.

Robbers, a Keystone Kops-oriented attempt to flog orange chocolate with the likes of Inspector Clueless, Konstable Klod and Ratnose Fink? A great many people, clearly.

As a last resort, you could brighten up a young child's day with some entertaining spiel on the back of the wrapper. Okay, 'entertaining' often meant a rather dreary retelling of a TV episode, as with Nestlé's *Larry the Lamb* bars ('Part 3: Larry is fishing when he sees the Mayor approaching on a small raft'). Cadbury's Soccerbars featured tips on how to improve match fitness. 'Stop eating this chocolate' might have been a good one, but the writers gamely tried to link sportsmanship with Bournville brands ('Did you know that star footballers play leapfrog, Freddo's favourite sport?'). They really let their hair down for the descriptions of assorted unlikely critters on Monster Bars. ('The Murky Murgswump is a nasty monster that lurks about in murky swamps. The damp gives him nasty pains so that when he bends down he goes "OOH-AAH-OUCH!"') Perhaps the *Wombles* bar gambit was best: a short description of how the MacWomble can crush nuts with his bare paws, and a cheery exhortation to Keep Britain Tidy by chucking the wrapper in the nearest bin. Wait a minute, though: weren't you supposed to be collecting them? Once again, Tobermory hadn't quite thought it through.

# Here are some new Furry Friends for you to play with...

## ...can you guess what they're doing?

Pom-Pom the Panda

Daisy Dormouse

Monty Mole

Freddy Fox

Peter Polar Bear

Bill Badger

Six new lovable Furry Friends from Cadbury's. Real Cadbury's Dairy Milk Chocolate for only 2p.

Cadbury's

## * FREDDO

A true star among the largely anonymous chocolate animal milieu, Freddo began life in 1930s Australia when one Harry Melbourne, apprentice chocolate moulder for MacRobertson's, nervously queried his boss's decision to launch a range of choccy mice, suggesting that, as some children (and, of course, all women) were sent into fits of chair-scaling terror at the sight of a rodent, might a frog not be a less risky

**Opposite:** Egg-laying amphibians? Freddo confuses a generation of budding natural historians (circa 1978).

**Below:** A frog in one's throat? Cadbury's jolly green client (1973).

commercial proposition? Rather than docking him a week's wages for insubordination, Harry's bosses, in a fine example of old-school 'the boy might just be on to something' management, sent him away to knock up a few samples. The resulting amphibian sweetmeat, sporting a cheery countenance and sensible footwear, proved that gut instinct right from the moment it went on sale. When Cadbury took over MacRobertson's it was inevitable that their top-selling line reached the UK.

Launched in 1973 on a wave of cartoon anthropomorphism and creaky puns about leap years on the wrappers, the British Freddo joined such webbed stars as Kermit, Alberto and the intimidating Grog from *Vision On*, in what turned out to be a singularly froggy decade. By 1974 the lad was turning over £2 million a year. Cadbury's Bournville HQ was inundated with Freddo fan art and fan fiction. As one exec put it, 'he has a steady band of admirers who enjoy his special brand of humour as well as his eatability.' This estimation was revised upwards the following year to the level of 'national institution', and non-edible merchandise was rolled out, including Freddo soft toys, finger puppets and greetings cards. Then, unaccountably, at the end of the decade he hopped it from British shelves. Perhaps the fame had all become too much. And sure, he's been packing the arenas since his 1994 comeback, but somehow it seems like a soulless, money-raking shadow of former glories. Oh, Freddo, what happened? You used to be all about the chocolate!

## BEHIND BARS

Jargon alert! Ask any chocolatier or confectionery insider (and who doesn't know at least three?) and they will tell you: a substantial majority of their industry profits is generated by what are known as 'countlines', those smooth choc-covered treats, filled with nougat, caramel, ill-fated factory-floor rats and so on, designed to be eaten on the move.

This particular form of one-handed pleasure isn't easy to sell. Before the days of commercial television, kids were too busy up chimneys and picking pockets to buy their own sweets. The advent of advertising allowed brand leaders and their highly paid agencies to come up with increasingly ingenious campaigns to remind us that countlines were reliable, dependable and enjoyable (as opposed to the commonplace, lacklustre and dreary reality).

So, when Mars brought their popular candy bar over from the US to London in 1932, deliberately changing the recipe to suit European tastes (more sugar, less malt, sweeter caramel and, at first – unbelievably – Cadbury's chocolate), they were unwittingly helping a future slogan-writer (not Murray Walker, despite what you might read elsewhere) come over all expert practitioner: 'A Mars a day helps you work, rest and play.' While the tagline riffed nattily on the old apple/doctor-repellent adage (ousting the previous Bob Monkhouse-fronted 'Stars love Mars' campaign in 1959), TV screens could be filled with sumptuous close-ups of sugar, caramel and thick, thick chocolate slathering over a nougat slab, yet still reinforce the impression that the Mars bar was not only nutritious, but practically vital. Of course, any claims were medically

**Opposite:** The cash cow of Slough: Mars (1932) and the slogan that first appeared in print in 1959.

**Opposite:** The other M&Ms. Milky Way (1935) and Marathon (1968).

difficult to prove. (The reasoning went: milk 'to nourish you, while you relax'; sugar 'to give you the energy to work'; and chocolate, more exuberantly, 'to play'. Oh, and glucose – just sugar again, wearing a pharmacist's lab coat – which could do the work of the other three standing on its head.)

If they weren't insistently showing us bogus production processes (the interior of a Milky Way was apparently 'whipped over 1,000 times' by a hand-held Kenwood electric whisk, if a 1980 advert is to be believed), Mars UK were encouraging assorted tower-block-dwelling, new-town youth to extol the virtues of snacking 'without ruining your appetite'. Absent parents were replaced by older brothers or sisters dishing out chocolate purchased on the basis that it wouldn't fill them up (in which case, what's the point?). Lovell's of Wales also momentarily squeezed into the 'between meals' gap with the candidly named Milky Lunch, a crisped-rice revamp of their brazenly opportunist Milky Whip. However, when Milky Way's annoyingly ear-worm-laden red/blue car race animations were revived for a twenty-first-century audience, the relevant lines had been jarringly replaced – not because of health lobbyist complaints, but because market research had indicated no one was eating regular meals any more.

Marathon, on the other hand, was positioned firmly as a meal replacement: 'packed with peanuts', curbing and satisfying

hunger pangs like a chocolate dominatrix. As if to emphasise the Olympic origins of the name, all Greek honey and heroism, 1970s ads featured various athletic, bright-eyed teens (and Keith Chegwin) marvelling at the sheer magnitude of it all, while the bar itself repeatedly disassembled into slices, as if to demonstrate the efficient regularity of the internal peanut distribution. As any child of the era will recall, this practice inspired parents likewise to carve up and share out a single bar among brothers and sisters, each of whom would fight tooth and claw to be allocated a chocolate-heavy end piece.

Ever alert to consumer behaviour, Mars's product developers speedily introduced the 'fun-size' bar. From 1972 onward, everyone could have their own end piece. Pound for pound, they were more expensive than their standard-sized counterparts but such is the marketeer's sleight of hand. To allay mums' housekeeping money fears, some friendly adverts demonstrated how much more a bagload weighed than a box of posh chocs. 'Two bites big,' they said. Big! Not small. The scales couldn't lie.

Aside from the short-term profit boost, another side effect of the treat-sized revolution was an increased number and regularity of 'consumption occasions', making nonstop grazing start to feel more normal. Trade magazine *The Grocer* identified a trend for 'ambient snacks', i.e. ones you could eat without actually noticing. Rowntree issued 'pillow packs' – inflated, miniaturised bags – of Rolo, Aero and Lion. Meanwhile, Cadbury,

**Opposite:** Cheggers plays pep. Keith's over-excited ad for Marathon, circa 1976, and a more chilled approach for Safeway's tie-in fridge competition.

**Below:** What we're all looking for in our chocolate is neatness, right? Fudge (1948), Topic (1962).

who'd missed the first foray into mini-bar territory (lacking the manufacturing capability to produce smaller versions of their own products prior to 1986), fortunately had one veteran countline, and a corporately funded nursery rhyme, to fall back on.

After a 'new, more buttery taste' had failed to ignite interest in the early '70s, Cadbury set about reminding parents that their 'finger of Fudge is just enough to give your kids a treat', with a deliberately nostalgic, dust-laden advert. The school orchestra-style rendering of old regimental brass number 'The Lincolnshire Poacher', courtesy of former Manfred Mann singer Mike d'Abo, alongside sentimental scenes of grey-shorts-and-jumpered boys playing conkers, was calculated to set apron-strings a-tightening and purse strings a-loosening. Use of what a director of photography might call 'a limited palette', to belie the product's true vintage, helped Cadbury smash any upstart competition, such as Meltis's Fudge Finger.

When the long, hot summer of '76 decimated chocolate sales (as everyone raided their newsagents for ice creams, especially the all-new Cornetto), the Fudge similarly became a poster-boy for Cadbury's 'straight from the fridge' campaign, poking out of a glacier the following year, 'firm, cool and icily irresistible'. Even then, Mars beat them to the punch with a set of 'Cool 'em for a summer's day' ads featuring Topic (another bar keen to reassure us of its evenly distributed innards: 'a hazelnut in every bite') and Bounty among the usual suspects. The combined effort changed punters' shopping habits, and by the year 1984 exactly 84 per cent of consumers enjoyed their chocolate on the rocks, soggy wrappers notwithstanding.

A finger of Fudge is just enough.

Cadbury's

Fudge

In singles or packs of four.

**Opposite:** Cadbury promotes adequacy as a USP for Fudge's most enduring campaign, circa 1980.

**Below:** Stan Boardman's toffee Fokker never got off the ground, either. Triffik, post-Mike Reid, circa 1978.

The heat obviously got to the smaller, independent companies, who cast around wildly for celebrity endorsement. On paper, it made sense for Barratt to team up with comedian-turned-singer Mike Reid for their Triffik nougat bar: they shared a catchphrase, his 'Ugly Duckling' novelty record had swanned into the top ten, and *Runaround* was a hit with the kids on TV. But plastering a sweaty, bespectacled, working-men's club comic's mug on your wrapper does not a marketing strategy make and poor sales soon meant it had to g-g-g-g-g-go.

The difficulty was creating a countline with staying power. A deserted factory optimistically intended to fulfil national demand for Aztecs was hastily repurposed by Cadbury for the Welcome bar – more fudge, this time studded with hazelnuts – although it soon outstayed its own. The same fate befell the Rumba, which waltzed off without applause. Down south, Tottenham's own Jameson's Chocolate staked a claim for the niche, theatre-going market with their sophisticated, rich and dark raspberry Ruffle. Defiantly unplebeian, it wouldn't be their last experiment with 1979's evidently bumper crop of *Rubus idaeus*, but it would be the only one still sneaking through foyers into the Royal Box over three decades later.

As the indie companies bobbed and weaved, scrapping for the occasional title bout, heavyweights like Mars went all out to prove themselves in multiple divisions. Their countlines appeared in new wrappers: king size (regal, decadent, with its own state-funded armed forces) and snack time (instant, disposable, far less of a chore than its grown-up brother). No gap was too small or too large to be filled by confectionery. Then, as Britain lurched towards the European single market, the now-global brands sought to consolidate operations across continents. Why run separate ads for the same product in multiple territories, simply because the local names differed? Think of the poor, confused MTV viewers. Not to mention the money it would save. So, in 1989, Marathon began to carry little 'internationally known as' badges (soon swapped for 'the new name for') as Snickers' dominance asserted itself. 'All that's changed is the name' bleated the label, as if that were a mere trifle. Fifty-odd years of carefully accreted brand awareness obscured by a smokescreen: the entirely fictitious threat that Mars just might have dared meddle with the recipe. It had never been on the cards but it was a handy distraction from the fact that Snickers was, and is, a ghastly name.

## * TEXAN

The history of British sweets marketed by knock-off cowboys is long and baffling. When the Milky Bar kid first flaunted the only NHS prescription in nineteenth-century Nevada, kids did indeed still flock to the flicks for historically dubious tales of ethnic cleansing in fetching hats. By the time Rowntree Mackintosh launched their Mighty Chew on the knee-high populace, however, the

**Opposite:** Rowntree's much-missed Lone Star bar, Texan (1973).

**Below:** Rope 'em in. Move 'em out. Eat 'em up. TV's ten-gallon toffee-lover, circa 1977.

predominant Western image was of Gran dozing off in front of *The High Chaparral*.

Nevertheless, in the strong, silent, jaw-jutting mould of Eastwood and Wayne, the Texan Man was effective enough. But whereas Nestlé's bespectacled law enforcer was an Aryan-tressed riot of six-shooting roundup action, our cartoon friend's capabilities were limited to getting caught by a variety of racial stereotypes. Injuns and Mexicans alike tied him up, frugged wildly about, then foolishly granted him a last request: a chance to scoff his Texan bar. The resulting postponement of atrocities via the prolonged mastication of chocolate and nougatine eventually rendered his foes unconscious, whereupon he would untie himself, tiptoe over his dozing captors, and mooch off to bore the crap out of some other ethnic minority. He livened up in later ads, effecting daring escapes from ice floes and stagecoaches, and even performed a rather lasciviously chocophiliac hoedown ('Take your Texan by the hand/Strip it down! My, that's grand!'), but mainly it was a case of trudging about, sending foreigners to sleep and being, by cowboy standards, a bit of a useless arse.

Not that any of this dented the success of the bar itself. It may not have been the first nougat bar to sell itself on sheer longevity of the chewing experience (several children who purchased the short-lived Cadbury's Big One in 1971 are still finishing it today as they leaf through their unit trust portfolios), but the combination of that star-spangled wrapper and a block booking of ad breaks on *Tiswas* enticed a generation to 'bite through the chocolate and chew... real slow'. Just don't mention the suffocating tedium.

**'In the strong, silent, jaw-jutting mould of Eastwood and Wayne, the Texan Man was effective enough.'**

## * DIME

The Scandinavians, for some reason, have never been in a hurry to export any of their consumer goodies. There's a fish-canning company in Göteborg who, had they shown more international ambition in the '70s, might now not be the world's second-most well-known Abba. Similarly, the UK had to wait nearly thirty years for the affordable home accessories and tricky-to-assemble furniture of IKEA to

**Opposite:** Brother, can you spare a Dime (1953)?

**Below:** Ruddy hell, it's Harry and... Harry? Enfield coins it in, circa 1993.

arrive in its giant, out-of-town industrial parks. So it was that, in 1982, Barker and Dobson (of Victory V fame) and Marabou of Sweden finally brokered a historic deal to distribute the latter's crunchy, buttery, almondy sliver of a bar to a grateful British public. The Dajm had arrived, in the scantiest of chocolate coats. (Hurrah! Schnapps all round, etc. Although, er, we're going to have to take another look at that name, guys.)

Impossible to describe to anyone who hadn't yet eaten their first, a fact later exploited for Harry Enfield's winning television campaign, the rechristened Dime materialised in tuck shops almost entirely without branding 'push' but with an attractive 15p price tag attached instead. It proved to be a cracking success, so an emboldened Marabou raided their cupboards for other lines that might yield a high exchange rate on the confectionery currency converter. However, neither the twenty-two piece, prosaically named Milk Chocolate Roll, nor the sickly sweet butter-cream crisp Delight bar caught the public imagination in the same way. Disillusionment set in and, after a skanky American drive-in-themed ad ('Dynamite Dime') failed to blow up, Marabou took their business elsewhere.

Barker and Dobson fell immediately into bed with Ritter Schokoladefabrik of West Germany and began supplying the unusually filled, but resealable, Sport brand chocolate blocks to off-licences ('snaps open for action, folds back for protection'). United Biscuits sealed the deal for UK Dime distribution and, within years, had the nation shouting, 'Oi, nutter!', 'Armadillos!' and other such advert catchphrase nonsense. They never did quite nail the product description, though. Current Norwegian owners Kraft's website probably comes closest, putting it, via Google translation software, as 'the small bent piece of chocolate glaze'. Quite right too.

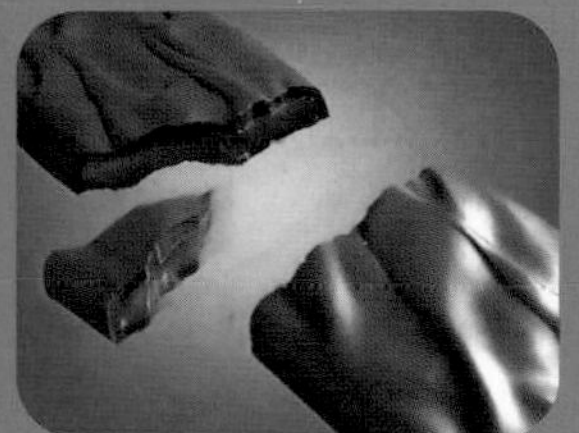

**'Dime materialised in tuck shops almost entirely without branding 'push' but with an attractive 15p price tag attached.'**

## ✻ CRUNCHIE

Honeycomb, cinder toffee, call it what you will, it's as old as the hills. It's easy to make: get some sugar and corn syrup extremely bloody hot, bung in some baking powder, stand well back, and there you have it. Or rather, there you have irregular lumps of it. It's how you tame the fragile honeycomb into a sleek polyhedron that's the tricky part.

**Opposite:** Land of milk (chocolate) and honey (comb). Cadbury's Crunchie (1929) is foiled again.

**Below:** Long, cool and bubbly. TV's 'champagne bar' campaign, circa 1978.

Aussie manufacturer Hoadley's started squaring the brittle in 1918 with the Violet Crumble. The down-under spies at Fry's reported this back to their Keynsham HQ, and a race was on to replicate it. Early attempts were unreliable, Fry's having to employ women specially to solder snapped bars back together with bunsen burners, but eventually a nifty system of cutting the slabs with a high-pressure jet of oil solved the problem. Add a distinctive heavy foil wrapper to stop the honeycomb going soft, and it's Crunchie ahoy.

It was slow to take off, despite some early product placement in horsey kids' book *National Velvet*, though after the Second World War it was popular enough for Rowntree to float a short-lived rival, Cracknel Block. The '60s saw it really embed into the national psyche – by '68 *Observer* hacks were writing 'that's the way the Crunchie crumbles' when casting about for a with-it-sounding cliché.

By the '80s it was everywhere, repackaged in shiny gold and sponsoring Five Star and Billy Ocean. Though what really got it noticed was a strange daily ad campaign in 1987, wherein an automatic wall-calendar sombrely recorded the changing days of the week, as a rather glum voice mused, 'Not long till Friday.' Come the weekend, this low-key teaser was revealed as the beginning of the Thank Crunchie It's Friday campaign, which gave rise to two decades of frenetic fun in the name of burnt sugar. Modern advertising, you see, all very clever. And slightly more appropriate than associating children's chocolate with the man who sang 'Get Outta My Dreams, Get Into My Car'.

**'Early attempts were unreliable, Fry's having to employ women specially to solder snapped bars back together with bunsen burners. '**

## ✻ WISPA

It's a lazy journalist's dream: a chocolate bar from the 1980s that was a triumph of marketing over substance. The Wispa's Aero-meets-Flake texture didn't exactly spark a confectionery revolution when the fluffy ingot made its debut in the Tyne Tees area. What raised eyebrows were the TV ads: wry chunks of two-handed banter between famous celebs of the day. Even so, it wasn't a Zeitgeist-surfing triumph from the off. Picking the

**Opposite:** Blue velvet? Cadbury's Wispa (1981).

**Below:** 'That's the most pleasurable experience I've ever had.' Summoning the spirit of Maplins for a TV advert, circa 1983.

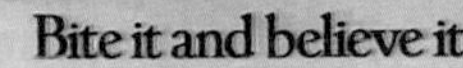

stars of *Dad's Army* and *The Sweeney* was an odd gambit in the days before retro chic turned every old brown sitcom into a nostalgic goldmine, while the choice of the third show, *Shoestring*, was just plain weird. A shabby regional detective with mental health issues – he'll tell us what to eat, right, kids? By the time of the bar's nationwide roll-out two years later, they'd perfected a more contemporary line-up: *It Ain't Half Hot Mum* and *Yes, Minister* may not have been trendy, but they were at least current, and the *Hi-De-Hi* ad, with Ruth Madoc and Simon Cadell in full sexually charged character, but cannily using each other's real names to avoid legal hassles, tapped a rich seam of chocoroticism mined further by Paul Nicholas and Jan Francis, and real-life bedfellows Rula Lenska and Dennis Waterman, set off by the nudge-nudge strapline 'Bite it and believe it'.

By the end of the decade, Cadbury were packing the edgier likes of Peter Cook and Mel Smith off to ramble in front of a black cloth at Shepperton Studios, under the banner 'You're thinking chocolate, you're talking Wispa', while Noel Edmonds, rather worryingly, demanded, 'Know someone who just has to keep doing it?' While all this was going on, the brand diversified into the sickly Wispa Gold, the Wispa Mint and the biscuity Wispa Bite. This expansionism proved a bit much, as sales declined through the '90s, until all varieties were discontinued in 2003. But you can't keep a good marketing man down, and within a few years Cadbury, overwhelmed by 'grassroots public demand', reinstated the bar following a suspiciously well-orchestrated Internet campaign. This is what's known in the trade as 'doing an Arctic Roll'.

## * AZTEC

This is a tale of two cultural cornerstones. On the one hand, the mighty Quetzalcoatl, feathered serpent god of the ancient Aztecs, who gave his people the sacred gift of chocolate via a beam of heavenly light, bringing them universal wisdom and Type 2 diabetes. (Sadly, the one bit of knowledge that might have been some use, namely 'If you see these Spanish blokes with big shiny helmets, run like the clappers,' slipped

**Opposite:** A sign of civilisation. Aztec (1967), swiftly sacrificed to the gods of tuck shop nostalgia.

**Below:** Instigating a Mexican crave. Safety-pin propaganda on behalf of Cadbury's.

the feathered one's mind.) In the blue corner, there's the equally legendary rival to the Mars bar, opportunistically cooked up by Cadbury in a lean period and promoted with a travelogue-swish TV campaign filmed at one of your actual Mexican temples, only to vanish mysteriously four years later. The former lived on for centuries in folk memory and overpriced Acapulco gift shops. The latter enjoyed a similarly fertile afterlife, becoming the de facto nostalgic touchstone for the first wave of alternative comedians (Ben Elton's swing-top bin was so long unemptied it had 'Aztec wrappers in the bottom').

It's perhaps fair to say that Elton's championing of fair-trade didn't tally too well with the Aztec's imperialistic undertones, a state of affairs not helped by the life-size cardboard warrior chieftains installed in newsagents the nation over, to the innocent delight of kids who'd gleefully perform a culturally inaccurate whooping war dance around them. All this happened, of course, while the Milky Bar kid was doing his bit for the Native North Americans. To complete the continental clean sweep, the 1980s, when you'd have thought people would have calmed down a bit, saw the launch of the otherwise unremarkable Rowntree's Inca. We could, of course, all be very smart and ironic about such things by the time the Aztec made the slightest of slight returns in the year 2000.

**'Ben Elton's swing-top bin was so long unemptied it had "Aztec wrappers in the bottom"'**

## * CADBURY'S CARAMEL

Cadbury had a big year in 1976. On the downside, there was the Rowntree's Yorkie. More positively, there was the Montreal Winter Olympics, all over which the Goodies appeared in TV ads urging hungry kids to swap ten Cadbury wrappers (oh, and £3.60) for a transistor radio in exciting blue denim! Then there was the launch of the Cadbury's Caramel.

**Opposite:** Hare necessities. Cadbury's Caramel (1976).

**Below:** 'Hey Mr Bee, why are you buzzing around?' A Baloo-influenced work ethic for the dole age via the Cadbury's Caramel bunny, circa 1979.

You could tell this was a classy bar. For a start, it was frighteningly expensive, even in those times of vertiginous price rises. It was also very neat, each section being a little sculpted pillow of chocolate, delicately engraved with the Cadbury livery. Let there be no idle talk of 'chunks' here. All terribly sophisticated, very grown-up... and a tad dull, to be honest. This product needed sexing up.

Enter five-foot jobbing actress Miriam Margolyes, who took one of the least promising briefs ever ('Right, so you're this lazy, but saucy, West Country rabbit with a chocolate obsession...') and turned in thirty seconds of sub-Bristol vocal smouldering that was destined for immortality. The cartoon blurred the line over who the product was aimed at slightly. Was it responsible to tell children 'arses are there to be sat on, have some chocolate', via a buck-toothed erotic trade unionist? Nevertheless, a surprisingly timeless campaign was created.

Cadbury took their own advice and took it easy, letting the anthropomorphic amour carry the weight. The bar's sales never troubled the top ten, but the 'exclusive' price kept it afloat. In 1993, enter the Galaxy Caramel. Panic on the streets of Bournville! Well, okay, a bit of a rebadge and a new recipe. It saw off the competition, but it's hard not to view this most successful of also-ran bars as a bit too much in temperament like its skiving mascot, and too little like her industrious, if slightly thick, woodland pals.

## LUNCHBOX HEROES

In the bright, razzle-dazzle world of confectionery, the chocolate biscuit (and here we mean the individually wrapped, chocolate-coated type) has always had secondary status. While it's unquestionably the best bit of any packed lunch you may care to throw together, it never quite reaches the giddy glamour of confectionery proper. This might be something to do with the bakeries: all stout provincial yeomen, imposing brick factories, brass bands on a Sunday, that sort of thing. Not a potential Wonka in sight. Still, they did the job, and after Rowntree got the Kit Kat up and running, they wasted no time in targeting the Tupperware.

An early Kit Kat rival was Glaswegian baker Gray, Dunn and Co.'s Blue Riband, named for some reason after a transatlantic shipping speed record trophy but otherwise conforming to the same anonymous, slightly plain-wrappered image as many a lunchbox chocolate wafer since its debut in 1936.

Nothing changed this sensibly clad state of affairs – not the changing of brands to Rowntree in 1967, or the drafting in of Mike Berry to provide some tuneless Dylan-esque dad-rock for the omnipotent early '80s Blue Riband Blues TV campaign.

Even when the formula was jazzed up with a layer of caramel, as with McVitie's deceptively succulent Taxi, the result still hid behind stark, two-colour, designed-by-local-authority cellophane.

The same firm's Bandit, which made a layer of chocolate cream its USP, at least had the guts to strut out onto the counter in eye-catching scarlet foil, even if the claim made by the TV ad's excitable Mexican stereotypes that 'great big bar Bandit is as big as a door' could be accused of pimping the truth.

**Opposite:** Communion wafers from McVitie; all hail Taxi circa 1971; bought it, ate it, Bandit (1957).

**Below:** Bartered breaktime biscuit bullion. Cadbury's Bar Six (1965), versus Jacob's Club (1932).

Moving into more solid territory, Dublin bakers W&R Jacob's Club range was nothing fancy, but stood out from the rest by means of its dinky-yet-sturdy dimensions – a little ingot of chocolate-heavy joy, wrapped in amusingly oblique wax paper sleeves, featuring visual puns on the name (a golf ball, a playing card... er, and the word 'PLAIN' when they couldn't come up with a pun for plain chocolate – how hard can that be?). This winning combination of gnomic design and plentiful cocoa brought it to within spitting distance of Kit Kat's throne,

Okay then, how about a bit of demographic targeting? In 1963 Cadbury entered the wafery fray with the groovily named Bar Six, aimed at the moped-riding, coffee-slurping Mod set, who could thrill to its sextuple snappable delights in a happening Carnaby Street boutique. Taking the standard Kit Kat construction and altering the shape, it featured one fab solid wafer slab coated in segmented chocolate. This novel way of getting Rowntree's lawyers off their back raised problems of its own, though, when a conflict of the properties of chocolate and biscuit gave rise to warped wafers and bald patches on the back. Kids forgave Cadbury the odd mutant bar, and even found the randomness quite endearing (to this day, a child who possesses an all-chocolate Kit Kat attains the status of a playground prophet), but it never got close to pole position. This wafer biscuit lark was clearly harder than it looked.

**'Jacob's Club was a little ingot of chocolate-heavy joy, wrapped in amusingly oblique wax paper sleeves, featuring visual puns on the name.'**

but not even a squadron of stage school kids trilling 'If you like a lot of chocolate on your biscuit, join our club,' could topple the two-fingered tyrant. Nor could the arrival in 1980 of the Trio, Jacob's toffee-in-triplicate backup plan, which shot to third place in a matter of months on the back of an ad campaign that cast John Peel and Derek Griffiths in an old Stan Freberg comedy sketch about Harry Belafonte's recording levels to devastating effect.

In 1970 Rowntree upped the ante, spearheading a 'two-pronged assault on the chocolate biscuit market'. Prong number one – the Fingammie – was destined for the grocer's dog's dish, but the Breakaway, a good, solid biscuit bar set in chocolate, engraved with a neat lattice pattern and wrapped in saucy yellow, was destined for great things, especially after 1972 saw Eric Idle reformat his Python 'Nudge, Nudge' sketch to come to its televisual aid. There were no such marketing certainties for McVitie's United bar, which augmented its biscuity base with sprinkled honeycomb pieces. The obvious footie theme was developed into a confusing commercial wherein a substituted player bit into a bar, only to be momentarily teleported into various unlikely situations, insisting to his coach that 'it was the candy crisp wot did it'. This was later junked for a more straightforward scarf-waving oompah singalong.

**Opposite:** 'No three things are quite as good together as a Trio.' Self-assembling flip-top excitement and that eardrum-challenging ad.

**Below:** From wholemeal to goal meal. Rowntree's Breakaway (1970) and McVitie's United (1976) are up for the (tea) cup. Burton's noble Viscount is full of surprises, circa 1978.

The marketing triumph of the biscuit world must surely be the transformation of William Macdonald and Sons' chocolate-dipped bourbon derivative, made since 1932 and cursed with a stupid name, from plucky also-ran into the sort of 'cult' national institution marketing departments fantasise about to keep their marriages intact. The advent of ITV brought the first tentative knockings – a chirpy chant of 'Hurry, hurry, Penguin's on the way!' – but it wasn't until 1966 that Derek Nimmo was called in to provide sub-Noël Coward talky-singy duties over footage of quizzical sphenisciformes let loose in public places. Granted, 'P-p-p-pick up a Penguin' couldn't match Frank Muir's Cadbury songs for ingenious wordplay ('What's bigger and best for you?' indeed), but as a consciousness-invading fruity irritant, it was matchless.

But enough of the cuboid. How about something round and creamy in your lunchbox? McVitie's were happy to oblige with Yoyo, the minty digestive in a green foil ballgown, but it

**Opposite:** Warning: may contain gender stereotypes. Burton's were in no doubt about who wore the trousers in British homes, circa 1978.

**Below:** Wagon Wheels (1948) in Big Country guise. Simple Minds and Aztec Camera varieties just didn't taste the same.

was yet another old-timery baking firm that led the way in biscuit discs. Burton's Gold Medal Biscuits – based in Corporation Street, Blackpool – could match the Yoyo bite for bite with the more regally named (though almost identical) Viscount. Far more important, to Burton's, the kids and society as a whole, was the Wagon Wheel.

Out of the ovens just as the Cold War began heating up, the marshmallow biscuit sandwich impressed all who saw it by its sheer, austerity-busting size. This duly increased over the years but, aside from the original wax paper envelopes mutating into the regulation foil pack, nothing else was changed for decades. Nothing needed to be. It was the biggest biscuit out there, and so clearly was the winner. The odd advertising campaign helped: 1985 saw Wagon Wheel Week in your super soaraway *Sun*, and telly ads memorably claimed 'It's so big you've got to grin to get it in'. Perhaps one of the older boys at the back would like to explain what's so funny about that to the rest of the school. But the sheer totemic size carried the day.

Not so many of the old guard fared as well at that time, though. A big cleanout at McVitie's in 1988 saw Taxi and Bandit come a cropper, though the latter briefly lived again in the late '90s. The Trio's reign faded, and the Club mutated beyond all recognition after Danone got their yogurty grasp on it. Some old-fashioned 'factory gates and cobbled street' wafers eventually came to the fore, most prominently Tunnock's, with its olde worlde stat-packed wrapper, but elsewhere it was weird Euro imports and lob-anything-into-the-dough American-style cookies a-gogo. The golden age of biscuitry was over. Insert the sad bit of music from the Hovis ad here.

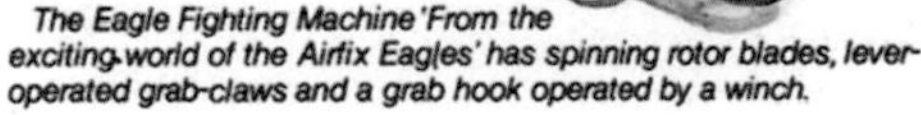

The Eagle Fighting Machine 'From the exciting world of the Airfix Eagles' has spinning rotor blades, lever-operated grab-claws and a grab hook operated by a winch.

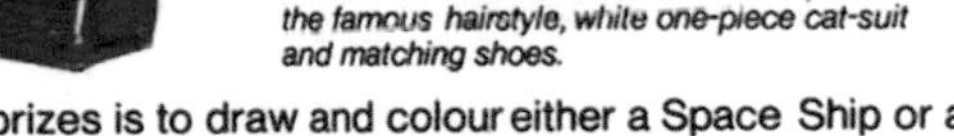

This 12" Farrah Fashion Doll is complete with the famous hairstyle, white one-piece cat-suit and matching shoes.

Just imagine yourself combating the forces of evil with this amazing all action Eagle Fighting Machine. Or dressing Fabulous Farrah the Hollywood film star, for one of her sensational engagements!

All you have to do to win one of these super prizes is to draw and colour either a Space Ship or a Film Star's dream house in Hollywood.

For full details of how to enter, see the special packs of Burton's Bowlers, Burton's Coconut Mallows and Burton's Snowballs.

**Get your mum to look for the special packs**

## ✻ KIT KAT

Launched around the same time as the Aero, the Rowntree's Chocolate Crisp made much less of a splash. It was just as innovative as its porous counterpart, a chocolate-encased double wafer of the like never seen before. 'The biggest little meal in London' was its original selling point, equating those two snappable fingers to a two-course meal (of, presumably, pudding and pudding). In 1937 it

**Opposite:** Golden. Delicious. Kit Kat (1937) celebrates 50 years as a four-fingered favourite.

**Below:** Eats, shoots and leaves – that *Who Dares Wins*-indebted panda ad, circa 1989.

became the Kit Kat Chocolate Crisp, and shortly after the war those last two words were finally dropped. The Kit Kat had arrived.

Problem was, it had arrived pretty much unnoticed. Its humble ambitions - 'the perfect companion to a cup of tea' went the early slogan – hardly marked it out for greatness. Thank heavens, then, for advertising giants J. Walter Thompson, who hatched the 'Have a break' slogan in 1939 and stayed with the bar, and those words, for the rest of the century. Never have three words proved so durable, whether accompanied by Bernard Cribbins as a chatty fisherman, Arthur English as a security guard, or a hapless New Romantic outfit destined to go 'a long way'. In the first half of the '70s, sales rose by over two-thirds on the back of such economical publicity, and seldom faltered afterwards.

Kit Kat statistics make for giddy reading. By 1984, Rowntree were shifting 24 million bars a week. In 1987, forty were said to be eaten every second worldwide. Even so, it never got higher than number two, always the bridesmaid to Mars's bride. Then came Euro expansion: travel to France or Italy in the '80s and you could amaze your school chums by returning with, respectively, five- and three-fingered mutant Kit Kats.

The rise wasn't inexorable: March 1985 saw the GLC react to Rowntree's lack of transparency regarding disclosure of equal employment opportunities by summarily banning Kit Kats from school tuck shops in the Greater London area. Well intentioned perhaps, but you don't play politics with the kids' lunch, Mr Livingstone. Mrs Thatcher, herself no stranger to snatching dairy produce from the mouths of babes, dissolved the GLC the following year, like a Kit Kat finger in a hot cuppa, just in time for the bar's golden jubilee.

**By 1984, Rowntree were shifting 24 million Kit-Kats a week. In 1987, forty were said to be eaten every second worldwide.'**

## TEA BREAK TIME

We humans are an essentially primitive species. Our flabby, wasteful brain is easily fooled. At its heart, there's the reptilian core, reminding us to breathe, stand upright and open our mouths to put snacks in. Over that, we've grown the limbic system, which controls emotions and reminds us, often unconsciously, which snacks we like and which we don't. Then, finally, there's the neocortex, responsible for imagination, language and abstract thoughts like 'Ooh, it's got two bars! That must mean I get to eat twice as much!'

This, in a nutshell, is about the right level of neuroscientific knowledge required to work in a chocolate factory. Start pointing and naming things like the amygdala and you're probably over-qualified. But arrange your chocolate bars like schoolchildren in a newsagent's, two at a time, and the keys to the kingdom will be yours.

Mars was most successful at foxing our equivocal minds with the introduction in 1967 of the Twix, a heady double cocktail of chocolate, caramel and shortcake biscuit, surely the most inoffensive of ingredients.

But if it's a biscuit, then what's it doing here? According to the VAT-man, it's not a biscuit, which means it can't be taxed as a luxury item. But it's not entirely a chocolate bar either. It can only be described as a confection, decided Mars; a law unto itself; a snack. Hence the unusual name, so called not only because of its twin-bar nature, but also because it occupies a no-man's-land 'twixt biscuit and bar. Initially, it was marketed with a 'longer lasting' promise, although that could easily be misinterpreted as a thumbing of the

**Opposite:** Is that a ladder in your stocking or are you just pleased to see me? Bored 'Eighties office girls get their kicks with Twix (1967)...

**Below:** ...whereas moody loners prefer Drifter (1980): 'Speak English, boy!'

nose to sell-by dates. Then, as if genuinely trying to flaunt its tax-exile status, Twix tried to insert itself into that bastion of biscuit consumption, the Great British tea break.

Traditional nibbles were mocked at every turn. The everyday goings-on of the working class in warehouses, offices and bus queues, already looming large in the adverts, now came with a magic sprinkle of Twix-y dust. Innuendo abounded. The window cleaner couldn't drop by an open window without offering to share a finger with the secretary. Girls couldn't meet their fella in the park without giving him one.

It was like the *Confessions* films re-edited for the under-eights. Ironically, these scenes were almost exclusively populated by soon-to-be-stars of children's television. Jobbing actors they may have been but, look, there's that girl from *Hickory House*. And isn't that the ponce off *The Tomorrow People*? And her from *Blue Peter* with the pop star daughter? Indeed, like a pregnant Janet Ellis,

Twix just kept getting bigger through the '80s, gaining extra length and an additional ten grams in 1984 to keep up with some of its arch-rivals.

Rowntree's Drifter, after a slow start, had finally taken off on television. Its 'real mouthful' attributes were reinforced by a stereotypically fly Huggy Bear-style dude jive-talking to an old lady shopkeeper 'for something to jaw on, crispy in the mainstream, and wearing top to toe his Sunday best'. English subtitles were provided for anyone who hadn't already seen the same schtick done better in the *Airplane* movies, though the high-fiving 'skin there, little blood' coda with a tiny schoolboy was suitably slapstick enough to ensure hilarious playground repetition. The bar itself was nothing more than a predictable, sub-Lion, chewy caramel and wafer affair, though it was unarguably sizeable and sweet enough to floor a diabetic at ten paces. Ain't no pimp fo' sho', but the jive ass bro' sure is a sugar daddy.

Almost identical in looks, but a country mile behind in flavour, Banjo had the air of a bar that put all its money on the horse called 'nuts', only to see it romp home in last place. The problem was actually whatever covered the outside of the bars, clearly artificial and lacking in real milk chocolate. No claims were made as to the provenance or pedigree of the 'flavoured coating' by makers Mars. Instead, emphasis was firmly on 'nutty cream filling', wafer and nuts, more chopped nuts, 'plus roast nut flavour too'. Like Bounty before it, and lard come to that, just two varieties were offered: blue or red, the latter rumoured to contain toasted coconut.

A cheap-as-chips TV spot reworked jaunty bluegrass standard 'Oh! Susanna', as performed by the Christy Minstrels (that's the vaudeville blackface outfit, not the chocolate in a crisp shell), but with clunkingly different lyrics. Do not ponder the massive creative leap involved in getting from 'Alabama with a banjo on my knee' to 'Banjo, Banjo, Banjo is brand new', because this fondly remembered '70s bar actually hides a dark past. Originally introduced by Mars during post-Second World War rationing, the original Banjo carried even less subtly racist undertones, with the 'O' on the wrapper depicted as the thick, red lips of a singing minstrel who was, to use your grandmother's vernacular, as black as a tinker's pot.

Far from brand-new, Banjo had also been previously revived as Trophy, a name that would have fitted more congruently with Kevin Keegan's Match Winners competition, Mars's first land grab on football sponsorship. Reasons for the change are unknown (the best playground-sourced explanation was 'it sounds like a swear word in French'), though it may have been to avoid

**Opposite:** Strum candy talking – going nuts over Banjo (1978). Nobody mention *Deliverance*.

**Below:** Trøffel – for Norsemen of the a-choc-o-lips.

confusion with Trøffel, two big chocolate-coated bars of truffle and roasted hazelnuts longboated over from Norway by cartoon Vikings. Ja!

Dubious foreign nomenclature also applied to Balisto, a North Rhine-Westphalia export whose name, far from implying incoming rockets, missiles and bombs (even the Germans aren't that insensitive) alluded to the dietary fibre within: '*ballaststoffe*'. Small and efficient, this bar packed a lot into its short, stubby fingers. What the Americans would call granola, and the Brits would call digestives, Balisto called 'wheatmeal biscuit'. Adverts for honey-almond or muesli flavours alternated prominently on Dairy Crest milk bottles. Why? Because this Teutonic teatime trespasser arrived on the crest of an '80s health food wave – which also brought us breakfast-cereal-replacement bars Cluster, Tracker and Jordan's Crunch – even if its second-highest ingredient was hydrogenated vegetable fat. Defending these shores from German invasion, Sharps of York failed to win over the muesli-munching masses with a wheat, nuts and raisin mix masquerading as Swisskit. The similarly single-fingered Rowntree's Novo launched in 1986 as a 'healthy Double Decker' and rival to Cadbury's extant Go bar – chocolate, raisins, rice and cornflakes on the bottom layer, sesame seeds, oats, rice, coconut and honey on top. But it was too much, too little, too late. You had to get up pretty early to catch Balisto out, as the towels on the sun loungers around the pool proved.

'The original Banjo carried unsubtle racist undertones, with the 'O' on the wrapper depicted as the thick, red lips of a singing minstrel.'

Cadbury's first crack at Twix's crown came in the shape of Skippy, exhumed from its '60s grave and revived with a bright, colourful

wrapper and a low, low price of 12p. Demand was poor, however, for 'a crunch in the biscuit and a munch in the middle', and Skippy's threat proved as empty as its calories. It even looked like the interloper as part of a combined Cadbury's Nat West bank account promotion – kids in the '80s were always opening bloody bank accounts – offering a £2 starter in return for posted-in wrappers.

Authentic two-fingered salutes were finally flourished Twix-ward after Cadbury invested in new technology and development in the mid-80s, specifically in the field of chocolate texturing and extrusion. One of these, declared the Bournville boffins modestly, would be 'the next Wispa'. The results were kept as far out of sight as possible during the test phases, with Spira (in search of a 'young and active' teenage market) only available in the Granada region and Twirl banished to Ireland.

Initially sold as a solo bar, the latter eventually went two's up in 1990 to make it appear less like a Dipped Flake, and survived by virtue of an execrable 'can't top the taste of a Twirl' campaign. In stark contrast, Spira and its 'clean, crisp taste' went toes up.

Cadbury's final roll of the dice was Time Out, the teatime break with Flake in the middle, although even then it was only launched after a stuttering redesign process to make it

**Opposite:** One snack for the outback, one for the rucksack and one overdue a comeback – Tracker (1985), Twirl (1987) and Spira (1987).

**Below:** Fickle fingers of fate – Time Out (1992), and KP's Toffee Dips, circa 1981.

'modern' and 'chocolatey' enough. Invented by Craton, Lodge and Knight, Cadbury's go-to hothouse of product development (and just how many blue-sky brainstorms did it take to think of sandwiching 78 per cent chocolate between two wafers?), the product came long after the name, which had been registered for years in the hope that the rise of American sports in the UK would give it some traction.

Time Out was positioned firmly in grown-up territory, fully formed and ready to dunk in your tea. Choc Dip, on the other hand, exhibited an altogether more hands-on ethic for primary school kids. Biscuit fingers and chocolate again, but separated into constituent parts by Halifax-based KP Foods for messy DIY snacking. (Portion-pack servings of Ferrero's Nutella provided similar fun, unless the tuck shop fridge had solidified the spread into a dense, unyielding block. In which case: chocolate lollies!) In 1990 Choc Dip's entire TV advertising budget was binned and the money instead spent on a ninety-foot hot-air balloon shaped like the cup container which travelled the country on a Phileas Fogg-style two-month tour.

By this time, even Twix had stopped going on about its superior binary qualities, preferring instead to rattle on about abstract ideas like the 'snack gap' and its suitability to fit therein. Accordingly, our primitive brains had wised up and were no longer taken in by the twin-pack trick. It was, sadly, now just our waistlines that had grown flabby.

## ✻ BOUNTY

There was always something indefinably odd about the Bounty. It wasn't the bar itself. 'Tender coconut, moist with pure syrup, lavish with thick chocolate.' Nothing unusual about that. We'd been here before in 1950, with Rowntree's ill-fated Cokeroon bar. Maybe it's the way the Bounty featured two bars in one pack, without making a song and dance about it. Always suspicious when a chocolate bar keeps something like that

**Opposite:** Dessication's what you need. Bounty (1951).

**Below:** Phew! What a scorcher. Sweltering scenes circa 1978, the year of Bounty's sales peak.

to itself. And the way it did it – not side by side, but in series, with a little jerry-built piece of black waxed cardboard guttering underneath to take up the inevitable slack, leading uncertain youngsters with fond memories of the rice paper on the bottoms of macaroons to try to digest the whole thing. All most irregular.

Then there were the adverts. 'A Taste of Paradise' had been around since the mid-'60s, and was fairly self-explanatory. Coconut = tropical. Dead posh, like. Fair enough. The problems began in 1977, with the 'Bounty hunters' TV campaign, showing a weird tribe of well-groomed, lightly tanned Caucasians lounging about on a tropical island somewhere, having left civilisation behind. How could they look that good out there? Especially when they existed entirely on Bountys?

Not only that, they made the bars themselves. Somehow. We saw a coconut being deftly cleft in twain. Then a sheaf of perfectly wrapped bars floated down a limpid stream on a raft of palm leaves, for the tribe's womenfolk to pick out and chew absent-mindedly under a waterfall. The intervening stages of manufacture were missing. Where were the grunts shredding the coconut? How did they get hold of the syrup? Whither the glycerol processing plant? And the guttering mystery remained. Worse still, the original flute-led musical backing from Howard '*The Snowman*' Blake now featured scene-setting lyrics. 'The Bow-own-tee-hee HUN-ters, are here/They're searching for PAR-a-dise...' trilled a woman who sounded constantly worried she'd chosen a falsetto too high to sustain. This explained nothing.

After 1978, this fair-trade wonder had to compete with the Rowntree's Cabana, which added caramel and chopped glacé cherries to the coconut mix, testing the retentive powers of even the strongest stomach. So they made attempts to assimilate into the real world, acquiring catamarans and scuba gear and moving into the more general 'sun-kissed lifestyle' aspirational bracket loved by lazy Martini account holders and Duran Duran. Structural improvements in wrapper engineering rendered the guttering redundant. The tremulous falsetto became a schmaltzy cover of 'Try a Little Tenderness'. The message was: 'Hey, it's okay! We're not strange at all any more!' Nevertheless, the Bounty is still looked at askance by your average British consumer. Still, it could have been worse: in America it's called Mounds.

## KNOBBLY NIBBLES

So, you've got your basic filled chocolate bar template: an inner core of some stout substance (biscuit, nougat, toffee) covered in chocolate. To jazz it up, you can play variations on a theme within that core. Or, alternatively, you can stick stuff to the outside. Bits and pieces. Nuts. Raisins. Rice. Cornflakes. Anything the machinery and the food and drug laws will allow. Do that, and you've got one of the family of odd-shaped chocolate bars that aren't, but perhaps should be, known collectively as 'the knobblies.'

The family has its origins in the venerable, if slightly lumpy, shape of the Rowntree's Nux. Seven long years in development, what started as a chewy chocolate bar laced with peanuts and raisins finally surfaced in shops in 1957 coated in hazelnuts and Rice Krispies. The extended gestation period, sadly, didn't prepare it for the harsh realities of the 1960s snack market, and after several under-performing years it finally passed on in 1965.

Chief among its reasons for collapse was the Fry's Picnic, which appeared within a year of the Nux. This went for the peanut and raisin combo rejected by Rowntree, but built it around a sturdy caramel wafer chassis, and dolloped a generous amount of Cadbury's milk chocolate over the whole shebang. Later came the addition of the inevitable puffed rice to the mix, bringing it closer to its stablemate from 1963 onwards, the Mackintosh's Toffee Crisp.

Time for Cadbury themselves to have a go. The Bournville posse intended 1971 to be a year of great things. In a blaze of publicity, they launched nine new confectionery products at once. There was Fresca, a chocolate wafer with a lemon sorbet centre. Harmony, the marbled chocolate bar. The self-explanatory Stroodels, Yoggets and

**Opposite:** Raisin 'arris owner. The changing face of Cadbury's Picnic (1958).

**Below:** Fudging it. Picnic's doomed rivals – Mackintosh's Prize (1972), Rowntree's Nutty (1973), and Cadbury's Amazin' Raisin (1971).

Coffee Irish. And Husky, an attempt to cross over into the cheesy snack market. None of these, perhaps unsurprisingly, lasted the distance. But the Amazin' bar, a raisin-stuffed lump of nougat, looked like a winner. Squat and solid, it burst onto the TV screen with a cockernee knees-up testimony: 'It's Amazin' what raisins can do!' And it was, up to a point. But in an already crowded marketplace, the bar soon went the way of the Aztec.

Then things got confusing. In 1972 Mackintosh launched the Prize, which aped the Picnic's peanut and raisin coating, but applied it instead to a core of fudge. This they brought out at exactly the same time sister company Rowntree unleashed the Nutty, which was what you got if you took a Prize, removed the raisins and chocolate, injected it with caramel and wrapped it in transparent brown cellophane. And if you did that, you deserved what you got. Fortunately the ad campaigns allowed a distinction between the two products: Prize pitted a hapless commuter against the zany antics of hunger-creating cartoon supervillainry. Nutty, meanwhile, cleverly drafted in Kenny Everett to make a selling point of the bar's irregular shape, to wit: 'It's got so many knobbly bits it can't stand up on its end!' Unfortunately, it turned out it could accomplish that feat perfectly well, so the oddest USP of the 1970s had to be faked by the use of a magnet under the table.

Then five years later they were at it again. This time, though, they played the long game. The Lion bar was, to all intents and purposes, one scoop of peanuts short of a Picnic, but instead of going for the wacky branding angle, respectable wrappers and ads showing noble beasts in majestic repose gave the knobbly genre an altogether classier, more adult image. (Whether or not this move into maturity was done to counter the alternative image of these bars, as exemplified by a common pub trick based around their similarity to a freshly voided human turd, remains unrecorded.) Alongside the Yorkie, it helped Rowntree bite a hefty chunk out of Cadbury's market domination, notwithstanding the contemporaneous launch of their similarly upmarket knobbly effort, the Nunch bar.

Licking its wounds, the beast of Bournville retired to its laboratory for an extended period, leaving the knobbly market in a steady state for the rest of the '70s, save for a reshuffle in 1979 when Nunch became Star Bar, and Jameson's brought out the Nudge (hazelnuts and fudge, natch), and the Oh Yes! Bar, a nougat 'n' peanut creation with the totally uncalled-for addition of a layer of raspberry jelly. In 1980 Cadbury finally emerged with a concoction of biscuit, peanuts and raisins they considered a world-beater. The public didn't agree, and the Ticket went straight back to the depot.

Tinkering and testing for another few years, they finally got it right in 1985 with the Boost, a log

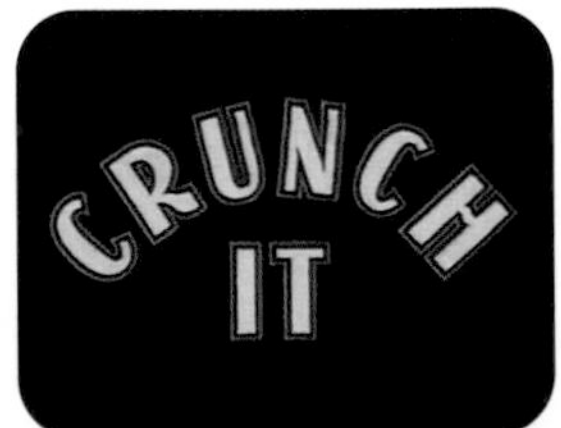


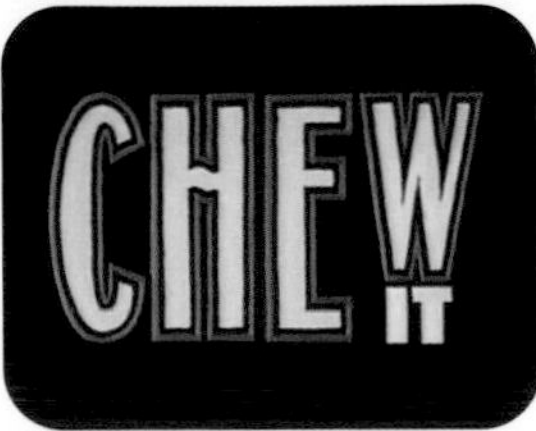

**Opposite:** Wild thing. Lion Bar (1976), originally designed by Rowntree's Allan Norman.

**Below:** 'When you wish upon a Nunch' doesn't have quite the same ring to it. Star Bar (1979), via Nunch (1976), and the cheapday return Ticket (1980).

of coconut and caramel, swiftly joined by biscuit and peanut variants, which cleverly purloined the ancient Mars bar tenet: 'It's absolutely packed full of sugar therefore it'll have you bouncing off the walls – but in an entirely productive fashion.' Give Your Ego a Boost, suggested the sharp-suited salesmen. Although Cadbury's collective ego benefited most, as the new bar overtook the Lion within six months of its national launch. Its place was consolidated in the '90s when Reeves and Mortimer lent their capering personae to a campaign that probably best describes this whole misshapen family: 'slightly rippled with a flat underside'.

'Respectable wrappers and ads showing noble beasts in majestic repose gave the Lion Bar an altogether classier, more adult image.'

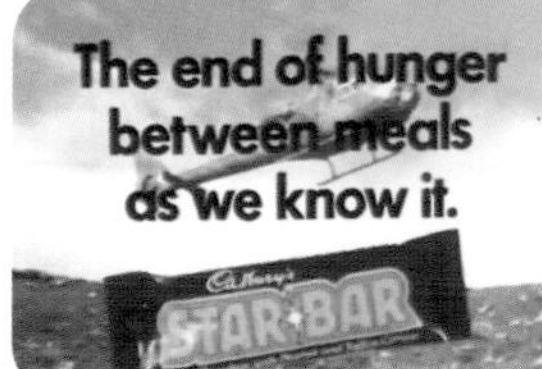

## * DOUBLE DECKER

Meals on wheels, as the giveaway badge would have it. Double Decker was yet another sortie into what the product developers termed 'substantial' snacking territory. A slightly coffee-flavoured nougat layer floated above a palate-gouging base of cornflakes, rice and (until the mid-'80s) raisins suspended in a chocolate matrix. Clearly the name was a marketing retrofit to the technology that

**Opposite:** Brum brum. Birmingham's Double Decker (1976), featuring the original raisin recipe.

**Below:** Room for one more up top? Opportunities for double entendre are criminally wasted in a 1983 ad.

enabled such choccy bar apartheid but it immediately invoked a definitive symbol of Britishness. Tall, uniquely constructed and recognised all over the world. Not buying one was bally well unpatriotic, what?

So who better to embody such sterling stoicism than satirist, comedian and actor Willie Rushton, jabbering his way through a solo 'crunchy or chewy?' debate on the TV ads? Well, er, maybe Cliff Richard. Or Melvin Hayes. Or anyone else from *Summer Holiday* that the public might more immediately identify with a rear-loading Routemaster to help promote this between-meals bus fare. (Typical! You wait ages for a likely celeb to endorse your product then three come along at once.)

In 1983 there emerged Dougie, the Double Decker dog, a predictably furry man-in-a-suit mascot who toured the country giving away bars at the likes of Pontin's, before it was decided he should go away 'to live on a special farm'. The concurrent telly campaign featured the incongruous arrival of a Cadbury-liveried bus at unsuspecting punters' places of work just when they felt 'a bit peckish'. Convenient for elevenses, yes, but pity the poor pensioners already aboard, hawked hither and thither on their journey to the post office.

Sold as 'the double filling bar for the double filling feeling' Double Decker was no doubt the favourite of innuendo-loving bus drivers everywhere. Yet, where were the specially designed chocolate bars for other RMT union members? London Underground staff arguably had the tube of Smarties, and road freight was all wrapped up in Yorkie, but mainline rail, shipping and offshore, or any number of other transport-sector workers, were criminally ignored. In fact, it may only be comic association with the cheeky clippies and malingering conductors of LWT's *On the Buses* that allowed the Double Decker to remain in service. Although the TV show was long gone by the time Double Decker rolled up, Cadbury's PR bods more than missed a trick not reuniting Stan, Jack, Olive et al. for one final excursion to adland, especially considering Blakey even came equipped with his own snack-friendly slogan-cum-gag, i.e. 'Did you eat that Double Decker, Inspector?' 'No, I 'ate you, Butler!'

**'As "the double filling bar for the double filling feeling" Double Decker was no doubt the favourite of innuendo-loving bus drivers everywhere.'**

## ✻ CURLY WURLY

Cadbury entered the 1970s in reflective mood. Mars was the problem. Their big-hitters – filled bars in the Marathon, Mars or Milky Way mould – were cleaning up, while Cadbury's sedate blocks were primarily successful with only the older, and significantly less impulsive, customer. No one bought and scoffed three bars of Fruit 'n' Nut in an afternoon break. (Or at least, if they did, they kept quiet about it.)

**Opposite:** Cadbury's make with the 'miles of chewy toffee.' Curly Wurly (1970).

**Below:** They really should've called the kid Short. Curly the moose and pal seek Curly Wurly Club members in 1982.

Cadbury already had the Crunchie under Fry's imprimatur, but recent innovations had met with varied results. Their best shot was the Aztec, but even that was losing to the celestially named behemoths from Slough. Cloning Mars products was a fool's errand, so Cadbury's technicians started thinking outside the bar. One outlandish design, a braided lattice of three caramel laces, seemed to fit the bill. A pleasingly wacky shape inside, and it dwarfed its rivals on the shelves by dint of sheer scale: as Malcolm Tucker reminisced in *The Thick of It*, 'the size of a small ladder'.

This was the confectioner's Holy Grail: give them less, but convince them it's more. It worked a treat. A focus group of 100 children were given a bar to munch, then asked if they'd rather have a sixpence or another Curly Wurly. Only seven plumped for the cash, but history doesn't record whether that was due to the new bar, or the knowledge that, with decimalisation round the corner, chocolate was probably a better investment than a moribund tanner.

The bar launched in a blaze of publicity. TV ads featured Terry Scott as a Bunterish schoolboy causing good-natured, sugar-fuelled havoc in assorted public buildings, in every commercial break ITV had to offer between noon and teatime. Never before had chocolate been so heavily marketed: the sweet old days of George Lazenby stomping down a gangplank with an outsize replica Fry's bar had given way to an orgy of mass media exposure, making the Curly Wurly, in Cadbury's humble estimation, 'the success story of post-war confectionery'.

Such success, inevitably, spawned imitators. Within two years, homages appeared in Canada, Germany, Japan and the US (where Mars confused a generation of holidaying Brits by naming their faux-Wurly Marathon). Nothing could beat the original, though, not even the 1980s scrapping of the decreasingly schoolboyish Scott in favour of a frankly bizarre campaign featuring a moose in American football gear and a spookily silent child. All very odd, but the Curly Wurly was now the institution Cadbury had longed for, and the kids wrote off in their thousands to East Molesey for Curly Wurly Club packs and badges. You only needed ten wrappers to join, too. Terry Scott could've managed that in an afternoon.

## * FLAKE

Here come the girls! Some twenty-odd of them down the years, in fact; each one winsomely wrapping her lips around a fat, ribbed shaft of sweet, delicious chocolate in a series of adverts increasingly intent on steaming up the glasses of nervous, starch-collared middle managers the land over. Such simmering sensuality may have been lost on runny-nosed rug rats, but dads were

**Opposite:** Breaking the mould. Flake (1920) – as unique as a fingerprint, they say. But tastier.

**Below:** The Lady of the Flake? Cadbury's adds very little to the Arthurian canon, circa 1970.

reportedly consumed on the spot by a terrible lust, which must have been quite off-putting if you were trying to make a cuppa in the middle of *3-2-1*.

In fact, back in the early black and white era, Flake girls fantasised about nothing more exciting than waterfalls, pony-trekking and 'sixpence-worth of heaven', which is hardly bonkbuster territory. (No mention of a tuppence, for starters.) It took the creative muscle of Norman Icke (also responsible for the Curly Wurly and Milk Tray ads) and Ronnie Bond (not the Troggs ex-drummer) to forge the cast-iron classic 'Only the crumbliest, flakiest chocolate' jingle and remind us it 'tastes like chocolate never tasted before', although they singularly failed to point out that it also drops crumbs down your shirt and onto Mum's best cushions like never before. Presumably the Flake girls took to so seductively unwrapping their choc bars al fresco 'cos they were sick and tired of being nagged about leaving tell-tale specks on the sofa.

Thenceforth, colour television was treated to a heavy rotation of soft-focus semi-erotic vignettes set in fields bursting with poppies or sunflowers, and plots involving runaway gypsy caravans, untethered rowing boats, and sudden summer downpours. (All the better for drenching those doe-eyed beauties in their clingy, sheer and see-through clothes, eh, lads?) Through the '70s and '80s a succession of sultry models succumbed to the Flake's mouth-watering chocolate charms, including former Miss World Eva Rueber-Staier (whose ad was pulled, such was its perceived lasciviousness), royal squeeze Catrina Skepper (trading in Prince Andrew for something slightly less ostentatious) and, in 1987, Debbie Leng, scantily clad and draped, legs akimbo, in the window seat of a chateau while a gecko scuttled inexplicably across an unattended phone. (The lizard 'suggested the exotic' claimed Icke later. Leng herself went on to marry Roger Taylor of Queen fame. Draw your own conclusions there.) Arguably the best-remembered of the ads, however, featured Scouse Lisa Stansfield lookalike Rachel Brown luxuriating in an overflowing bath. Prime spoof-fodder for the likes of Jasper Carrott ('Here's your problem, love. It's Flake wrappers in the plughole'), the ad also attained legendary playground status when

rumours circulated that 'the girl in it overdosed on Ecstasy and ended up in the nuthouse'. (Chinese whispers, as it turns out: Brown was hospitalised after allegedly being spiked with Class As at a birthday party and made a full recovery.)

However, that flooded Venetian bathroom coincidentally harks back to Cadbury's initial inspiration for the Flake, as it was a lowly factory employee who spotted that excess chocolate spilling from the moulds cascaded down in a stream of thin sheets, creating a distinctive texture. Never, it must be said, has an industrial accident been repackaged so successfully and sold so pruriently. Mars's similarly phallic chocolate log, the Ripple, failed to chop down the mighty Flake, possibly because it didn't have a powerhouse creative marketing team behind it, possibly because it was noticeably that bit smaller, or possibly just because it rhymed with 'nipple'. A rebrand in 1987 saw Ripple embraced into the premium Galaxy fold, and 1992 added further length and girth to the bar, making it immediately more popular with women. Tsk! Typical. And, though even Cadbury have long since axed A-rated allusions to fellatio from their branding campaign, it will be a good while yet before those Flake ads drop out of any bloke's top ten sexiest/sexist formative moments.

---

**'Flake girls fantasised about waterfalls, pony-trekking and "sixpenceworth of heaven", which is hardly bonkbuster territory.'**

---

**Opposite:** Like water for chocolate. Flake ads get steamy circa 1991.

**Below:** Maltesers (1936), Mars Ltd's brown ball substitute for mini-snooker tables.

## BAG 'EM UP

Milton Hershey, straw-boatered, moustachioed caramel toffee manufacturer of Pennsylvania, had toured Europe's great chocolate manufacturers in the late 1800s, and, upon his return, built a factory of his own. Rather than sensibly nicking the recipe off the Swiss like everyone else in the trade, he set about reinventing the wheel and tried to create a chocolate blend from scratch. This trial and error period lasted for years and, even then, the product ended up – at best – a little sour. (Or, at worst, a little cheesy, vomity and baby-sicky; to this day it remains at odds with British taste buds.) One of his earliest successes, however, was the small, teardrop-shaped Hershey's Kiss (named after popular Italian chocolates, Baci). In 1907 they started shipping across America inside bags intended for sharing.

Back in Blighty, Cadbury had already introduced a similar product, Choc Drop (later to be rebranded as Cadbury's Buttons, coyly positioned as 'chocolate for beginners', and pushed via cosy, *Jackanory*-style adverts starring Felicity Kendal or some other woolly-jumpered fairytale-narrator). Moreover, Hershey's entire *mode d'emploi* was an homage to the Cadbury family: the garden village built to house employees, the schools to educate their children, and the museums of chocolate production. Though, while the British chocolate manufacturers were faint in condemnation of the foreign slave labour that brought cocoa to their factories, Hershey's response was to build another, equally altruistic version of his 'chocolate town' in Cuba. He was a generous bloke.

Not so generous the punters munching their way through countless chocs, though, eh? So much for 'share and share alike', a phrase largely credited to Daniel Defoe, writing *Robinson Crusoe* in 1719. But surely even his famous island castaway would have baulked at going halves on a bag of Revels. If you bought your choccies on Thursday, there's very little chance you'd save some for Friday.

It's a human failing the confectioners capitalised on: for good reason are these so-called 'sharing' bags known in the trade as selflines. Add to that the fact that anything sold bagged-up means the consumer is paying for 50 per cent air, and you have an irresistible recipe for profit.

It isn't entirely mercenary, however. There's an element of alchemy involved. Small morsels of chocolate melt more quickly on the tongue which, in turn, affects the taste. Bung a coating of sugar on the outside and they can be carried around for a lot longer than a horrid, melty choccy bar. An observation not lost on Forrest Mars, inspired – so the official story tells – by Spanish Civil War soldiers eating pellets of chocolate that 'did not melt in the hand' on the long walk to the front line. (Cynics might point out that Rowntree's Smarties had been on the scene a good forty years by then and even they were unlikely to have been the first of their kind.) While fellow American Hershey lacked a foothold in the European market, Mars turned his eyes on Britain and slowly, surely drew his plans against us.

For a start, his Maltesers were already rolling off the production lines. (Sometimes literally: the factory cleaners' preferred solution was to stamp on them before sweeping up the mess.) Light, chocolate-covered malt balls, they were originally marketed as 'non-fattening' Energy Balls intended to 'deliver the taste of malted milk'. Nice. A later campaign concentrated on 'the honeycomb middle that weighs so little': so little, in fact that in 1967 Mars Ltd found themselves in trouble with Trading Standards' weights and measures division for overestimating how heavy the packs actually were.

**Opposite:** 'Chocolates? No, Maltesers!' A tut-tutting advert circa 1981. But it's a lifetime on the hips for Galaxy Counters (1967).

**Below:** Men from Mars. Minstrels (1976).

Just round the M25, George Payne was preparing to dispatch the first consignment of chocolate-covered sweets from his Croydon factory. Poppets (a nickname he'd given his daughter) hit the nation's cinema lobbies in 1937, in boxes designed for vending machines although not, it seemed, for human hands to open. By the rock 'n' roll heyday of the '50s, teddy boys and girls could break their flick-knives trying to hack into more than twenty variant flavours, among them the all-nut assortment, cherries, nougat, jellies and brazils (yet to acquire the 'Just' prefix).

The Poppet name faded in and out of favour over the next few decades (memorably returning as Skokets rice puffs in 1970, Super Poppets in '76 and Toffets in the '80s) before rallying in time for a 1985 advert featuring a Max Wall-voiced octopus who encouraged us all to 'get shaking'.

As had Rowntree before, with their 'cool milk' Cabanas, one of many fleeting attempts to harness the power of the portable chocolate drop. See also: the early '70s casualties, Golden Wonder Chocomates (buttons, nuts and raisins, advertised by a maniacally gobbling Benny Hill) and Trebor Pips. Galaxy Counters fared better, bunging animal characters on the packets and giving away origami kits (Olly Owl, Percy Penguin, Geoffrey Giraffe, etc.).

At a stretch, they could even be pitched as a learning tool, because each chocolate disc had a different number printed on it: 'Look, Mummy, I've got this many fillings.' Smarties also encroached into the classroom, commissioning Spanish painter and architect José María Cruz Novillo to create animal alphabet posters. Lucky they didn't choose Salvador Dalí – those clocks he painted had a tendency to melt in your hand, in your mouth, over landscapes, or anywhere.

With the candy-coating problem solved, Mars's attack on Britain began with Treets. Their three-pronged assault in 1976 took on Rowntree at the toffee, peanut and chocolate fronts. Treets appropriated the 'melt in the mouth' slogan lock, stock and barrel from their Yankee cousins, while fellow travellers Minstrels ('They sound candy crisp, they taste chocolate smooth') would also occasionally benefit from the same tagline. It was a time of great uncertainty. Toffee Treets became Relays in 1983, Minstrels were saved only by a move up to the floor marked 'Galaxy' and Peanut Treets were quietly scrapped at the tender age of eleven. Mars, it seemed, had been playing the long game. Its early M&Ms adverts had tested well, in the Tyne Tees region, for a full two years before the official launch in 1987. The balloon went up. The other chocolate makers readied to shoot it down.

Cadbury immediately set to work on a new project, codenamed Minder. Sadly, this wasn't to be an Arthur Daley-endorsed chocolate delicacy for 'Er Indoors, but instead a 'new, adult, functional, profusion line' (an obfuscating industry term for what were basically coated caramel, biscuit and raisin titbits).

**'If it can be crammed into a big pouch and priced for 'sharing', it's in the shops before you can say Toffee Buttons.'**

**Opposite:** No meen feet. The indomitable Treets (1976) hold their own against M&Ms into the 21st century.

**Below:** Cadbury's suffers from Stroller blindness (1991), but Buttons (1960) survive the baked-in-a-pie treatment.

Four long years later, they finally emerged; the appositely named Strollers, casually wandering into sweet shops to the tune of Black's 'Wonderful Life' (truly the most depressing song ever to feature in an advert), and sporting a revolutionary foil bag to ensure an unprecedented nine-month shelf life. In the end, a lack of popularity ensured nine months was about all they needed.

Nestlé, too, thought they had it in them to provide a 'point of difference', with white chocolates in a dark candy shell, and vice versa. But the British public were not in favour of such continental meretriciousness and steered clear in their droves. Neither a drop in price, nor the offer of 10 per cent extra free could tempt them, so Vice Versas were taken out of circulation. A similar fate also beset Bassett's Quirks, a chocolate mint developed, as these things so often are, as a result of an agreement with a Finnish chocolate company. Though, in fairness, it probably didn't help that they were described in public by the Bassett chairman as 'panned chocolate lentils'.

These days, if it can be crammed into a big pouch and priced for 'sharing', it's in the shops before you can say Toffee Buttons (another '60s frippery rebranded and relaunched in recent years as the assorted droppings of the Cadbury's Caramel bunny). Buttons have turned giant, Galaxy Counters and Payne's Poppets live on to fight another day. Even Hershey's, roundly critical of advertising practices until the 1970s, finally made it overseas, with Kisses materialising on UK supermarket shelves in 2011. Which just goes to show, all good things come to those who wait. As do all things cheesy, vomity and baby-sicky.

## ✻ REVELS

In the confectionery business, you're onto a winner if you can give the impression of offering more for less, and Mars took that precept to the limit with Revels, which must have been the cheapest product to launch in sweet-making history. After all, Maltesers and Galaxy Counters were already going, and the peanut and toffee varieties would be recycled as Treets a few years later. The only 'true' Revels were the coconut and

**Opposite:** Let the revels commence! Mars' motley medley (1967)

**Below:** : Bags more for everyone? Bagsy those uneaten chocs, more like. TV ad, circa 1978.

orange (later coffee) cream-centred chocs, which, perhaps tellingly, are the ones that compete for status of 'most hated flavour' in folk mythology.

The thriftiness extended to the advertising campaigns, with cheeky newsagents admonishing, 'You can't buy a box of chocolates for sixpence, sonny!' Post-decimalisation, the comparison was eked out in a recession-busting commercial wherein a half-pound bag of Revels was poured into an empty chocolate box, filling it to the brim in a most satisfying way. (The inconvenient truth that boxes of chocolates have always been pretty rotten value for money was tactfully ignored.)

As well as the impression of abundance on the cheap, Revels got into the underage public consciousness via the many opportunities their multifarious nature offered for juvenile mucking about (for kids, food you can fart about with invariably sits higher up the cultural pecking order than food that's only good for stuffing in your gob). Peanut-allergic comedian Milton Jones reminisced about school bullies forcing him to play Russian roulette with a bag in the playground, a gag which Mars, thrifty to the last, 'borrowed' for a *Deer Hunter*-parodying ad in 2002. You can't buy an ad campaign for sixpence, sonny...

**'The only 'true' Revels were the coconut and orange (later coffee) cream-centred chocs, which, perhaps tellingly, are the ones that compete for status of "most hated flavour".'**

## * SMARTIES

In common with most British confectioners of the nineteenth century, Henry Isaac Rowntree, cocoa merchant and denizen of York society, also acquired and published a newspaper. Preoccupied thereafter with matters of the fourth estate, he decided, in 1881, to entrust his brother, the philanthropist and social reformer Joseph Rowntree, with building a new chocolate factory. The first new

**Opposite:** 'How many tubes would it take to go round the Underground?' Only Smarties (1937) have the answer.

**Below:** Bean feast. Smarties Eggheads are a hollow victory, circa 1977.

products to roll off the conveyor belt twelve months later were small, colourful beans modelled on French dragées, sold loosely in bags to little tykes and bigwigs alike. Unfortunately, Henry died within a year, while Joseph's business went from strength to strength; proof if any were needed that chocolate is good for you, whereas journalism can be fatal.

Fast-forward to 1937 (the peak of snack food's very own age of light and innovation) and the beans were now being packaged in cardboard tubes and familiarly trademarked as Smarties (in the UK only, short-sightedly letting an American candy maker hijack the name across the Atlantic). Skip forward again, to 1959, and someone had the bright idea of introducing a plastic cap with a random letter of the alphabet on as 'an attractive plaything for children'. Strangely, the nation's letters to Santa that Christmas still resolutely favoured Barbie, Frisbees and Sea Monkeys. The real stroke of genius was taking out the disgusting coffee-flavoured ones the year before: take note, Revels.

In the following decades, a generation of swinging '60s kids learned to 'buy some for Lulu', while the hyperactive, multicultural, singing and dancing 'Smarties scene' did for the '70s (at least until the International Trade Group insisted on the removal of the phrase 'chocolate beans' in order to avoid confusing those few French people who were spoiling their cassoulets). In the '80s, Rowntree threw in their lot with the British National Book League to offer the Smarties Prize for Children's Literature (igniting another 'is it all right to rot your teeth, as long as you're expanding your mind?' ethical debate among metropolitan middle-class commentators). Monster-sized tubes, square sharing boxes, Easter eggs (and Eggheads) all made an appearance, as did hyperactive, multi-channel, singing and dancing CGI adverts courtesy of top pixel-wranglers Robinson Lambie-Nairn. Then, as the '90s dawned, not long after the introduction of blue Smarties, the ultimate tribute: a rubbish chart hit by a rave outfit styling themselves 'the Smart E's'. The similarity between Henry Isaac's chocolate beans and house music's disco biscuits has often been questioned, particularly by the tabloid press he'd so keenly wanted to be part of. It just goes to show: chocolate can be good for you, but techno is fatal.

## ✻ REESE'S PIECES

If you asked any British kid in 1982 what E.T.'s favourite sweets were the chances are they'd tell you they weren't allowed to talk to strangers and run off. Hooray! Those public information films weren't a total waste of money, then. But ask the same question in the States and you'd receive an ebullient reply: 'Reese's Pieces!' Spielberg's interstellar goblin conquered cinemas and hearts clutching a

**Opposite:** Exquisite. Exotic. Extra-terrestrial. Reese's Pieces (1978), arguably the first truly intergalactic product placement.

**Below:** Rich E.T. biscuits. Britain's altogether more urbane take on the 'phone home' phenomenon (1983).

handful of Hershey's own peanut butter 'candies', though they would remain unknowable to the UK until 1996.

To add to the confusion, William Kotzwinkle's novelisation of the film was worked up from an older draft of the screenplay and so made prominent mention of M&Ms (which, themselves, wouldn't debut in Britain's sweet shops proper until the late '80s), because it was originally intended that the bug-eyed gastronaut would chomp on those instead. Oh, for want of 'find and replace', eh, Bill? It's a small inconsistency but one that throws some light on a huge behind-the-scenes battle for supremacy in the market for tiny chocolate beans.

But who copied whom? Forrest Mars had originally taken his proposition to the Hershey factory and, while he couldn't convince the company to buy his idea, soon bagged himself a business partner in R. Bruce Murrie, son of the then president. With borrowed machinery and a contract to supply American GIs with bags of the candies for war rations, production began in 1940 on their eponymous M&Ms. Murrie, not having much of a taste for the chocolate industry, didn't stick around for long, though his initial lives on.

Hershey-Ets were M&Ms' nearest rival, though ironically not in the eyes of the Extra-Terrestrial, who favoured the 'peanuche' middle of Reese's Pieces. Mars, of course, had turned down the opportunity to be associated with the all-conquering alien and famously lost out on a killer product placement deal. It later transpired that Jack Dowd, marketing manager for Hershey, had signed the contract with Universal Pictures sight unseen and had no idea how ugly the creature was until it was unveiled at a private screening for his staff much later. Though, after trebling sales in a matter of weeks off the back of the movie's endorsement, it's no surprise that Hershey bosses were happy to go on record as saying E.T. was quite, quite beautiful.

**'E.T. conquered cinemas clutching a handful of Hershey's peanut butter 'candies', though they would remain unknowable to the UK until 1996.'**

**Opposite:** Everyone likes a box of chocs that can keep schtum. The discreet Rowntree's Black Magic (1933).

**Below:** 'All the fun of the share.' Quality Street (1936); big, round and purple. Milk Tray; tall, dark and handsome. Auntie Joan; full, fat and queasy.

## AND ALL BECAUSE...

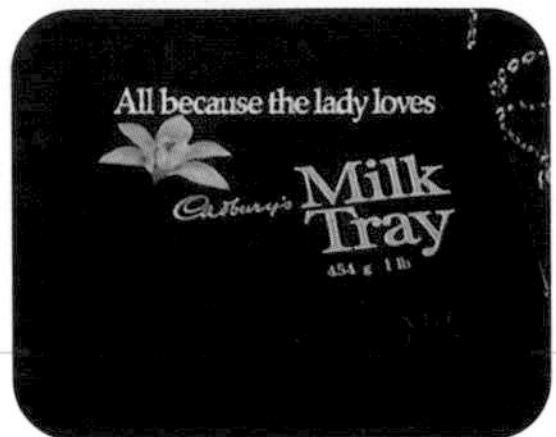


It's no shock that the boxed chocolate assortment was an invention of those ever-sentimental Victorians. It's perhaps a little surprising to see how much of the standard formula was in place from the very first British attempt. The Cadbury Brothers introduced their tempting Fancy Box in 1869, four ounces of sensuous creams with come-hither titles like Chocolat du Mexique, or Chocolat des Delices aux Fruits. To top it all off, Richard Cadbury himself provided cute paintings for the lids, including, yes, one of a small girl holding a kitten.

Exotic variety, poncy names, cutesy artwork: the mould was cast. Soon, familiar names appeared: Cadbury's Milk Tray in 1918 (formerly the Savoy Assortment), Terry's All Gold in 1931. Rowntree, not being quite at home with chocolate making, came relatively late to the party, but made up for tardiness with canny marketing. A thrown-together box, Tried Favourites, stiffed in 1927, sending them back to the drawing boards, during which they planned, sifted and market-tested their follow-up for six years.

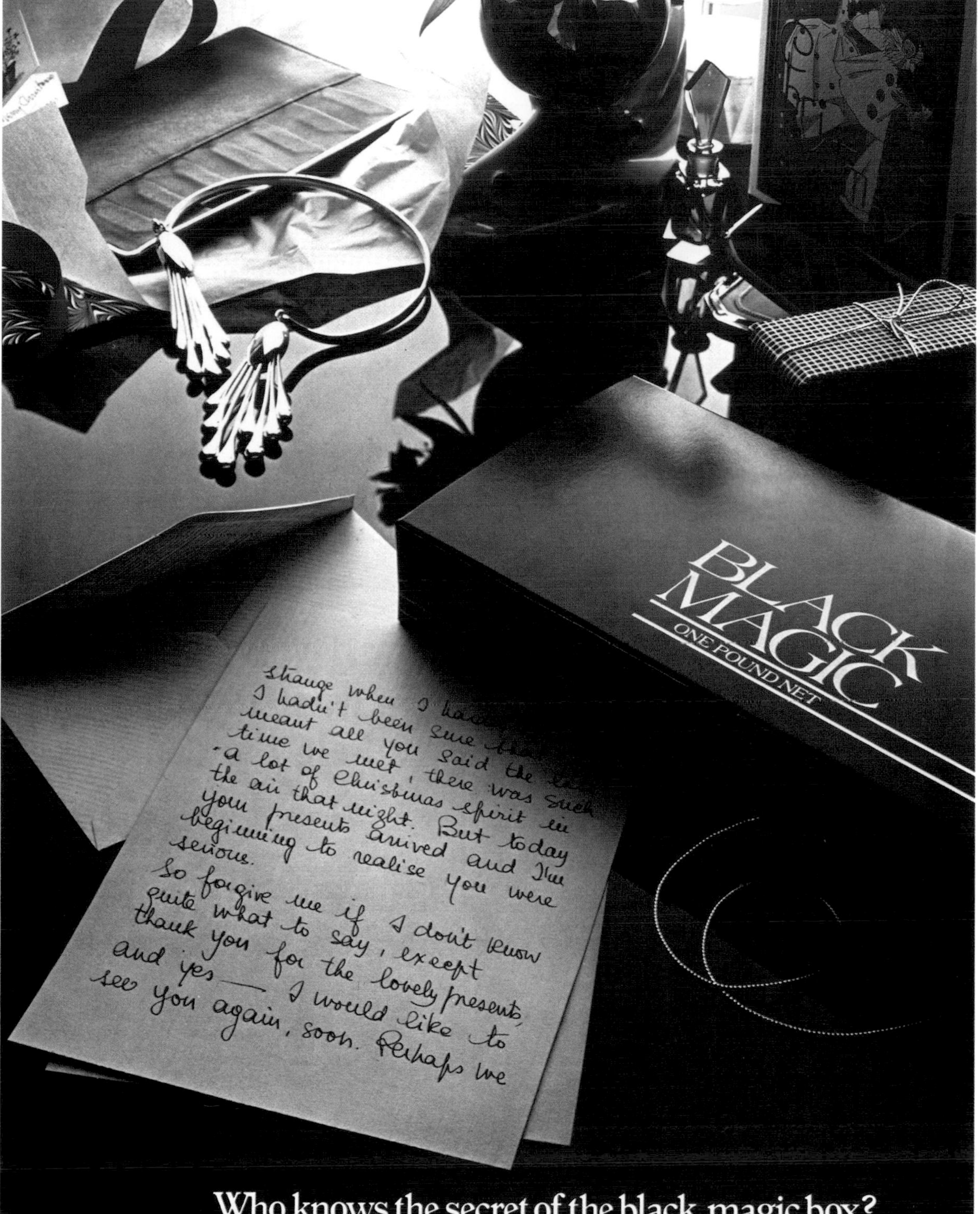
BLACK
MAGIC
ONE POUND NET
strange when I
I hadn't been sure
meant all you said the
time we met, there was such
a lot of Christmas spirit in
the air that night. But today
your presents arrived and I'm
beginning to realise you were
serious.
So forgive me if I don't know
quite what to say, except
thank you for the lovely presents,
and yes — I would like to
see you again, soon. Perhaps we
Who knows the secret of the black, magic box?

The all-plain Black Magic was the result of nationwide surveys of 7,000 people and 2,500 shops, which established that these things were indeed bought mainly for women by guilty men. Three years later, the milkier Dairy Assortment, later Dairy Box, went directly for Milk Tray's crown. Both were promoted by advertising campaigns of astonishing ferocity. Suddenly everyone else was playing catch-up.

Mackintosh opened up a new front in 1936, with the release of Quality Street. Two innovations were notable here: the mixture of chocolates and plain toffees with individual cellophane wrappers, cheaper and more cheerful than the usual chocs; and the start of nostalgic packaging. The assortment was named after a fluffy West End hit from the pen of J.M. Barrie, concerning the romantic fiddle-faddlings of society girl Phoebe Throssel and the dashing Captain Valentine Brown during the Napoleonic Wars, who were pictured en promenade on the box, albeit renamed Miss Sweetly and Major Quality.

**Opposite:** 'She'll love it if you bring her chocolates. She'll love you if they're Dairy Box (1936).' She might be slightly less impressed by the Milk Tray bar, mind.

**Below:** The end of milk and plain apartheid is ill met by Terry's Moonlight (1972). Roses (1938), on the other hand, grow on you.

A film of the play with Katharine Hepburn serendipitously came out the following year – and tanked. But the chocolates sold enough for Cadbury to launch their twisty spoiler, Roses, in 1938, starting a two-way battle that's been a seasonal fixture ever since. Others have tried to get a foothold, like Rowntree's short-lived Tokens in 1962, and Harlequin, Terry's 'assortment of magical tastes' in 1985, but whether in cardboard trapezoid or massive great tin, the two giants held sway.

Chocolate boxes proper, meanwhile, were resorting to variations on a theme. Cadbury hit upon the idea of combining milk and plain in the same box, though this being 1962, Contrast still segregated them onto separate trays. (When Terry's created the similar Moonlight ten years later, they shared the same tray, but were still kept very much apart.) For Mackintosh, it was a quest for the ever-fancier assortment.

Their Week-End of 1956 presented a Technicolor spectacular under the lid, enlisting hot pink cup cake cases, green fondant and candied peel segments to jazz up the standard brown brigade. In 1960 Good News featured a similarly exotic line-up on the inside of the lid, as immortalised by George Harrison in the lyrics for 'Savoy Truffle'. Terry's, meanwhile, looked back, using their 200-year history as a springboard for the antiquated 1767 assortment, all done out like a sealed royal parchment. This lavish box, with its sturdy build and sliding trays, had a serviceable afterlife as the 'secret gubbins' hideaway of many a '70s child.

**'Exotic variety, poncy names, cutesy artwork it's no shock that the boxed chocolate assortment was an invention of those ever-sentimental Victorians.'**

Mainly, though, it was the big three of Milk Tray, Black Magic and All Gold. Milk Tray tended to top the seasonal charts, helped by a James Bond knock-off ad campaign instigated in 1968 by the Leo Burnett agency, which peaked with a jaw-dropping helicopter-to-ocean dive that put stuntman Alf Joint in intensive care, and even inspired Waddington's to launch a *Man in Black* board game. From 1947, the brand was supplemented by the Milk Tray bar, eight popular centres wodged together into a misshapen block, a ploy Rowntree copied for a ten-segment Dairy Box bar in 1975. (A later Black Magic bar cheated, by being just plain chocolate.)

The fanciful names given to individual chocs, the better to tempt those indecisively wandering fingers, are the stuff of legend. The Quiet Beatle may have favoured 'a ginger sling with a pineapple heart', but this was the tip of the romanticised iceberg. Some, like Dairy Box's Caramont, aimed for sophistication, but ended up sounding like a retired couple's Broadstairs bungalow. Others were on surer footing: Black Magic's Montelimar is named after southern France's 'world capital of nougat', you know. The occasional bit of anti-sophistication was soon ironed out: Quality Street's Toffee Penny laboured for years under the apt, if less enticing, moniker of Toffee Pat.

The 1980s brought a new variation: the un-assortment. Terry's Neapolitans had introduced the idea in the '70s, a tapered box of identical chocolate segments wrapped up like bars, but at least the flavours varied. Once you'd eaten one Ferrero Rocher, however, you'd eaten them all, although that didn't stop the nutty ball invasion from taking off in no uncertain terms in 1982. Within three years British rivals were punted out, but neither Rowntree's hazelnut and praline Eclipse, nor Cadbury's Wishes, a self-confessed 'quick and nasty' response to Ferrero in rum and almond, did much to dent the inexorable rise of the diplomat's favourite.

**Opposite:** Terry's Neapolitans (1922), clearly an everyday kind of sweet. Whereas Mackintosh's Week-End, circa 1957...

Even in the reliable world of the assortment, things were moving on. Cadbury drafted suction-tipped robotic arms to stoke their chocolate trays, which worked fine until confronted with the rugged topography of the nut cluster. Quality Street did some hefty market research in the middle of the decade, altering the flavour mix as a result, to howls of anguish from many. (Twenty years later they backtracked slightly, releasing a limited edition bag of 'lost flavours', including the chocolate octagon and the sainted gooseberry cream.) Others fared even worse: Rowntree put the ailing Good News and Week-End out of their misery in 1988. The odd new product such as Cadbury's Biarritz, an unremarkable assortment that stood out by dint of its awkward triangular box, scarcely took up the slack, eventually bowing to angry shopkeepers by going rectangular in 1995 before vanishing, Bermuda-style, in '96.

Outliers came and went, the big names lumbered on, but the romance was fading from the chocolate box. Packaging was rationalised, with well-loved fripperies like the loose-leaf layer map and inter-layer corrugated divider phased out. Cadbury's Inspirations briefly revived the 'secret drawer' box, but it was too little, too late. Perhaps worst of all, the things could now be bought in petrol stations. Where's the romance in that? As any gentleman knew, nothing showed class and panache quite like a Woolworth's Price Blitz sticker.

The only serious rivals were Payne's no-nonsense Just Brazils and August Storck's hazelnut-in-caramel-cup line Toffifee, which was German in origin, and as a result prone to confused pronunciation, exacerbated by differing ad campaigns which called it 'Toff-eef-ee' or 'Toffi-fay', depending on the affluence of the demographic they were chasing that Christmas.

## * TERRY'S ALL GOLD

Though for years your bog-standard half-pound box o' chocs had been sold primarily to chivalrous, guilty or desperate men, never had the boat been pushed out further than by Terry's All Gold. Buying was no longer an act of obligation, it was about responding to a modern woman desirous of opulence and an altogether better class of chocolate. Just reading the names of the individual sweetmeats was an

**Opposite:** 'Alchemy! Alchemy! They've all got it alch...' No, that doesn't work. Terry's All Gold (1932).

**Below:** An admission of gilt? The posh chocolate payoff, circa 1982.

exercise in extravagance: Honeycomb Jewel, Russian Caramel, Chartreuse Bullion. The words themselves rolled around on the tongue long before the cocoa butter, invert sugar syrup and soya lecithin.

A cosmopolitan – some might say ecumenical – selection nestled in among the various kegs, ingots and clusters as were found in lesser assortments. No pick 'n' mix, this. If anything, Terry's All Gold aspired to exclusivity, conjuring up allusions to bespoke art collections, haute couture pieces, eclectic jeweller's windows... or some such other pretentious guff. The long-running ads only served to reinforce the sense of heritage, entitlement and implicit worth of the product. An upper-crust crooner of the Peter Skellern school entreated the viewer to 'see the face you love light up' as a porcelain-skinned chatelaine in an emerald organza dress ran lacquered fingernails across the box lid. Her tuxedo-clad beau remained at a respectful distance, half in shadow, confident in the knowledge he'd eventually be called upon to eat the one with the brazil nut in it. (The literal 'lighting up' of the loved one's face, a muted cascade of candlelight bouncing off metallic embossed cardboard, was an effect undoubtedly pinched wholesale by Quentin Tarantino for *Pulp Fiction*. What's in the mysteriously dazzling briefcase? Is it Marcellus Wallace's soul? No. It's the Lemon Barrel.)

Never more than in the acquisitive '80s, with its Spandau Ballet records, futures trading and Leeds Building Society savings accounts, was gold so much a symbol of ostentatious elitism and luxury. Nowadays, platinum is the new standard, but that's inflation for you. The phrase Terry's All Gold, on the other hand, has been relegated to the back pages of tabloid newspapers for use as a cheap headline about footballers. (Footballers called Terry, usually. That's how tabloids work.)

**'Terry's All Gold aspired to exclusivity, conjuring up allusions to bespoke art collections, haute couture pieces, or eclectic jeweller's windows.'**

## BEST-LAID PLANS

Which came first, the chocolate, or the egg? It may seem like it has been ever thus, but we have a relatively young industry to thank for this supermarket shelf-hogging symbol of Easter. Sure, people had fluffy yellow chicks and daffodils coming out of their ears each spring, but archaic traditions of egg painting and rolling had largely died out with the Victorians who chased them downhill (and most likely for that very reason). The pious old Quakers of British chocolate, on the other hand, saw an opportunity to marry their religious and commercial proclivities by resurrecting the egg in cocoa form. Luckily, the Society of Friends benefited from a lack of formal ministry, plus an increasingly vague definition of Lent when it came to the renunciation of chocolate. After all, there was nothing in the Bible about it: St Paul's letter to Ephesians didn't decree that their home-made Turkish Delight was off the menu, but then it was written some fifteen hundred years before Montezuma and Cortés traded cocoa beans and gold for Christianity and cultural oppression.

Also, the Quakers weren't particularly ones for observing religious festivals, preferring instead to adopt a policy of everyday simple living. Fry's first Easter egg, in 1873, was therefore a low-key affair, two welded halves of dark chocolate containing fruit-flavoured sweets. Cadbury replied two years later with a hollow milk chocolate effort, although both were still crumbly, sandy and somewhat harsh. Over in Switzerland, Rodolphe Lindt had found a way round that, an innovation he called 'conching' (kneading and blending chocolate to remove the grittiness and transform it into something altogether smoother). This technique almost single-handedly established the Swiss reputation as maître chocolatiers which, from 1952, also witnessed an annual, seasonal exodus of jingling, red-collared gold bunnies. Though let's not forgive them for inventing the cuckoo clock, eh?

**Opposite:** Bigger on the inside. Suchard's TARDIS-shaped Easter egg (1982).

**Below:** Inspiration for hidden DVD menu items since 1967. Cadbury's Easter eggs go Mini.

Suchard, which clearly regarded itself as the Carl Gustavovich Fabergé of Easter eggs, took to releasing a 'Spring Collection' brochure each year, featuring such mouth-watering objets d'oeuf as the Royale, the Elegance and the Privilege. The latter contained an assortment of dark chocolates and liqueurs inside a box emblazoned with a mandolin-strumming, bone china statuette, which either reeks of refinement or the flea market, depending on your upbringing. Less distinguished were the expedient '80s tie-ins with Peter Davison-era *Doctor Who* (particularly as the packaging graphics contrived to furnish the ancient Time Lord with a generous electric erection when viewed from certain angles) and the similarly phone-box-dwelling British Telecom mascot, Buzby.

Britain responded to the onslaught of Europe's chocolate soldiers with a spirited Easter uprising of its own. The big players established a reliable and regular range of crazy-paving-patterned eggs housed inside child-friendly cardboard animal shapes, masks and so on, alongside spherical iterations of their bestselling grown-up chocolate box lines. For the kids: Cadbury brought us the broody triumvirate of Henrietta, Harriet

'Traditions of egg painting and rolling had largely died out with the Victorians who chased them downhill (and most likely for that very reason).'

and Hilda Hens (all set to lay an abundance of candy-coated Mini Eggs); Rowntree filled their circus-themed eggs with Jelly Tots, Tiger Tots (liquorice allsorts) and Candy Tots (dolly mixtures); and Terry's hooked up with die-cast toy manufacturer Matchbox to conceal free hovercrafts, tractors and combine harvesters within a chocolate shell (any resulting broken teeth were to be considered a bonus). For the adults, highlights included: a paltry ration of five chocolates under the inaptly named Rowntree's Reward; the plastic vac-formed moon capsules of the Bournville Selection by Cadbury; and the utter metallic lunacy of Terry's Moonlight.

Competition was rife; each package more environmentally unfriendly than the one before, each cardboard construction more complex than the last. For a few short months every year the battle raged, like the World Wars preceding it, intense, bitter and richly flavoured. Mars, true to their American parentage, entered the fray late, sitting on the sidelines until finally dropping their own-brand eggs into confectionery's own Hiroshima in 1976.

Lest we forget, luxury was not solely the province of the Swiss. Home-grown high street outlet Thornton's lured a few continental chefs across *La Manche* and cornered the market in personalised, piped-icing eggs nestled in no-frills, paper-streamer-lined baskets. The '70s saw the rise of 'alternatives' to chocolate, including hideous soya and carob concoctions for vegans that bore only slim resemblance to their cocoa cousins. Neither could the poor escape the tyranny

**Opposite:** You do not want to see the hens that these bad boys came out of. Mackintosh's Toffee & Mallow and Rowntree's Fresh Minty Eggs (1982).

of the 'chocolate-flavour' egg, a market-bought, mug-bound impostor that failed to approximate either the taste or the texture of genuine chocolate and whose vendors must have been laughing all the way back to the waxworks.

The decade that restraint forgot further brought us the profit-driven, Easter-all-year-round appeal of filled eggs. Glimpsing Cadbury's indecently soft-creme-core steady seller, Mackintosh introduced small boxed selections of milk chocolate eggs stuffed full of soft toffee in 1977. Sister company Rowntree stuck with clown-covered chocolate cream eggs at first although, post-acquisition by Nestlé, eventually lobbed a Rolo Egg into the mix. Increasingly, it was an industry that was starting to resent limiting itself to the days between Holy Week and Whitsun. In the '80s, John Bradley, brand manager at Cadbury, carefully removed all explicit Easter identifiers from his product's boxes to prolong their shelf life: no more 'Good Friday feeling' for Crunchie, just a couple of bars under a generic milk chocolate egg.

Salvation was on its way. Back in 1972, Robert and Beryl Foskett, a Telford-based couple whose summer-only trade in freeze-pops was leading to lean darker months, had established the white-label Magna Foods company to license children's TV and toy names in egg form. Triumph soon rolled along in the shape of *Rupert Bear*, *Mr Men* and the *Munch Bunch*, while Norfolk rivals Kinnerton secured a lucrative Disney character deal. Between 1984 and 1989 alone, the UK market grew 77 per cent and, by 1990, Magna was shifting 18 million units a year. Britain had turned itself into another Easter island.

Suchard, now merged with Tobler, aimed to get back into Britons' good books (and, indeed, the record books) with the world's largest egg. It stood, tall as a double-decker bus and twice as delicious, throughout Liverpool's Spring Festival in 1987, before being melted down and dished out as smaller pieces in aid of Save the Children. Waddington's were drafted in to create novelty cartons that would appeal to the British sense of play. Even the annual catalogue displayed less ostentatious, more pastoral names: Medallion, Springtime, Reflections.

Then, in 1991, Britain finally gave in to the allure of Le Deux: dark truffle filling, cream and gold livery with, crucially, a Belgian chocolate exterior. Our foreigner-owned, sell-out, domestic companies had long since despaired. Belgian chocolate was the final nail in the crucifix. Yes, they could keep the punters shelling out for the familiar, uniform lines forever, but never in a month of Easter Sundays would they be able to come up with such an awesome egg-beater.

## * KINDER SURPRISE

The premise was set out in one of this notorious product's many ads. 'What do you want from the shops?' asks Mother, her flashing white teeth and badly dubbed voice indicating she is not of Bermondsey stock. 'Something exciting! And a toy!' reply her equally un-British offspring. 'And some chocolate!' Does she sit them down and give a one-hour lecture on the harsh realities of domestic economics? No.

**Opposite:** Kinder Surprise (1974), illegal in the States due to having 'a non-nutritive object imbedded.' Presumably they don't mean the white chocolate.

**Below:** Buy one, or he will dine on your very soul. Ferrero accidentally commissions Hieronymus Bosch to develop its TV campaign, circa 1984.

'But that's three things!' she instead responds, in the unfazed, bubbly laugh of someone who's mixing her prescriptions in cavalier fashion, and merrily trips off to satisfy their exorbitant demands.

The solution comes in the form of Ferrero's happy creation, which arrived on these shores in 1975: a semi-edible ovoid matryoshka in which a two-tone chocolate shell concealed a Mexican jumping bean-like plastic capsule, which in turn held the pieces of a rudimentary self-assembly plastic toy (always a pirate galleon in the early years, it seemed). It was the archetypal jack-of-all-trades: the chocolate was okay, the toy inevitably ground into the carpet within minutes, and the capsule itself was handy for filling with gravel and throwing at dogs or, for advanced users, gastro-intestinal contraband smuggling.

At first the UK egg market proved hard to crack, thanks mainly to the mighty presence of the Cadbury's Creme variety. A steady war of attrition commenced, boosted by unmistakable ads such as the above, and a nightmarish effort that was to live on in the long, dark nights of an entire generation's soul, featuring a boggle-eyed Humpty homunculus speaking in a gobbledegook patter that must have made Stanley Unwin consultibold his solicitaro. 'Doubly chockadooby!' was the freak's endorsement of the continental treat, only slightly undermined by the qualifying statement, 'Me screwball now!'

Still, it got people looking in Kinder's direction, and the little orange and white critters took their place in a popular culture that was just entering its ironic sweet-mocking middle age. The '90s saw a move away from the generic DIY playthings to a cannily collectable range of anthropomorphic zoological gangs. The Teeny Terrapins, Crazy Crocos, Leoventurers, Happy Hippos and their assorted descendants have filled summer holiday ad breaks with their head-slapping singalong antics ever since. Kinder Surprise: it's a state of mind. Unhinged, to be precise.

**'It was the archetypal jack-of-all-trades: the chocolate was okay, the toy inevitably ground into the carpet within minutes, and the capsule itself was handy.'**

## ✻ CREME EGG

Though various fondant-filled eggs had been produced by Cadbury since 1923, it wasn't until decimalisation that the Brummie confectioners finally cracked it with the consumer. That consummate assemblage of foil wrapper, chocolate shell, thick sugary albumen and all-important yolk centre debuted amid precious little fanfare. (Readers in Scotland had their own chocolate-filled egg.)

**Opposite:** Easter bon-bonnet. Cadbury's Creme Egg (1971).

**Below:** Resistance is useless. The Obergruppenführer of seasonal advertising, circa 1984. Plus Cadbury's chocolate-filled Border Creme Egg, circa 1977.

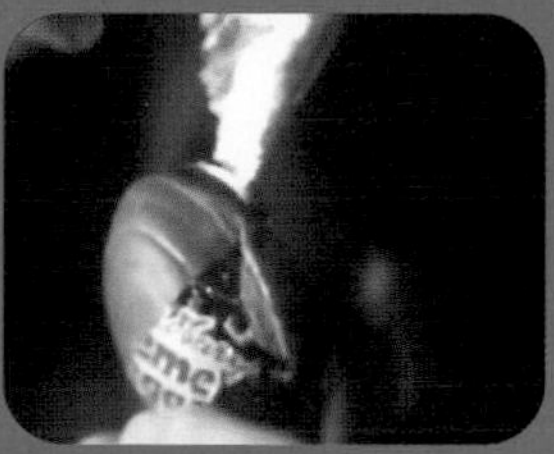

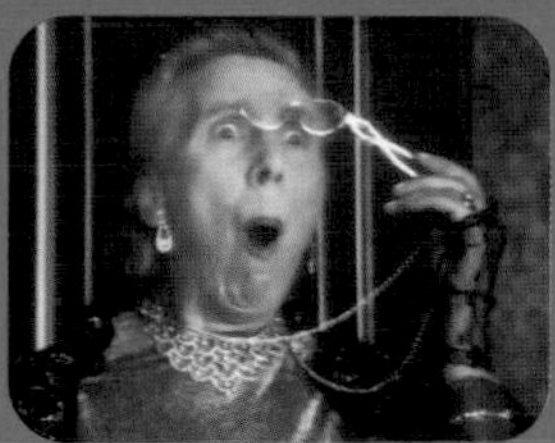

A short TV spot encouraging the customary Jennings-like schoolchildren to overwhelm shopkeepers with demands for '6,000 Creme Eggs, please' failed to take into account the limited means of the audience. But the marketers persisted and eventually hatched a television campaign based around a reworking of Cole Porter's genteel and only slightly racist song, 'Let's Do It', which saw all manner of shy debutantes, maiden aunts and girls in France falling for the irresistible charms of the ovoid snack. Impressionable kids scrambled to empty their piggy banks and helped boost sales from around 50 million in the mid-'70s to nearly 200 million by the early '80s.

In 1984 Cadbury's creative agency, Triangle, no doubt spurred on by the success of *Masquerade*, Kit Williams's kids' book, conceived an unashamedly derivative national treasure hunt for twelve golden eggs. Caskets were buried in far-flung corners of the countryside (though one, discovered accidentally, nearly blew the lid off the whole enterprise) and Creme Egg fans were invited to send off for, and solve, the *Conundrum*. Within three months, Cadbury had to call a press conference to halt overzealous punters digging up stone circles, hill forts and Christian burial sites in search of the £10,000 ('Garrards certified retail value') eggs. As far as slogans go, 'Stop looking on or around Pendle Hill and the Wrekin' is about as off-brand as you can get.

However, all this hedge-hopping hadn't gone unnoticed and Cadbury's rivals soon poached the egg idea for their own retail lines. Rowntree introduced both the Toffee Mallow and Fresh Minty Egg (in 1982), and Terry's hit back with the Nutcracker (ostensibly the same shape, only wrinkled, filled with caramel and nuts), then, in 1988, the ill-advised 'indulgent novelty' that was the Pyramint. Aimed at an older market, and fabulously advertised by the voice-artist dream-team of Leslie Phillips and Kenneth Williams, both hamming it up for all they were worth with an Egyptian mummy, it was a massive flop.

Too large, too unwieldy and too messy to eat, Pyramint barely survived three years before being resurrected in a four-segment bar format and then quietly interred for a million years. The Creme Egg, however, continued to grow (not literally, it has genuinely always been the same size). In 1986 the question 'How do you eat yours?' was raised, backed by an in-store promotion inviting shoppers to collect fifteen wrappers and send in for a free 'computer-produced personality analysis'. (`RESULT: YOU ARE BEREFT OF LOVE AND FILL THE ACHING HOLE THAT REMAINS WITH CHOCOLATE.`) Then, in 1992, Cadbury's very own Easter Bunny laid her first Caramel Egg (again, not literally; that would be the weirdest cartoon ever). The nest, as they say, is history.

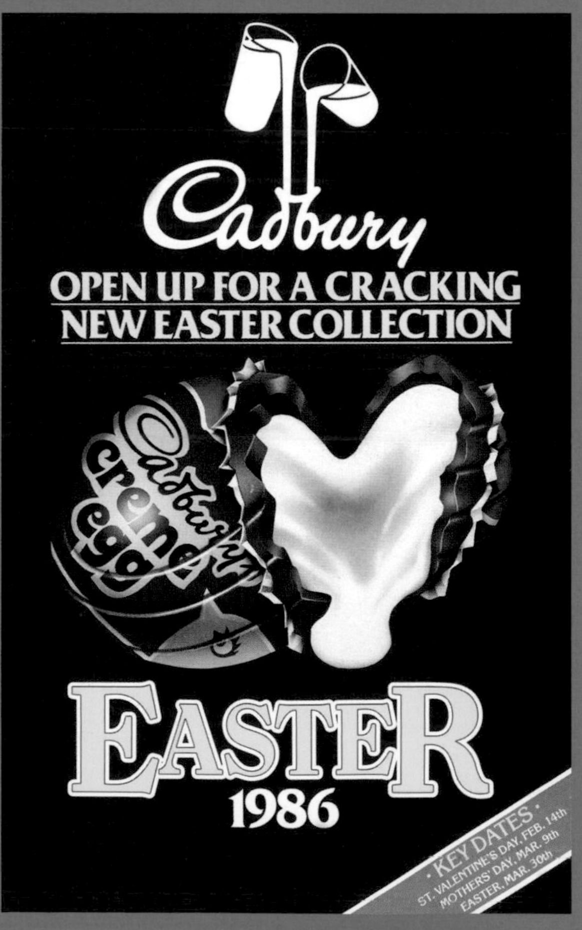


**'Cadbury had to call a press conference to halt overzealous punters digging up stone circles, hill forts and Christian burial sites in search of the £10,000'**

**Opposite:** From the author of *Clough's War*! Don Shaw's Creme Egg mystery, *Condundrum* (1984), and Cadbury's Easter catalogue, still employing 'cracking' puns two years later.

**Below:** Tout ça parce que l'homme n'aime pas Milk Tray! Bar Noir (1970).

## A TOUCH OF CLASS

Chocolate. It's too good for kids, isn't it? Not that you'd have come to that conclusion in the early 1970s, as the all-out Technicolor assault on the eyeballs of your unsuspecting newsagent browser demonstrated. With new printing techniques doing to sweet wrappers what they'd done to the Sunday papers a decade before, the shelves of your average confectioner looked with each passing year increasingly like a test card on a Philips colour set with the contrast turned all the way up. All sound marketing for the industry's staple army of knee-high nutters, but the garish outer casings often worked in the same way, for the discerning adult, as a wasp's stripy arse did for a chaffinch: 'You think this is doing your eyes in? Wait till you see what I'll do to your teeth!' The grown-up palate demanded a bit more class, and so chocolate folk threw as much invention into marketing posh, adult chocolates as the scruffy schoolboy kind.

Chocolate bars could be given a post-adolescent makeover in several ways. Plain chocolate was the simplest gambit. Take Cadbury's Plain Six, a dark version of the familiar Bar Six wafer, with its erudite credentials underlined by a series of ads riffing on Shakespearean tragedies; Richard III and Hamlet sneaking off mid-soliloquy for a crafty nibble. Plain Six later became Bar Noir, on the basis that two words of French were as good as the entire Shakespeare canon in the sophistication stakes. Class similarly abounded in Cadbury's Special Recipe, a rum 'n' raisin confection advertised on one of those silver serving dishes with the dome-shaped lids that are so posh you only ever see them in cartoons. If you couldn't be classy, you could always be cosy. Cadbury shifted a walnut variant of their Dairy Milk bars by renaming it Winter's Evening, sticking a barometer on the wrapper and claiming to 'capture the feeling of those cosy, pre-Christmas evenings at home'. If that wasn't soporific enough, there was always the Ovaltine chocolate bar to knock you out of a night – a shipping forecast in a foil wrapper.

It helped if you had a genuinely old-fashioned brand to start off with. No one knows much about the life of Elizabeth Shaw, doughty West Country inventor of the chocolate-covered honeycomb-centred Mint Crisp in the 1930s, but by the start of the 1970s the

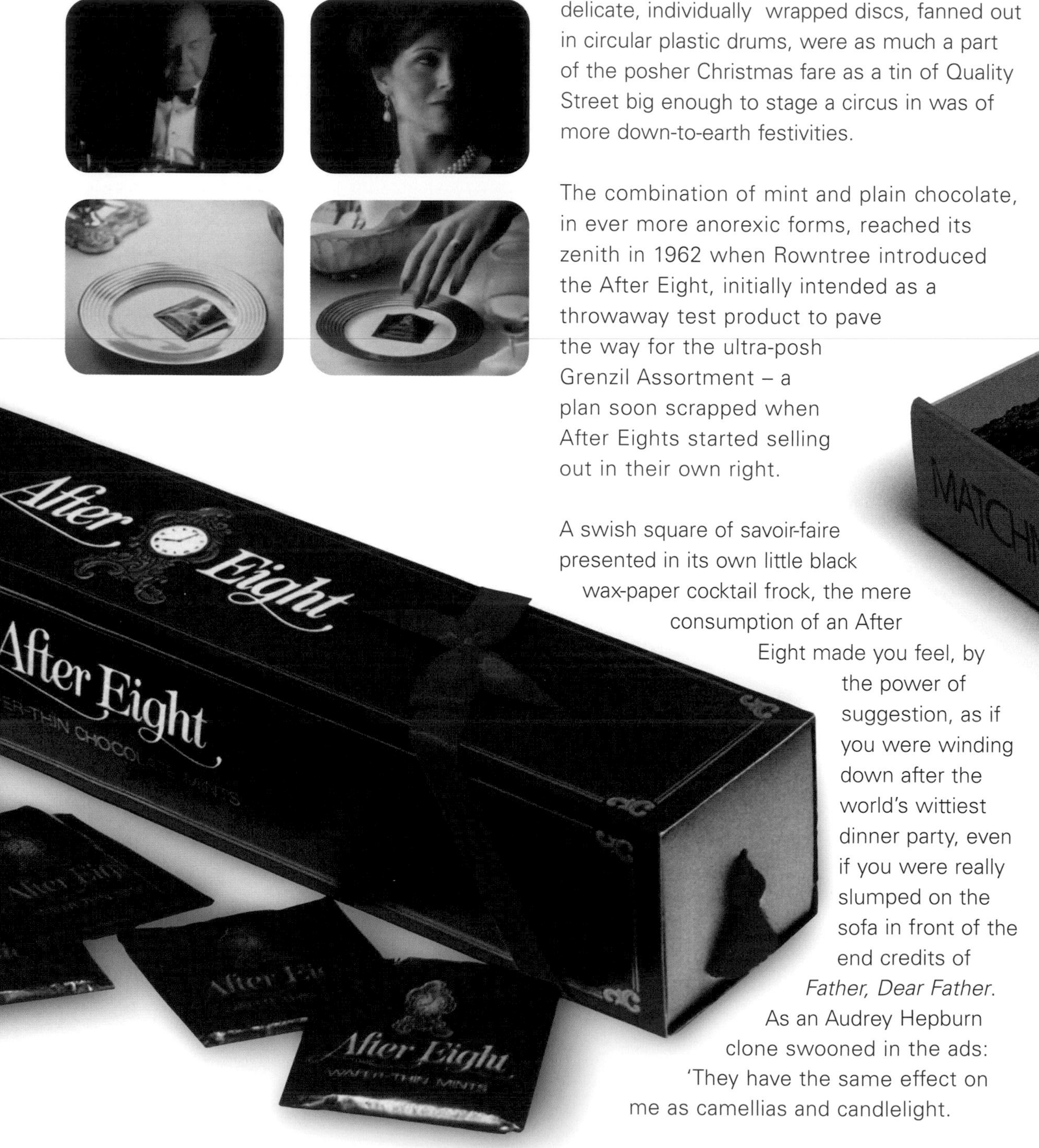


delicate, individually wrapped discs, fanned out in circular plastic drums, were as much a part of the posher Christmas fare as a tin of Quality Street big enough to stage a circus in was of more down-to-earth festivities.

The combination of mint and plain chocolate, in ever more anorexic forms, reached its zenith in 1962 when Rowntree introduced the After Eight, initially intended as a throwaway test product to pave the way for the ultra-posh Grenzil Assortment – a plan soon scrapped when After Eights started selling out in their own right.

A swish square of savoir-faire presented in its own little black wax-paper cocktail frock, the mere consumption of an After Eight made you feel, by the power of suggestion, as if you were winding down after the world's wittiest dinner party, even if you were really slumped on the sofa in front of the end credits of *Father, Dear Father*. As an Audrey Hepburn clone swooned in the ads: 'They have the same effect on me as camellias and candlelight.

**Opposite:** Slipping lissomely between the Mandate and Bisodol ads at Chrimbo – After Eight (1962). Rule one: do not put the empty envelopes back in the box!

**Below:** Top drawer. Matchmakers' first of many festive outings (1968).

They make me feel expensive, pampered and gay.' A new market was created, into which Mars stumbled in 1968 with their Royal Mints, while Rowntree did it rather better with Matchmakers, boxes of seventy-odd knobbly mint, orange and coffee crisp chocolate sticks built along the same lines as, and far outlasting, their cracknel bars. The easiest, and many would say best, way to take chocolate into the adult world is, of course... bung in some booze. Liqueur chocolates, usually shaped like globular whisky bottles and wrapped in Christmas tree-friendly foil, mouldered in a dusty corner of the sweet shop for ten months a year, but gloriously took centre stage in November as a miniature harbinger of the country's annual festival of Christ-honouring liver abuse. Indulgence was literally the flavour of the month. Fancy a Boucher's Celebration Cream Sherry? Then perhaps something from Anton Berg's Queen of Denmark range: this marzipan-coated plum in Madeira should warm your cockles. As the evening draws to a close, why not round it off with Poulain's pineapple chunks in rum, or prunes in Armagnac? What's that? Oh yes, first door on your right.

Usually, however, the accent was on sophistication, and it was often French. Long before Ferrero stormed British embassies with their Rocher task force, they had the black tie community in their firm grasp with the ubiquitous Mon Chéri – glacé cherries liberally doused in brandy and covered (or rather, enrobed) in plain chocolate. Meanwhile, Tobler's Old Masters range collected a bunch of whisky-sodden cocoa capsules in a big posh box with a Rembrandt emblazoned on the lid, as if to suggest the contents were as finely crafted as a Renaissance painting.

**'After Eight made you feel, by the power of suggestion, as if you were winding down after the world's wittiest dinner party.'**

Bisquit
COGNAC

Captain
Morgan

**Opposite:** No need to raid mum's cocktail cabinet. Happy hour for Hobbits with Sharps liqueurs, circa 1971.

However, the kings of the Cointreau selection box weren't continental interlopers, but Bristolian chocolatiers Famous Names, who realised all that chocolaty 'enrobing' and 'lavishing' was by the by: it was the booze that mattered. Thus, they enlisted the manufacturers of the biggest brands to provide the liquid centres for their bottle-shaped treats: Harvey's, Bailey's, Drambuie, Malibu and notorious Christmas indulgence De Kuyper cherry brandy, the drink that lines and churns your stomach simultaneously. By 1985 they were claiming 58 per cent of a liqueur market worth £24 million. They celebrated in style: by making Warnink's Advocaat available 'for the first time in chocolate form'. Yeah, thanks for that.

In 1986 they tinkered further, and in the process inadvertently brought the golden era of the chocolate liqueur to an untimely end. Traditionally, the delicate envelope of chocolate had to be protected from its 30 proof contents by a thick, tangy wall of crunchy sugar, lest the Famous Grouse eat through the walls of its dairy prison and make a mess all over the Highland toffee. The sensation of biting through that sugar crust, to let loose the alcoholic syrup within, was a key part of the liqueur experience. So what did Famous Names go and do? Introduce a revolutionary technique called (wait for it) 'crust-in-situ', which did away with the need for those naughty sugar walls and provided 'improved eating quality'. Their words, not ours. Those Harvey Wallbanger truffles never dangled from the tree quite so temptingly after that. ✻

## * TOBLERONE

You know you're talking about continental chocolate when you have to censor its origins for the under-twelves. Get your Toblerone history from *Blue Peter*, and they'd tell you a quaint tale of Swiss chocolatier Theodor Tobler being inspired to shape his new nougat, honey and almond-laced creation by rugged Alpine scenery. Ask someone closer to Tobler, and you'll get a less edifying yarn about the old

**Opposite:** Toblerone (1908). Considerably more successful than Toblertwo or Toblerthree.

**Below:** Love triangle. A soft-focus effect for Suchard's 1982 product catalogue.

man getting so turned on by a pyramid of derriere-thrusting dancers at the Folies Bergères he recreates the memorable pile of women's arses using the brown stuff. Depends what you go for in a story, really.

Granite or gluteous, the saw-toothed prism shape set the Toblerone apart from other chocolate bars, most of which didn't get to travel about in a special snug-fitting box. In Britain, though, it had additional cachet. Possession of any of the bar's bigger sizes (and, boy, did they get massive, up to a whopping ten-kilo edition) meant one thing: check out the flash git who's been abroad. Though not strictly foreign fare – Crosse & Blackwell had the licence to make them in their Newham factory from 1929 onwards – it was seen seldom enough, and never in such gigantic dimensions, that it became a totem for the well-travelled child of the world.

Fine for junior showboating, not so good for UK sales. To get the bar out of the duty free and into supermarkets, the boys from Suchard spent potloads. Televisual whimsy about triangular bees providing the honey surfaced in 1984. White chocolate came in 1985, and an affordable 18p snack size in '86. The Toblerone slowly adapted itself to the unforgiving British climate. Then Suchard went too far: they tried to buy out Rowntree, losing to those other mountainous Swiss chocolatiers, Nestlé. Moral: the British are up for new ideas, but don't push your luck. Especially if your flagship product provides the most uncomfortable eating experience in the Western hemisphere.

**'The saw-toothed prism shape set Toblerone apart from other chocolate bars, most of which didn't get to travel in a special snug-fitting box.'**

## * ROLO

Romance and chocolate have always walked hand in hand, like a pair of soppy-gobbed love-muffins. They speak a common language, all sweetness this, sugar that, and syrupy the other. Maybe it's the Freudian link between the filling the mouth and giving pleasure. Maybe it's the oft-identified, though scientifically disputed, chemical mix of theobromide and phenyethylamine (the 'love drug').

**Opposite:** Rolo (1937), marketed as 'a chocolate cup-o-toffee' circa 1972. Which is an improvement on 'a chocolate conical frustum.' But less geometrically accurate.

**Below:** Romper chompers. Munchies (1957), and Mintola (1955), recently spotted working undercover as After Eight Bitesize.

Certainly, even Casanova himself was said to partake of a bite or two prior to bedding his conquests. Whatever the truth, it's a relationship advocated by chocolatiers – as any spotty teenager trying to impress the object of his or her affections has learned over time.

Chief among the culprits is the otherwise unassuming Rolo, forged in an auspicious union of 'soft, chewy toffee in a milk chocolate cup' by Caley-Mackintosh. The two companies had themselves entered into a marriage of convenience in 1932 which meant Halifax's self-proclaimed Toffee King no longer had to rely solely on butter and molasses products to turn a pretty, gold-foiled penny. Bite-sized, chocolate-coated creations rolled off the drawing board and into the sweaty paws of lovestruck youth. Rolo was the entry-level brand, joined in 1955 by the cool and cultivated, plain chocolate Mintola (at the time, identical in size and shape to its older brother), and shortly after by radically square biscuit luxury, Munchies. All were packaged in 'the perfect pocket pack' to encourage sharing, that pre-Internet equivalent of viral marketing, and thus commenced many a back-row courtship under dimmed cinema lights.

Only a quarter of a century later did anyone back at HQ think to make use of the amorous association. Late '60s 'Rolo Sensation' adverts made brief stars of Danish kazoo-and-comb rockers Sir Henry and His Butlers and their international hit, 'Camp'. But it was on the back of their 'Do you love anyone enough to give them your last?' campaign that Rolo truly tugged at the nation's heartstrings. In 1986 the selfish-seeming Large Rolo was quietly withdrawn, and an extra 'last' Rolo was added to standard-sized tubes. A successful series of animations featured an existential young suitor who became increasingly self-aware as he was illustrated on the page, bashfully offering his final toffee to a beautifully drawn girl. Saatchi and Saatchi even pulled a stunt, placing appropriately painted Rolo posters along the route of Prince Andrew and Sarah Ferguson's royal wedding.

Munchies and Mintola meanwhile were left behind. An attempt to broaden the range with Rum Truffles, Wholenut in caramel and you-know-what-ish Delights failed. Rolo even trumped their rare opulence with a boxed, solid silver incarnation intended for Valentine's Day gifting (not for consumption), although Fergie probably does chomp her way through a fair number of these. Hence all those money worries.

## * WALNUT WHIP

Around since time immemorial but reinvented for a new, late '60s generation by Rowntree (they immediately removed the interior walnut and have since stealthily upped the outer-gloss factor on the chocolate body), the Walnut Whip is deeply ingrained in popular snack culture. Perhaps not a delicacy to be purchased on a whim – for who would want a Walnut Whim anyway?

**Opposite:** One Walnut Whip (1910). The exact cost per London resident of the Olympic Games 2012, according to Ken Livingstone. Remember him?

**Below:** What's the betting this was pitched as 'a kind of Alice In Walnutland' by the ad agency? Lose yourself in impenetrable symbolism, circa 1986.

– it was something that had to be carefully planned for. Newsagents could only stack them in boxes of three, thanks to the unusual beacon shape, square cardboard footprint and unhelpful cellophane wrapping, so they would seldom be seen in the house other than on special occasions.

To be frank, associations with highly polished Jaguar dashboards, strange pickle jars at the back of a grandparent's pantry, and that *Fawlty Towers* Waldorf salad episode already lent anything walnutty an air of specialness. Dads, typically cracking their way through a Christmas Eve bowl of nuts, would often be called upon to dispose of that top-mounted kernel (an acquired taste by anyone's standards), so that the remaining foam fondant funnel could be devoured unsullied. The altogether less innocent act of licking out the cream was wilfully transplanted by Ann Summers party organisers into their repertoire of saucy fun 'n' games, the cheeky monkeys.

Television advertisers, however, struggled to convey the Walnut Whip's unique appeal. A '70s attempt at volcano-centric, cloud-swirling psychedelia was supplanted by bizarre, office-based 'most fun you can have on your own' farce, before the usual chocolate ad fluff of whirling skirts, spiral staircases and a wistful Pan's Labyrinth montage took over in the '80s. Ultimately, immortality was ensured not by absorption into Cockney rhyming slang (it apparently translates as either 'acid trip', 'the snip' or 'kip', which must make conversation dahn the Auld Bull and Bush a constant challenge), nor as a literary simile for anything roughly conical in cheap novels ('60s women's hairstyles, Madonna's brassieres, or men's doo-dahs), but by a name-check in the 2002 top ten hit, 'What's Your Flava'. Because you know when you've made Craig David 'sick to the point of throwing up' you're at the top of your game.

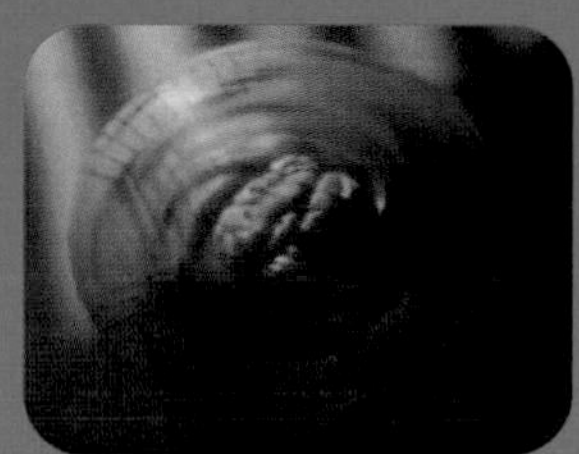

**'The act of licking out the cream was wilfully transplanted by Ann Summers party organisers into their repertoire of saucy fun 'n' games.'**

## ❋ FRY'S FIVE CENTRES

Dark-coated, crescent-shaped and elegant beyond measure, Fry's fondant bars are a product with pedigree. Back in 1853, the Fry brothers boiled up a cauldron of minty fondant and coated strips of it in plain chocolate to make Fry's Chocolate Cream Sticks. In 1866 the 'sticks' fell out of use, some gentle score lines were added for enhanced snappability, and one of Britain's poshest chocolate

**Opposite:** Centre spread. The changing face of Fry's Five Centres (1934).

bars set out on its long life, adverts depicting it in the dainty hands of hat-wearing women of means, often seen buying something dead pricey at an auction, backing a winner at Ascot, or just lounging about being Twiggy.

Well, that's the hat-wearing woman-of-means market sewn up, but what about the kids? In 1934 the first of what would be many incarnations of the more colourful Fry's Five Centres bar came to pass – raspberry, lime, vanilla, coffee and orange fondant centres abutting each other in the plain Chocolate Cream casing. Sadly, the war put this little luxury out of action within a few years.

In 1960 it was reborn. This time the chocolate was a more kid-friendly milk, and the flavours had been slightly altered: now pineapple, raspberry, lime, strawberry and orange centres jostled for position in a new seven-segment bar, the raspberry and strawberry flavours doubling up to fill the gaps. To confuse things further, the wrapper changed design seemingly every year. For a while it was even renamed the Medley. Then in 1982 it vanished again, only to revive, this time back in plain chocolate form, two years later. This final incarnation carried on until 1992, after which it really was no more.

Despite being rebadged more often than the Austin Metro, one thing remained a familiar constant. No matter how precision-engineered Fry's equipment, the different fondant segments never quite matched up with the dividing grooves in the chocolate shell. Thus a snapped-off chunk may look like pineapple, but the majority turned out to be boring old strawberry. Such intrigue and suspense helped make the Five Centres one of the most fondly recalled sweets of all, even if no two people remember quite the same bar.

**'No matter how precision-engineered Fry's equipment, the different fondant segments never quite matched up.'**

## * TURKISH DELIGHT

Hardly extinct and, at any rate, never really a candidate for that impulsive tuck shop purchase, Fry's Turkish Delight is nevertheless inherently nostalgic. Bristol-based apothecary Joseph Fry began churning out slabs nearly 100 years ago at his Small Street premises, yet it lingers on shelves like an almost shameful secret to this day. Indeed, Cadbury seems to have forgotten that it

**Opposite:** Sheikh, your moneymaker. Turkish Delight (1924).

**Below:** Epic veil. Model Vivienne Lynn, kissing Valentino by a crystal blue CSO screen, circa 1981.

makes the bar, which still bears the Fry name and a packet design that hasn't changed in five decades. The recipe remains a classic Anglicised version of *lokum* (boiled sugar syrup simmered with starch and cream of tartar), the likes of which would turn up at Christmas in suspiciously hexagonal boxes jam-packed with icing sugar and gooey, gummy, rose-flavoured lumps of unknown origin. Fry's chocolate-coated variety took many forms before settling on the now familiar block, roughly the size, shape and texture of a human tongue, for the more discriminating Anglo-Saxon palate.

Though historically associated with temptation (via Narnia's White Witch), Turkish Delight was invariably the Friday night treat of choice for any mum in search of what the industry deemed 'a slow, savoured eat' and the chance to put her feet up after a day's slaving. (Her personal ottoman empire was just that back bedroom storage divan for spare blankets and bedding.) The name itself hinted at the kind of carnal pleasures one might only experience in the non-Christian East – what Alan Whicker called the 'mosques, minarets and mayhem' of Istanbul (not Constantinople) on behalf of Barclaycard – and which Cadbury more than happily alluded to from the 1950s onwards in a series of television ads 'full of Eastern promise' (whatever that is). A succession of mysterious, raven-haired beauties reclined to receive the attentions of brooding, dark-skinned Bedouin men on horseback, though the desert scenes often owed more to Acton than Ankara. This was an era when belly dancers were thought the very height of exotic sophistication, and the merest hint of a pierced navel would send men giddy with desire.

In 1981, however, Cadbury dispensed with any attempt at realism and commissioned 'Shifting Sands', a lavish, eerily lit montage of vaguely Middle Eastern imagery, featuring a snake, Saudi sand dunes and the dulcet tones of Anthony Valentine over Cliff Adams's haunting pan-pipe soundtrack. As other companies found out to their cost (whither the Tobler Turkish, for example?), the product was peculiarly sensitive to advertising, and so Cadbury took a scimitar to the Turkish Delight budget, slashing it Gordian-knot style. In the thirty years since, not a penny has been spent on updating the campaign. Thus it remains, languishing at the very back of their back catalogue, a mirage-like reminder of an altogether more indulgent age.

# COLLECT FOUR FREE COMICS WITH KP SKIPS

*Collect four free comics with KP Skips.*

You'll find a Skips free comic token in any of your nine favourite comics: Buster, Eagle, Whizzer and Chips, Tammy, 2000 AD, Tiger, Battle Action Force, Roy of the Rovers, and Whoopee.

Just send off four of these tokens and ten KP Skips wrappers together with 12p in coins in an envelope to the address shown at the top of the next column.

KP Skips 'FREE COMICS' OFFER,
P.O. Box 100,
MEASHAM,
STAFFS. DE12 7HQ

And we'll send you the money for your four free comics.

*But hurry, you'd better get to your newsagent before Colin does!*

# CRISPS & SNACKS

**Opposite:** He's not the enemy of society! He's just a bit clumsy! Colin the punk/metaller/biker prior to hiring a few Skips (1985).

**Tough luck, Brits: the potato chip (as it should be correctly referred to – none of this crisp nonsense) is an American invention. Or is it?**

The popular story, as related in many books and TV shows, dates back to 1853 and tells of George Crum, a part-Native American chef at a Saratoga Springs resort hotel. Angered by a fussy patron's repeated requests for thinner, crispier French fries, legend has it, Crum retaliated by deep-frying a plateful of paper-thin potato shavings dusted with too much salt. Far from spiting the customer, however, the new chips took off, soon becoming a local delicacy and enabling Crum to found his own restaurant.

Depending on whose history books you read, diners who ordered a portion of the Saratoga chips thereafter included Herman Lay (a travelling salesman who popularised them as a snack in the southern States), a Frenchman called Cartier (who ultimately sold his grocery firm to Britain's crisp pioneer Frank Smith) or a gormless, red-tongued monster on a worldwide hunt for the biggest snack pennies can buy.

However, what often gets ignored is a book by the name of *The Cook's Oracle; and Housekeeper's Manual*, published in New York, which included detailed instructions for frying potato slices cut 'in shavings round and round, as you would peel a lemon... till they are crisp'. Unmistakably potato chips, this recipe by Dr William Kitchiner is dated 1832 and – what's more – admittedly freely adapted from the original English edition of 1829. Stolen, you might even say. So, as with the World Cup, the Internet and *The Office*, the potato crisp (as it should be correctly referred to – none of this 'chip' nonsense) is a British invention that the US just happened to lay claim to. Oh, and while the potato itself might have originated on American soil, it was Sir Walter Raleigh who popularised it.

**Opposite:** Planters flog us the all-American goober (circa 1983) while Lineker plugs a slice of Lincolnshire (1986).

**Below:** Beauregard, Smith's answer to Bob Dylan, and Pork Crackling crisps, Smith's answer to the British Heart Foundation.

Whatever the provenance, it's fair to say that the crisp as we know it has been less than 100 years in the making. The earliest, handmade crisps were generally sold loose off the back of a cart. Like a dry martini, an Agatha Christie story, or Tanita Tikaram's sobriety, they came with a twist: a simple, single serving of salt, in a thumb-sized wrap of paper. As recently as the 1960s, most potato crisps were still sold in tins, rather than bags, for freshness. Yet by 1987 Burton's were shifting bucketloads of the most un-potato-like bacon and bean flavour Piglets puffs, part of their 10p-a-pack Farmyard Friends range. (The others were the improbably named Chicklets and Beeflets.) That we came so far so quickly is down to the perfect marriage of a plentiful, cheap crop and ingenious industrial processes.

TV programmes 'For Schools and Colleges' chronicled the meticulous and mechanised detail of crisp production for generations of primary school kids sitting cross-legged in front of the Ferguson TX television. Conveyor belts, storage hoppers, rotating drums, water jets, scanners, slicers, pallets and boiling-hot vats of hydrogenated vegetable oil: these make up the highly automated reality of the twenty-first-century crisp. If there's one thing the Brits do well, it's replacing men with machines.

So much for the artisan, Kettle Chip fantasy. As George Crum would no doubt agree (and John Ford almost certainly said), when forced to pick between truth and legend, print the legend.

## DEEP-FRIED FOUNDERS

Crisps began knocking around British pubs shortly after the First World War, when Frank Smith and his wife started bagging them up in their Cricklewood garage. For decades, Smiths was the country's only major crisp company, on the stock market since 1929 and corporate to a fault. Up and down the country, though, nearly 800 tiny backroom outfits were nibbling at their heels, many started by grocers and butchers augmenting their tough, ration-hobbled trade with a cheap sideline assisted by a demob grant.

Initially, production was crude and dirty, with crisps fried in batches in much the same way as fish suppers. Toiling workers became so saturated with oil fumes that their bosses had to lay on special buses to take them home, to keep public transport free of the stench of stale chip oil. That all changed in the late 1950s when newfangled continuous fryers were imported from the States, Tudor being the first recipients in '57. These automated wonders could provide a constant stream of crisps, at the rate of eight tons of spuds an hour. British crisps were about to become big business.

The main challenge to the Smiths monopoly was Scottish outfit Golden Wonder, started by William Alexander as a sideline to his bakery business. They gained plenty of local kudos, but really took off when they were bought by Imperial Tobacco in 1961. The new Golden Wonder's objective was nothing less than national domination. While Smiths were still farting around with booklets wherein fictional radio matriarch Doris Archer doled out recipes for scones and fudge featuring a handful of 'delicious Smiths potato crisps, crushed to farthing size', Golden Wonder went

**Opposite:** Golden Wonder's 'crackle-fresh' flavours, circa 1978.

**Below:** A cheek-pouch filler for Chipmunk (1972). Smith's forelock-tugging flavour (1981).

for broke. They built three new crisp factories including the 'world's biggest' in Corby, and replaced old-fashioned waxed paper bags with a long tube of glossy cellophane. These were filled with crisps, sealed and snipped off into instant, moisture-proof packs with reassuring little windows onto the product itself: 'Crackle-fresh!' as children's entertainer Mr Pastry put it in the adverts.

Noting that Smiths had the traditional crisp market – old blokes in pubs – locked down, the Wonder team shipped their glossy offerings off to grocers, supermarkets and newsagents. What was a dreary post-war meat substitute became a fun family snack. Smiths' management reeled under the weight of unprecedented competition. Imperial Tobacco even tried to buy them up too, but the Monopolies Commission weren't having it. The '70s began with Smiths knocked into second place for the first time in crisp history.

Britain's third biggest crisp maker was, of course... Meredith and Drew. Hardly a household name, but they were behind nearly all the own-brand supermarket crisps of the day, as well as their own Crispi Crisps which, after 1975, were gradually brought in line with their nut-based sister brand KP. Regional manufacturers were being incorporated left, right and centre. Chipmunk Crisps were bought from their parent company Liebig, makers of Oxo, and assimilated into Golden Wonder in 1969. Tyneside's venerable Tudor had been a Smiths subsidiary since 1962, while Burton's of Doncaster (makers of Crown and XL Crisps) and Lancashire's Rishy were absorbed by the colossal Associated British Foods Group. Oh, and US monolith Frito Lay sought a bit of British action by buying up tiny Scottish firm Crimpy Crisps, but nothing came of that.

Through all this upheaval a few indies held out, like Bradford's dauntless Seabrook Crisps, and an operation that spent the 1970s slowly but surely expanding from its command centre at 4 Cheapside, Leicester.

It's fair to say no one saw Walkers coming. Instigated in 1949 by butcher Henry Walker and sandwiched geographically between the Smiths and Golden Wonder head offices, they eschewed going national in favour of slowly but steadily conquering their local market. By 1973 they accounted for over half the crisps sold in the Midlands, which was a lot of crisps. Walkers also renounced kid-friendly cartoon gimmicks. Not for them the unctuous, Nimmo-voiced likes of the KP friars, or the funny little bloke in the tam-o'-shanter who decorated packets of Golden Wonder. Nor did they try to compete with the likes of Tudor in the novelty flavour market. Slow, sensible and steady-as-she-goes was their motto.

The market for crisps was expanding as never before, but it was a choppy ride. Potato famines were, predictably, a dent in profits. The introduction of the breathalyser in 1967 hit pub sales so badly that Chipmunk had to put 200 workers on short time. Worse still, in 1974 Denis Healey stuck VAT on crisps, leading a *Daily Mirror* consumer report to conclude that 'the price per pound often puts these products in the steak class.' Novelties designed to distract customers from the ludicrous prices came and went. While the big boys knocked themselves out to stay on top, Walkers just carried on soberly divvying up the sales areas, sweet-talking the country's cash and carries

**Opposite:** Walkers' 'confuse an alcoholic' campaign, circa 1980.

**Below:** Try eating these on the streets of Belfast! Murphy's Crisps, circa 1974. Stop-motion spuds welcome oblivion for Smith's, circa 1982.

and plonking the odd Guinness world record on the backs of the packs.

Walkers were bought out by Shredded Wheat giant Nabisco. Soon afterwards, they swallowed up Smiths as well, and so began the long, painful process of Smiths and Tudor gradually vanishing under the unstoppable might of their former rival. Golden Wonder became distracted by their Pot Noodle, which was suddenly very successful, and then just as suddenly wasn't. Strikes and a factory fire didn't help matters. They never fully recovered their old pep. At the end of the decade, Walkers were sold on to the even mightier Pepsico, and the rest is jug-eared, *Match of the Day*-presenting, crisp-thieving history.

The crisp world is a ruthless commercial battleground, and no one should begrudge Walkers their hard-won success, but despite your Sensations, World Cup limited editions and Comic Relief flavour-related hilarity, it's hard not to shed a tear for that overcrowded, cartoon-festooned, pickled onion flavoured pantechnicon that was the 1970s crisp world. But that's probably the nostalgia talking. Or maybe the sodium benzoate.

'In 1974, a *Daily Mirror* consumer report concluded that "the price per pound often puts these products in the steak class".'

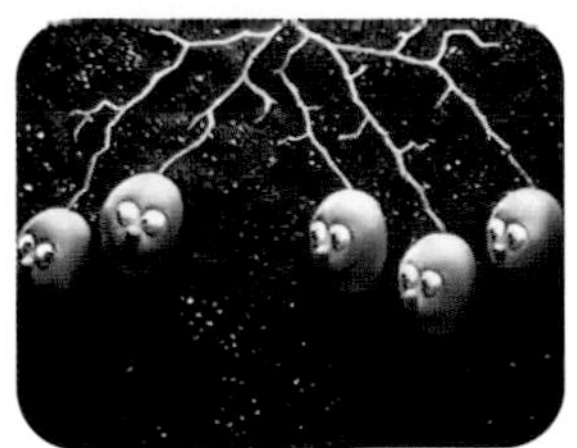

## * TUDOR CRISPS

A wily paperboy tricking his mate into taking the stairs to the top of a skyscraper. Billy Dainty gatecrashing a party with a suitcase full of crisps and becoming the life and soul. Terry the Gateshead Gourmet returning to his home town in a Rolls-Royce, nicking crisps off a hitch-hiking student along the way. For a defiantly local crisp company, Tyneside's Tudor produced advertising images every bit as

**Opposite:** Canny bags – lengthwise logo circa 1976, fried chicken circa 1983.

**Below:** The north-east's potato-based barter system in full effect, as another high-rise negotiation gets underway outside the Derwent Tower, circa 1980.

memorable as the big hitters and, some might say, even more memorable crisps. Being relatively young, their management was not averse to commissioning the sort of flavours an adult might baulk at, but kids wolfed down with glee. Never underestimate the power of a 'canny bag o' Tudor'.

By 1970 their distinctive bags, often featuring a smug-looking Henry VIII stuffing his face and – for a brief period – the name written lengthways down the front to make the bags seem bigger than they were, contained pickled onion, roast chicken, tomato sauce and 'b-fee' varieties. Throughout the decade, they added the increasingly exotic likes of hot dog 'n' mustard, roast lamb 'n' mint sauce, roast beef 'n' pickle, gammon 'n' pineapple, brown sauce and kipper. At its '70s height, Tudor's flavour laboratory in Peterlee turned out a new flavour every three months. Among the hundreds of crisp flavours attempted but never released to the general public were mushroom, mayonnaise, celery, peach, cherry, strawberry, lemon, banana and passion fruit.

Non-crisp snacks arrived, like nuts, Smokey Bacon Waffles and Wackys ('a potato-based pasta product with an intriguing grille shape'). Fries (a rival to Smiths' Chipsticks) could be eaten from the packet or, it was claimed, heated in the oven and served up with a fish supper. The grammatically suspect 'One's' range came in cheesey, onion and nutty varieties, as well as a sweet orange flavour, which bombed. Sweet flavours in corn snacks weren't what the people wanted at all – mess with the Green Giant's market at your peril.

With 99 per cent of the north-east's crisp market at their peak, Tudor had the potential to go all the way and become a national brand, but an ill-prepared incursion into the Midlands faced them with the quiet, calculating marketing might of Walkers, and victory was not to be theirs. Eventually the company would be subsumed by its Midlands rival, but it's tempting to imagine what the country's crisps would have been like had that decisive battle gone the other way. Maybe Terry would have actually owned that Roller.

**'Tyneside's Tudor produced advertising images every bit as memorable as the big hitters and, some might say, even more memorable crisps.'**

## * SQUARE CRISPS

If you want a reason why so many formerly dominant names in British snackery have gone to the wall, you need only look to the manner in which their flagship products were created. Smiths Square Crisps, for one, were rumoured to have been the responsibility of a junior engineer experimenting in his spare time with 'potato granules'. No doubt such industriousness among the lower ranks was encouraged

**Opposite:** Squares on the hydrogenated hypotenuse. Smith's Square Crisps (1976).

**Below:** Rectilinear relaunch (1983).

(as indeed was the maintenance of a surplus potato granule mountain) until the bean-counters took over in the '80s. No more happy accidents after that. No more improvisation, no more free-form jazz crisp invention, and certainly no more squaring the circle.

Initially something of a four-cornered flop for Smiths, Square Crisps' lacklustre advertising was blamed for the low expectations of the consumer, leading to poor sales. In short, these equilateral eats were seen as 'just an ordinary crisp' by Thick Jack Clot on the street, rather than the revolutionary reformed potato snack they really were. But with Smiths paying their Lincoln-based factory workers an extra £260 each to operate specially commissioned machinery, something had to be done, and fast.

In the wake of a successful Monster Munch TV campaign, Smiths enlisted the eye-rolling services of 'Mr Lenny Henry' (as the *Evening Standard* insisted on calling him) to promote the 'crisp that isn't a crisp'. The first wave of ads in 1982 riffed impudently on (i.e. thieved audaciously from) Roy



Jay's 'spook, slither' convict character, popular on kids' telly at the time, right down to the 'It's weird!' catchphrase. A second set pitted Lenny against animatronic co-stars in the shape of Tiddles the pig, and Dobbin the ostrich, while redefining the pack contents as 'more of a crunch than a crisp', although whether that affected Smiths' VAT return remains undocumented.

Bovril and spring onion soon joined the original triumvirate of flavours (a standard selection of salt and vinegar, cheese and onion or ready salted) and, by 1983, Square Crisps were second only in popularity to Golden Wonder's all-conquering Wotsits. Emboldened, Smiths increased the size of the squares, though this may have been too much for then deputy leader of the Labour Party, Roy Hattersley. Defeated once again in opposition by the Conservatives under Thatcher, he decried the very notion of square crisps as 'false wants' and proof of capitalism's excess. Really, Roy? Ideologically unsound savouries? Maybe if you'd stopped worrying about the catering you could have sorted out the Militant Tendency.

A final push came in the late '80s as, alongside the 'altogether more cultivated' sister product Crispy Tubes, Smiths went all-out to emphasise the snack's crunchiness. Unfortunately, the campaign coincided with the actions of an individual saboteur whose idea of extra crunch was to introduce shards of broken glass to the packets. Police intervention and a product recall pretty much stalled Square Crisps' relentless cornering of the market. But then, maybe that's what happens when disgruntled former junior engineers suddenly find they have too much time on their hands.

**Below:** Make mine meat! The manly taste of Smith's circa 1974, and Golden Wonder (1972).

## DO US A FLAVOUR

It's not clear who came up with the first flavoured crisps (ask any crisp company of sufficiently advanced years and they'll say, 'It was us'), but Ireland's Tayto have a better claim than most with their early-doors cheese and onion circa 1957, with Golden Wonder following suit soon after. Smiths, slow on the uptake but eventually sensing an emerging market, countered with salt 'n' vinegar, tested first by their Geordie subsidiary Tudor, and launched nationally in 1967. Though they did not know it, both companies had fired the first rounds in a battle that would become a two-decade-long flavour war. By the end of the 1960s, the crisp market had doubled.

First to notice was – who else? – renowned architecture and design critic Reyner Banham, the man who had helped define early modernism, brutalism and industrial megastructure. An unlikely commentator on the common 'tater, possibly, but an earnest one nonetheless. In a prescient 1970 *New Society* magazine piece entitled 'The Crisp at the Crossroads', no doubt knocked out over a weekend, he correctly identified a trend towards 'sundry aromas arising from the secret kitchens of [crisp companies'] research and development departments'. Later that year, the British Society of Flavourists formed, uniting food technologists and commercial enterprise in a common interest: giving every child in Britain really stinky breath.

It worked! In 1971, flavoured crisps accounted for 55 per cent of the industry's total sales. Tudor, for one, started to treat their consumers like some unofficial focus group, as they searched for new natural and artificial flavours to help widen market penetration. 'Special request' edition packets were introduced,

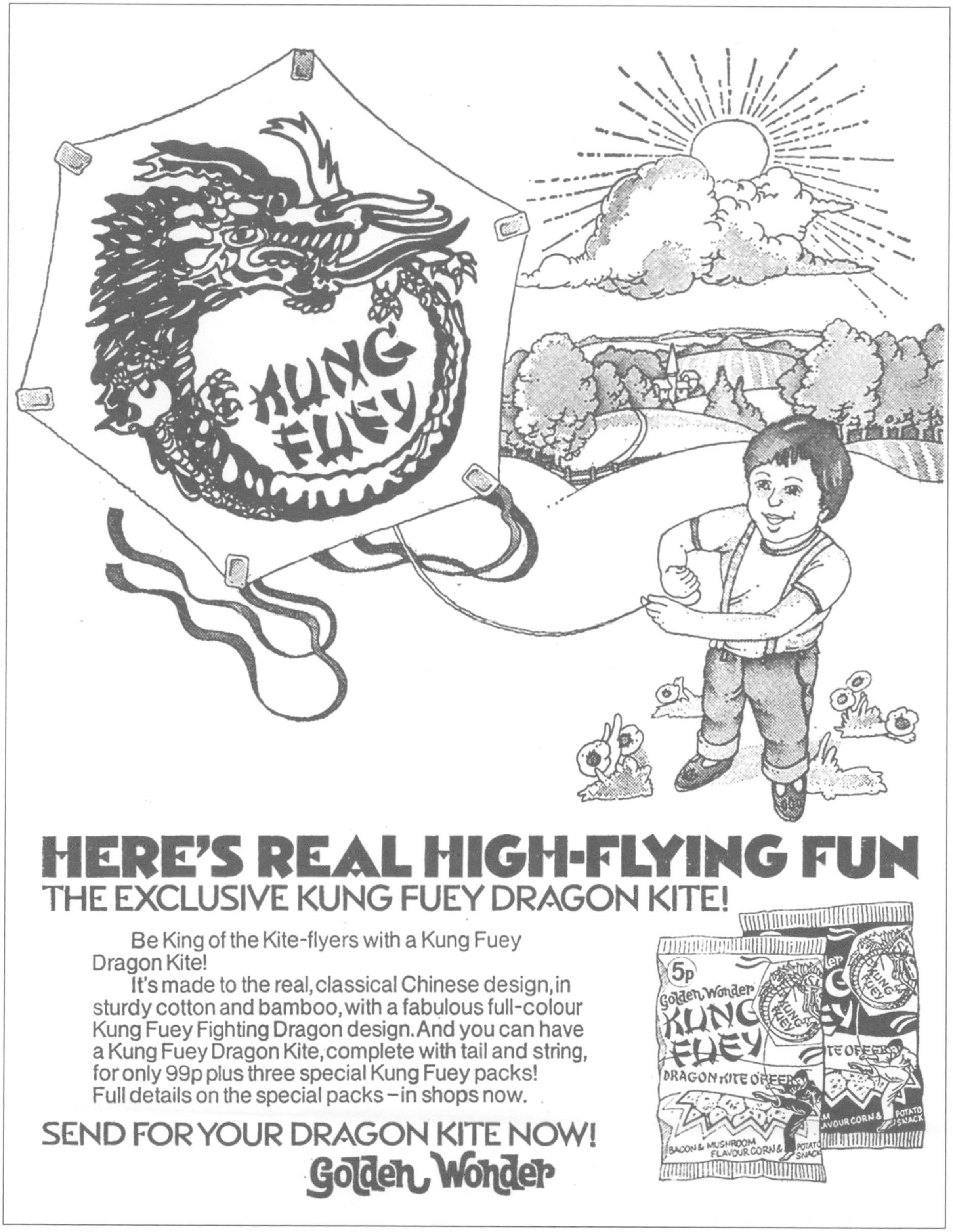

# HERE'S REAL HIGH-FLYING FUN

## THE EXCLUSIVE KUNG FUEY DRAGON KITE!

Be King of the Kite-flyers with a Kung Fuey Dragon Kite!

It's made to the real, classical Chinese design, in sturdy cotton and bamboo, with a fabulous full-colour Kung Fuey Fighting Dragon design. And you can have a Kung Fuey Dragon Kite, complete with tail and string, for only 99p plus three special Kung Fuey packs! Full details on the special packs – in shops now.

SEND FOR YOUR DRAGON KITE NOW!

Golden Wonder

apparently due to public demand and for overtly limited periods. Golden Wonder, meanwhile, were all over the shop. A baked bean flavour was loudly trumpeted, the product of 'a year's research and development'. It soon turned out a year wasn't long enough. More successful was a branded Oxo flavour (though that too quickly faced opposition from Smiths' Bovril flavour). Where Golden Wonder did excel was in the savoury snack category, a fact even arch-rivals Smiths had to accept begrudgingly in the face of Wotsits' domination. Non-potato vegetable proteins were cheaper and more plentiful, plus they could be aerated (thus filling a packet for less) and they suited the more esoteric flavours better than their subterranean counterparts. For inspiration, all Golden Wonder needed to do was look east.

Enter, in 1974, to the sound of a gong and that racist xylophone riff, Kung Fuey, 'crunchy corn and potato balls with an unusual bacon and mushroom flavour'. Golden Wonder's Oriental opportunism paid dividends, riding the crest of a wave of martial arts popularity: kids were already karate-chopping piles of wood and trying to kick down walls barefoot. Now TV ad breaks were filled with Chinese stereotypes doing the same in the name of snack food (leading one copycat eight-year-old in Acton to lose a toenail). Kung Fuey's yellow-packed, inauthentically flavoured original was joined later by a black-clad cheese and ham variety, though this was greeted less enthusiastically and, like Bruce Lee before them, the snack went the way of the dragon.

**'A baked bean flavour was loudly trumpeted, the product of "a year's research and development".'**

**Opposite:** British beef (1972) meets Kung Fuey (1975).

**Below:** Good old seaside fun from Chipsticks circa 1978, and good old casual racism from Quavers (1977).

Other companies also took their starchy corn, wheat and potato creations to the takeaway in search of a taste sensation – Smiths' Chinese flavour Quavers sort of approximated spicy beef, KP Skips dipped into a sweet 'n' sour sauce, and even Benson's attempted a rudimentary prawn cracker – but the real winners were to be found wrapped in newspaper down the good old British chippy. Smiths' much imitated Chipsticks took a patriotic approach, with packet design and TV advertising that riffed on saucy seaside postcard humour (initially aimed at an adult audience with lashings of innuendo but soon softened to kid-friendly Punch and Judy show standards).

Oily, yet moreish, these flaky, puffed-up sticks of potato and maize concealed often intense and acerbic flavours, the salt 'n' vinegar variety being particularly nasal. Tudor's version, Saucy Fries, mimicked the similarly piquant tang of a bottle of HP whereas, puzzlingly, Americans would have been more familiar with Andy Capp's Pub Fries, the distributor (Goodmark Foods) feeling that the Hartlepool-based layabout made for a good mascot. At least they weren't Mini Chips, KP's appallingly dry, solid spikes of potato, deemed so bland by marketers that they were sold under the tagline, 'You can hear the taste'. When your snack product cannot be enjoyed without calling upon the assistance of another sense organ, you know it's in trouble.

By the late '70s, the boffins in the food science labs were coming into their own. Chicken 'n' sage, fried onion and curry flavoured crisps were commonplace. Golden Wonder's crispy bacon flavour (created by the controlled burning of hickory sawdust) was among their top sellers, along with beef 'n' onion and sausage 'n' tomato, while a super-confident Smiths were game enough to risk a 'mystery flavour' for their astrology-themed snack, Zodiacs. In 1979 United Biscuits claimed they had over 200 flavours 'under review' for possible use in their crisp range, and the other big players were undoubtedly juggling similar numbers.

Many of them now outsourced their seasoning requirements to the likes of Glentham International of Twickenham (chicken tandoori, sweet and sour pork), Dinoval (Bolognese sauce, hamburger) or Griffith Laboratories of Derby (the inventors of salt 'n' vinegar, so they claimed, although how hard could that have been?). The first of these was about to drop a flavour bomb so big it would change the fried potato landscape forever. All thanks to a supercilious TV chef.

Fanny Cradock started the decade as the queen of British cuisine and ended it as a laughing stock. The success of her long-running cookery series had been undermined by one dyspeptic appearance as a celebrity expert on *The Big Time*, a documentary-cum-talent show for the Beeb. For years, however, Cradock was known as the champion of a certain sophisticated signature dish that would eventually become a byword for 1970s naffness.

**Opposite:** Out of the unknown and into the gob – Smith's Zodiacs (1979). Dubious rejuvenation claims ahoy, circa 1987.

**Below:** Shouldn't this offer have been on packets of McCoys? (1986). The acme of deep-fried daintiness, KP Skips (1976).

moment' and brought in gargantuan professional wrestler Giant Haystacks to act the ponce on TV. They never looked back.

Over in Bradford, a company that would later become synonymous with unusual and strong flavours had just relocated to a new factory in Duncombe Street. Seabrook Crisps (so named after a local photographer's shop misspelled owner Charles Brook's name) pioneered the use of sunflower oil and sea salt, as well as grammatically challenged slogans ('More' – Than A 'Snack'). From the mid-'80s their roster boasted 'Wuster' sauce, Canadian ham, roast garlic, sweetcorn, and bacon 'n' brown sauce among the usual array of onion, cheese and chicken flavours.

The prawn cocktail, transplanted from Las Vegas surf 'n' turf buffets, via Berni Inn and *Abigail's Party*, rose to epicurean eminence under her stewardship. Yet it wasn't until 1980 that Glentham managed to capture perfectly its seafood-in-a-marie-rose-sauce essence. Associations with retro kitsch didn't stop Smiths, Tudor and Golden Wonder releasing rival flavours within months of each other, and opening the floodgates for the prawn cocktail plague. KP Skips rebranded themselves as 'Britain's daintiest snack' with 'the flavour of the

Resolutely northern, their ongoing success gave the lie to the theory that only namby-pamby southerners would approach anything a bit fancy. Smiths remained poker-faced and commissioned some research into regional tastes: 'Northerners prefer barbecue chicken and other meaty flavours' they stated baldly. 'In the Midlands, cheese crisps take over, and down south the milder tastes are preferred.'

Another Seabrook advance was the use of the 'crinkle cut' for their crisps. The theory went that crinkles would enhance the flavour by increasing the surface area of each individual crisp, thus allowing more contact between tongue and titbit. In practice it was nothing more than a gimmick. KP's Crinkles launched in 1980, with an offer to obtain an 'I'm a KP Crinkle-ologist' badge that might just as well have read 'Please kick seven bells out of me'. Smiths' Crinkle Cut copycats claimed 'From now on ordinary crisps will seem a bit flat', which was a bit rich coming from the makers of Square Crisps.

**Opposite:** The KP friars swap pick 'n' mix belief for pick 'n' mix beef. Plus 'In what way is this not just, you know, "cheese"?'

Walkers leap aboard the 'finicky flavours' bandwagon (1989).

**Below:** Unnecessary inverted commas not 'pictured'. Seabrook's crisps circa 1984.

Flavour experimentation waned as the '90s loomed ahead, with novelty crisps rising and falling from favour in quick succession. KP Pizza crisps, apparently devised by clerical cartoon frontman 'Brother Angelo', were swiftly carried away to join the choir invisible. Walkers' spicy sausage flavour, the company's one ambitious attempt at something out of the ordinary, also long exceeded their sell-by date. And the less said about Benson's XL corned beef crisps the better. In 1991 *The Times* reported that the UK was home to forty-four different flavours of crisp, more than any other country, and an unsustainable high for the snack industry. The torch eventually passed back to Tudor ('the only crisp worth its salt') who introduced the fried potato/chocolate combo in – where else? – Scotland, sounding the death knell for the tasteful crunch and opening the door for the 'gourmet chip'.

Britain's favourite flavours faced assault-n-vinegar on two fronts. While American atrocities of the sweet chilli, nacho cheese and 'cool ranch' variety drifted lazily across the Atlantic on a Frito-Lay Lilo, further battle lines were being drawn in Brussels. The tabloids fingered German industry commissioner Martin Bangemann, 'the Eurocrat determined to ban our flavoured crisps' under a Common Market directive restricting the use of artificial additives. The British response was clear: you can straighten our bananas and stop us smacking our kids, but keep your hands off our sacred cheese 'n' onion, Fritz! It seemed that Reyner Banham had been right all along. For him, as for all Britons, the crisp was a 'ritual substitute for solid food, the kind of token victual that ancient peoples buried with their dead, the nutriment of angels rather than mortal flesh'. Good luck with those Scampi Fries in heaven, St Peter.

## ✻ SALT 'N' SHAKE

Don't bother trying to look up the origins of Salt 'n' Shake on the Internet. The definitive story is harder to find than a little blue salt bag in a bin full of catering plasters. What is it? A guilty secret? Some versions involve one-armed ex-servicemen, trade union disputes and early child labour. Others dwell on stolen salt cellars and layers of Holmesian intrigue. As in most cases, the likely answer is

**Opposite:** The second coming of the sachet. Salt 'n' Shake (1975).

probably the simplest: that Frank Smith came up with the idea, around 1920, of lobbing a small wrap of salt into each packet just to make the crisps taste nicer.

The original flavour enhancer, that unfussy twist of blue paper, served Smiths' Salt 'n' Shake well until 1965 when the company was taken over by General Mills. The new American-owned regime set about rationalising the crisp range, scrapping the in-bag superfluity in favour of ready salted, and concentrating instead on the invention of a whole variety of flavours. But what our colonial cousins, with their 200-year history and shoot-for-the-moon forward thinking, neglected to take into account was the nostalgic disposition of the Great British Public.

Ah, the Great British Public: what a contrary bunch! For the best part of forty years they'd grumbled into their plain bags of crisps from a dark corner of the snug or works canteen. Then, faced with a veritable smorgasbord of choice, they'd started banging on about the good old days of austerity, make-do-and-mend, and do-it-yourself crisp seasoning. So it was in 1975 that Salt 'n' Shake was reintroduced after a 'sustained campaign' by consumers. Who needs Facebook groups and online petitions when a spot of collective nationwide whingeing will do the job?

Having won the right to decide whether or not to give themselves high blood pressure, the Great British Public found something else to complain about. Instead of the old twist-wrap system, the salt now came in a small, hermetically sealed sachet. Smiths, explained a spokesman unconvincingly, had 'lost the blueprints for the machine that twisted the bags' during the takeover. Purchasing Salt 'n' Shake became something of a lottery, with salt distribution a hit and miss affair. Occasional double-bag bonuses were outweighed by crushing crisp-only disappointments.

Another change of hands, this time to Nabisco, led to a half-baked attempt at brand extension in Flavour 'n' Shake, a nine-pack selection of all-plain crisps packaged with ten envelopes of artificial salt and vinegar, tomato sauce, fish and chips or spicy flavours. Though popular with kids, particularly those who liked to mix and match or over-season their crisps, oldies suffering from chemical burns to their taste buds were less impressed. Flavour 'n' Shake didn't survive the final acquisition of Smiths by current owner Walkers. Salt 'n' Shake, on the other hand, are still available, but you needn't bother trying to look them up on the official company website. They're not there. What are they? A guilty secret?

**'Occasional double-bag bonuses were outweighed by crushing crisp-only disappointments.'**

## * HEDGEHOG CRISPS

It seems baffling now but, for a short while at the start of the '80s, hedgehogs were the last word in pant-wetting hilarity. *Not The Nine O'Clock News* was the trailblazer, where nary a week went by without Mel Smith stuffing his face full of freshly squashed hedgehog sandwich. The image was considered iconic enough to adorn the team's second LP sketch compilation and, as the audience's

**Opposite:** Not so much a bag of crisps, more a can of worms. Hedgehog crisps (1981).

ensuing, mock-horrified laughter faded, this small, spiny mammal emerged as a kind of shorthand for outrageous, boundary-pushing comedy. So it must have been with a knowing smile that Philip Lewis, landlord of the Vaults in Welshpool, served up his first batch of Hedgehog Flavoured Crisps to the regulars in 1981.

Invented at the request of gypsy customers – so the quaint story trotted out by Lewis had it back then – Hedgehog crisps, we were assured, were the closest thing to eating a real live Mrs Tiggy-Winkle. 'Old gypsies who used to eat baked hedgehog say it tastes something like veal,' he alleged, to a flurry of media interest. Esther Rantzen took to the streets in a blind taste test for *That's Life!*, gleefully recording the disgusted expressions of OAPs as she revealed what flavour they'd been enjoying. Kids, only too used to checking bonfires for hibernating hedgehogs and avoiding traffic lest they end up flattened like one, snuck off to corner shops for the controversial crisps deemed 'worth crossing the road for'. The RSPCA, being neither gruesome nor gourmet, flew right off the handle.

Bristling under pressure, Lewis finally admitted that no actual hedgehogs were harmed in the making of his crisps and the 'traditional country fare' flavour was actually a credulity-stretching combination of hedgerow herbs and hog fat. The Office of Fair Trading, alerted to the fact there was more of pork than porcupine about the product, insisted on some important point-of-law rebranding. Thus, 'Hedgehog Flavoured' became the subtly less misleading 'Hedgehog Flavour' and the rear of the packets gained a few lines of pro-wildlife waffle. Publican Phil ditched his Romany research team and eventually sold up to Benson's of Preston, who had a purpose-built manufacturing and distribution plant in Newport ready to meet public demand. By 1986, they were shifting 12 million bags a year.

Perhaps it was a humourless refusal to diversify ('We have no plans to make mole or curried rat flavoured crisps or anything like that,' claimed Benson's general sales manager), or a further attempt to reposition the Hedgehog brand as the world's first 100 per cent organic crisps, but the end, when it came, was swift. A downturn in fortunes at Benson's in the '90s sealed their fate as surely as any foil-fresh bag. Hedgehog crisps (by then only available in rather bland cheese and tomato or lightly salted varieties rather than the more obvious prickled onion) departed for the giant cardboard box in the sky. The humble hedgehog, naturally, went on to occupy its rightful status in the eyes of a new generation: as an anthropomorphic blue video game character. Sonic this new impostor may have been, for sure, but was he as tasty in a sandwich?

---

**'"We have no plans to make mole or curried rat flavoured crisps or anything like that," claimed Benson's general sales manager.'**

---

## THE ART OF MAIZE

The best thing about savoury snacks, from a kid's point of view, is the independence they represent. You buy them yourself with your own money, and eat them where and when you fancy (or at least can get away with). Best of all, they bear little or no relation to all that boring old 'proper' food your mum tries to shove down your gullet when you go home. If the flavours don't actually taste anything like their descriptions, that's surely a bonus. But snack firms have another trick up their sleeves to distance their liberating bags of fun from the everyday meat and two veg grind: the corn or potato puff, warped into a pleasingly wacky shape.

Large-scale corn snack cookery is nothing like any cuisine you'll have encountered. For one thing, it has a strangely sadomasochistic vocabulary all of its own involving twin-screw extrusion cookers, kneading zones, surge bins and feeder shafts. Essentially, the powdered potato or corn meal is mixed with water, squeezed through a heated tube by a long screw, cooked at super-high temperatures to create that mouth-melting puffy texture, forced through a metal die cut in whatever shape you choose, and cut to length by rotating knives. The resulting 'collette' falls into a big spinning drum to be fried and coated with whatever giddy numerical flavourings Brussels will allow, along with lashings of – as the accepted industry term has it – liquid cheese slurry. It's a maize-based abattoir, really. Best not to think about it.

**Opposite:** Years of the dragon – spicy tomato (1978) and original (1975) Walker's Snaps.

**Below:** Snack geometry basics – Smith's Quavers (1968) and KP Griddles (1982).

Still, what the nine-year-old eye doesn't see, the good folk of Ashby-de-la-Zouch get away with, and such munchable mutations became big sellers during the early 1970s. Phase one consisted of two basic shapes: the puffed-up cheesy lozenge, as exemplified by Golden Wonder's Wotsits of 1971, and the flattened shape that curled up at the edges, initiated by Smiths in 1968 with the Quaver, and enhanced by Walkers in 1975 for a rare excursion into shaped snacks, the Snap. The adverts for Snaps handily summed up the sensory experience of the ideal corn snack, laid out by the eponymous Harry H. Corbett-voiced dragon as consisting of, a) the crunch, b) the 'melt in your maahf' and c) the flavour explosion. Despite this canny technical dissection of the snacking experience, Walkers never ventured too far into multiform manufacture, the relatively straightforward flattened puffery of Say Cheese and Bitza Pizza being as daring as they got.

For everyone else, the game was afoot, and phase two was more topologically adventurous. For this, a more dense form of corn pulp allowed a greater degree of control, and the resulting snacks were crunchier. Simplest of these was the ring, pioneered in 1970 with Smiths Onyums, onion rings in maize form with an off-the-peg cartoon Frenchman on the pack, beating Golden Wonder Ringos to the shelves by almost three years, and KP's perenially popular finger-sized Hula Hoops by two. Last, and very possibly least, KP Griddles ('with the holes in the middles!') rolled up at the end of the decade.

DICK TURPIN
ENGLAND'S MOST NOTORIOUS HIGHWAYMAN WAS BORN IN ESSEX IN 1705. AT 21, HE OPENED A BUTCHER'S SHOP-WITH VENISON STOLEN FOR HIM FROM WALTHAM FOREST.
LATER TURPIN JOINED THE GREGORY GANG, STEALING DEER AND ROBBING STAGECOACHES.
IN 1737 HIS PARTNER TOM KING WAS ACCIDENTALLY SHOT AND KILLED BY TURPIN IN A STRUGGLE WITH AN INNKEEPER OVER A STOLEN HORSE.
TURPIN MOVED TO YORKSHIRE USING AN ALIAS. HE TRADED IN STOLEN HORSES BUT WAS ARRESTED FOR SHOOTING HIS LANDLORDS GAMECOCK. HIS IDENTITY WAS DISCOVERED.
TURPIN WAS SENTENCED TO HANG AT TYBURN GALLOWS ON APRIL 7th 1739. HE BOUGHT NEW CLOTHES AND EVEN PAID FOR MOURNERS.
YOU NEEDN'T COMMIT HIGHWAY ROBBERY FOR KP GRIDDLES! YOUR SHOP WILL SWOP THIS COUPON FOR ONE OF THE 18 PACKS IN OUR NEW SERIES!
KP GRIDDLES
Crisp potato snack
BEEF FLAVOUR
Kids will do almost any thing for Griddles!
GRIDDLES
COCKTAIL FLAVOUR
FREE KP GET A PACK OF GRIDDLES WITH THIS COUPON!
KIDS! Cut out this coupon and take it to your KP shopkeeper. He'll swop it for a FREE packet of Beef or Prawn Cocktail flavour Griddles. But hurry you must do it by the end of June 1982.
TO THE SHOPKEEPER
KP Foods Ltd., Dept. 30006, 34 Queens Square, Corby, Northants, NN17 1NN
FREE

**Opposite:** Your coupons or your life – dandy highway robbery from Griddles (1982).

**Below:** The Fabergé egg of moulded snacks, KP Wickers (1981).

As shapes became more ambitious, their quasi-geometric descriptions began to cause confusion. Smiths released their ground-breaking spiral-shaped potato puffs in 1974, heralding a new development which, as they modestly put it, 'could be as important as the invention of crisps'. Whether you called them Quirls or Twists depended, initially, on where in the country you bought them, until everyone settled down with the latter name. Things were simpler at the start of the decade when their intricately lattice-shaped Chekkers were called the same thing countrywide. Incidentally, the lattice shape was, for some reason, something of an obsession with snack companies, reaching its zenith in 1981 with KP's finely wrought Wickers.

These miniature wickerwork envelopes in modish prawn cocktail flavour were promoted, oddly, by adverts featuring an all-singing, all-dancing medieval court. This fierce high-tech one-upmanship soon established the shaped snack market as the Formula One of the tuck shop.

Snacketeers enlisted the help of good old industrial food dye to help define their vague wobbly forms. In 1975 Smiths showed off their bacon rasher-aping product Frazzles, blessed with an 'exciting flavour, superior to that of any bacon flavour product' by adding little brown streaks of Lord-knows-what concentrate.

It wasn't just the industry giants who were screwing that corn pulp. Tudor cooked up their knobbly Rustlers and Tags, and in 1972 their cheesy Rolls were being touted as 'a technological breakthrough in snack food production' – yes, there was a lot of this kind of talk – attaining unheard-of levels of melt-in-the-mouth bliss. 'Mouthfeel' was the daftly named but increasingly important quality that separated a light, fluffy savoury success from a rock-hard, misshapen catastrophe. Although one

**'This fierce high-tech one-upmanship soon established the shaped snack market as the Formula One of the tuck shop.'**

of the by-products of snack extrusion failure, namely the occasional lump of solid flavouring lurking at the bottom of the bag, became a prized delicacy among junior gourmets whose taste buds were living on borrowed time.

Once the basics of moulding were mastered, things got ambitious with a spate of representational realism.

KP's bacon flavour Whiz Wheels literally surfed the 1978 Zeitgeist by aping the little plastic cylinders to be found on those trendy new things called skateboards. They weren't the first to make wheels. The good people of Tudor had beaten them to it by two years with their similarly spoked Forty Niners, and the cash and carries of the north groaned under the weight of gigantic, squirrel-adorned packs of the supersized Nibb-It Wheelz.

None of those wheels, however, would have got you very far by the time the packet was opened. The higher snack artisans aimed, the harder they fell when contents settled in transit. KP's Outer Spacers were frequently scarred by some colossal intergalactic war that broke out halfway up the M6. Smiths' Farmer Browns, a hopelessly over-ambitious farmyard miscellany promising 'bags of moo, neigh, woof, baa and cock-a-doodle doo', looked more like an assortment of fossils straight from the primeval sludge. Most unfortunate of all, the plucky little daredevils in a packet of KP Sky Divers were prone to all manner of horrendous injuries, suggesting a product recall at the parachute makers was in order. Perhaps the way to go was towards abstraction: Golden Wonder's Atom Smashers were supposedly modelled on the contents of a particle accelerator, but looked suspiciously like bog-standard noughts and crosses to the physics-ignorant kid on the street.

**Opposite:** The culinary equivalent of Halford's – a big bag of Nibb-it Wheelz (1986); the dimension-warping snackery of Golden Wonder Odduns (1983).

**Below:** Lunchbox meltdown with Golden Wonder Atom Smashers (1978); a free coroner's report in every bag of KP Sky Divers (1980); Excelsior emulsified by Golden Wonder Super Heroes (1980).

Golden Wonder ducked out of the novelty shape market in 1978, dismissing it as faddish, but looked at the sales figures for Smiths' all-conquering Monster Munch and swiftly rethought. In 1983 they teamed up with DC Comics to launch Super Heroes: Spiderman and Superman symbols fully endorsed by the webslinger and man of steel. Golden Wonder fancied their chances, declaring Monster Munch to be 'nearing the end of its product life'. They were rapidly proved wrong.

The early 1980s saw the high-water mark of snack diversity. As the more outlandish varieties became extinct, it was clear that the classical forms were the most durable: the Quaver, the Wotsit, the Ringo; timeless shapes that exist outside fickle underage fashion. The only long-stay snack to have joined their ranks since the golden years is Golden Wonder's Nik-Nak, which made a virtue of its own deep-fried deformity, a scampi 'n' lemon flavoured Elephant Man. So popular has it become around the world in various guises, it's even earned the highest accolade of all: its very own dedicated extrusion cooker. So if you fancy making your own unlimited supply of Nik-Naks, get your hands on the JRJ Nik-Naks Extruder, a snip at £37,000. You might have to supply your own cheese slurry, though.

# COME FEBRUA
# BE RAIDED BY LI

# RY YOU WILL
# TTLE MONSTERS.

We have a launch situation.

A new crunchy snack from KP takes to the TV airwaves on 9th February.

It's called 'Space Raiders'. And it takes three forms: Cheese, Beef and Pickled Onion.

You would be well advised to stock up. Kids will materialise from nowhere.

## * OUTER SPACERS

*Star Wars* has a lot to answer for. In terms of the hasty badging of snack foods with a picture of R2-D2 (or, more likely, a picture of something sufficiently unlike R2-D2 to bypass the mighty 20th Century Fox legal team), its impact couldn't be underestimated. One snack, however, was ahead of the game. In 1976, while George Lucas was still pratting about at Elstree, KP launched

**Opposite and below:** 'My God! It's full of crumbs!' Outer Spacers: the first generation, prior to embarking on a face odyssey (1976).

their first wave of Outer Spacers, intergalactic spaceships rendered in puffy corn.

Inevitably, you had to use your imagination. The beefburger flavour rockets were possibly the most convincing, while the pickled onion space stations looked more like lifebelts than successors to Skylab. Bringing up the rear were the rather boring, unadorned cross shapes given that most evocative of monikers: chutney flavour starships. The results wouldn't have given Industrial Light and Magic's model makers any sleepless nights, but with the aid of a few artists' impressions on the packs, which cunningly retro-fitted radar dishes and laser cannons onto the basic, blobby chassis, they literally flew into the mouths of a generation of would-be astronauts.

Though never toppling arch-rivals Smiths' Horror Bags, Outer Spacers sold steadily for the rest of the decade. Then sales dipped, and mucking about commenced. In 1981 they were repackaged in voguish metallic bags. In 1982 those under-performing starships were decommissioned in favour of cheese and ham flavour aliens. This was just the beginning. The following year the extra-terrestrials took over, the renamed Alien Spacers featuring odd new shapes in salt 'n' vinegar, cheese and onion and prawn cocktail flavours. What happened? For many kids, this invasion was as big a disappointment as *Return of the Jedi*, but our alien overlords forged ahead undaunted. In 1985 came a rather nifty innovation: comic strips on the packs which continued on the inside of the bag. This still wasn't providing the shot in the arm KP's accountants were after, though, and in 1986 they started casting about for a fresh angle.

They found it in the unlikely form of daft cartoon punks Sigue Sigue Sputnik. The ludicrous techno-gonk stylings of Tony James and his melody-dodging chums were lifted wholesale by KP's artists, now let loose on virulent new strains of green and purple printer's ink. Behold the Space Raiders, a fugitive gang of bogbrush-headed renegades led by Astra, 'a ruthless female outlaw' cruising the cosmos for galactic booty in impractically funky garb. The garishness extended to the snacks themselves, now decked out in EEC-frightening hues of green and red. This was all achingly hip (for a corn snack at least), but improbably the brand kept going, and still exists today, though you might have to look hard for evidence – a bit like the space programme itself.

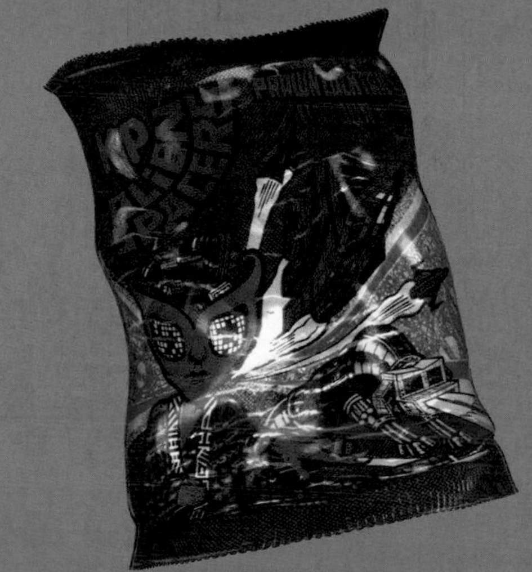

## ✻ HORROR BAGS

For the '70s child, horror was an obsession. It seemed to be everywhere yet nowhere at the same time: on late night ITV showings of Hammer films you were forbidden to watch, cinema releases of newer films like *The Omen* you hadn't a chance of getting into, or dog-eared volumes like the *Pan Book of Horror Stories* passed illicitly round the playground on days you were off sick. If a lot of

**Opposite:** Bite of the living dead – Horror Bags Fangs and Bones (1975), Claws (1976) and Ribs (1977).

it turned out to be a bit crap when you finally got hold of it, no matter. It was the thrill of that forbidden 'X' certificate that mattered the most: this was stuff we weren't supposed to see.

It's not a principle you can readily apply to food, but in the latter half of the '70s they had a good try. Sweet shops went mad for sugar skulls and Phantom Chews, while the freezer cabinet became chilling in all senses with a variety of vampire and Frankenstein-themed lollies. Nothing, however, had quite the impact of Horror Bags, a durable line of unsavoury savouries from Smiths launched in 1975.

Clad in the requisite red and black bloodcurdling horror livery, they were among the very first of the shaped corn snacks to actually try to look like something, namely bones and fangs in salt 'n' vinegar and cheese and onion flavours respectively. Masks and glove puppets were given away in competitions, and the whole concept was topped off by a series of TV ads featuring a crap Dracula 'who tries to be frightening but continually fails'.

All innocent fun, but Smiths had reckoned without the Great British tabloids, who railed against the '"X" certificate snacks', drafting in one Dr James Willis, psychiatric consultant at Guy's Hospital, for an academic drubbing. 'Using unpleasant stimuli as a selling line could disturb a child in the same way that a vulnerable youngster can be disturbed by early exposure to sexual things,' claimed the doctor. 'The feelings and fantasies of children should not be exploited.'

Rubber bats as bad as porn? What you talkin' 'bout, Willis? Smiths kept their heads, and fired back some common sense. 'Children like wearing the fangs, Dracula-style, before eating them,' said a spokesman winningly. 'It's good for children to be on fun terms with things which, in other circumstances, might frighten them.' This was enough to see off the curmudgeons, and Horror Bags soared to the top of the snacks market with a turnover of £4 million per year.

Buoyed by the emerging market in junior horror spearheaded by the likes of *Monster Fun* comic and *Rentaghost*, Smiths added a new variety each subsequent year: Freaky Bacon flavour claws, Vampire Vinegar Ribs, and finally 1978's Bats in Batburger flavour (all right, beef 'n' onion). The reign of terror only came to an end when Smiths chanced upon another monstrous snack that would become even bigger...

## * MONSTER MUNCH

The '70s fad for outlandish corn snacks reached saturation point in the decade's latter half. You name it, a factory somewhere had milled a metal die in the shape of it and shoved some pulped maize through it. Inevitably, returns diminished. It took Smiths to spot the obvious way to stand out from the pack: make it bigger. On its 1977 launch, everything about roast beef flavour Monster Munch was

**Opposite:** Mouth-watering misshapes – the original Monster Munch pair (1977).

supersized: the packs, the snacks, the wibbly-wobbly typeface. And all yours for a very reasonable 7p. 'An incredible bulk of snack,' enthused the man from Smiths, 'more for the price than ever seen before.'

Cannily, the realist fashion was jettisoned for a bit of abstraction. No attempt was made to explain what the contents represented. A paw? An eye? Some other orifice? It was 'said by children during research to resemble giant squashed spiders and Loch Ness monsters'. A child's imagination is a wonderful thing, especially when it does the marketing man's work for him.

TV ads built up a Muppet-like world of plush, googly-eyed freaks who hung about scoffing the snacks, conversing in a linguistic mixture of Captain Caveman and Bill and Ben. For seven-year-olds, these were aspirational figures. There was dissent, however, from the *Observer*, which got the wrong end of the stick entirely about a piece of packet-back whimsy concerning dragons eating little girls, and raged about this 'repellently packaged brand of potato crisp known as Monstermunch [sic]', only to apologise the following week after they'd calmed down a bit.

The adverts were sitcoms in miniature, complete with an expanding cast. The original red roast beef monster (goofy grin, lolling tongue) was joined in 1980 by a pickled onion pal (yellow, one eye). A year later came a 'saucy' cohort (blue, four arms, top hat, prone to posing as a doctor), and an orange shortarse with a shock of red hair who never appeared on the packs: a sort of Monster Without Portfolio.

They were a roaring, grunting success from the off, but Smiths did get carried away. In 1981 they also launched the doomed soft drink spin-off Monster Fizz: cola, cherryade and shandy flavours (not pickled-onion-ade, alas) sold in individual plastic bottles decorated with those same monster pals. It was trialled in the Southern TV area for a couple of months and, unsurprisingly, never heard of again.

The rest of the decade saw many reshuffles in the 'Munch' cabinet, with One-Eye temporarily losing his pickled onion post to the orange upstart, and much experimentation with giant prawn and sizzling bacon varieties. All hell broke loose in the '90s with new monsters, new flavours, 3D shenanigans and the like, diluting the brand and winning no fans. With a new century came the return of the old monsters, now garlanded with all the retro-ironic trappings pennies can buy, and lauded as grand old men of packed lunch show business. Saucy Monster is currently appearing in *The Government Inspector* at the Theatre Royal, Drury Lane.

## WHAT A GIVEAWAY

'Pester power', according to the *OED*, wasn't defined until 1979 (coincidentally the UNESCO International Year of the Child), though the *Observer* had reported on the phenomenon the previous Christmas. Cash-rich, time-poor parents were cut out of the loop as manufacturers devised 'pack-top' promotions that beckoned alluringly from supermarket shelves directly to their offspring. In the Queen's silver jubilee year, Golden Wonder took out a full-page newspaper ad targeting children with a pocket-money-saving coupon to 'cut the cost of crisps and snacks', going so far as to point out to any mums reading that this offer simply wasn't for them. The crisp cartel had found their ideal consumer base: solvent, yes, but also bored, easily distracted and dissolute.

Discounted samples or money-off vouchers were one thing but, household budgeting not being a concept kids could readily grasp (even Golden Wonder had promised the additional incentive of a pop poster 'of ABBA, Starsky or Hutch'), it was their magpie instincts marketers appealed to. Bright, shiny offers flashed across the packets, encouraging that crucial first purchase at 'point of sale' in shops, and validating repeat purchases through the collection of on-pack tokens. In a market traditionally dominated by short-termism, if the products themselves couldn't foster brand loyalty, then there had to be a secondary reward system – a whole heap of free stuff.

The instructions varied but most giveaways followed the same basic rules: find tokens on the reverse of the pack, print your name and full address in BLOCK CAPITALS on a piece of notepaper, enclose in an envelope with a stamp to cover postage, send to a PO Box somewhere in Kent and allow twenty-eight days for delivery (while stocks last).

**Opposite:** Bri-nylon beatitude – a heavenly KP friar offer (1981).

**Below:** Great big lumps – original Golden Wonder Wotsits (1971) and KP's Arthur Mullard-voiced 'Brother John' advert (1980).

For the rookie collector, an item gained thus might be a badge, sticker or T-shirt emblazoned with the brand's logo – 'I'm a Tudor flavour raver!' – although quite why such eBay-clogging promotional bum-fodder was prized is still a mystery. A full set of the KP friars in ceramic mug form, for example, could take months to stockpile, a task requiring the patience of a saint (or, at the very least, the riches of the Vatican).

Down the years, nearly every kid's hobby and interest was mined for gift potential. Tudor's greatest innovation was the decoration of packs with extra-curricular folderol, beginning in 1971 with the serialised adventures of Tudor Crisps and His Merry Flavours, a Robin Hood-like gang larking about in comic strips and quizzes. As a spokesman grandly put it, 'We are attempting to give an extra dimension to crisp eating by giving consumers the opportunity to have fun at the same time.' How terribly thoughtful of them. KP expanded into own-brand superheroes with a comic starring Captain Krunch – who, while he may have had the power of flight, failed to take off with punters – although most companies sensibly rode the coat-tails of established celebrities.

Cuddly Kenny Everett was one of the most entertaining, lending a giant foam hand to help hawk free 'Video Stars' posters from the front of Smiths crisps. He was later replaced by fellow Wunnerful Radio 1 DJ Sir Jim'll Saville and his Fix-It competition (which included the chance to win

YOUNG JIMMY WATSON WAS WALKING HIS DOG SHEP NEAR THE FLATS WHERE THEY LIVE, WHEN SHEP CUT HIS PAW ON A BROKEN BOTTLE LEFT LYING ON THE PAVEMENT BY SOMEONE:

-THIS IS THE PLACE

PDSA ANIMAL TREATMENT CENTRE

THE PDSA TREATMENT CENTRE IS WHERE HIS GRANNY TAKES HER OLD CAT TIBBLES - SHE CAN'T AFFORD TO PAY FOR A VET ON HER OLD AGE PENSION AND THE PDSA TREATS PETS FREE! THE PDSA EXISTS SOLELY ON VOLUNTARY CONTRIBUTIONS.

IN A FEW DAYS YOUNG JIMMY IS PLAYING WITH SHEP AS THOUGH NOTHING HAD HAPPENED.

## THE PDSA URGENTLY NEEDS YOUR HELP TO TREAT SICK & INJURED ANIMALS

OUR TARGET £15,000
2p FOR EVERY 10 EMPTY PACKS RETURNED

PLEASE HELP!

CHOICE OF 8

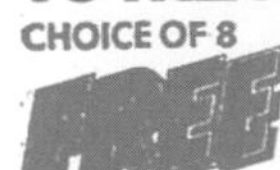


BADGES FOR EVERYONE WHO HELPS

The People's Dispensary for Sick Animals urgently needs YOUR help to treat sick and injured pets.
In Animal Treatment Centres all over the Country, the PDSA take care of nearly a million pets a year.
The PDSA give this help FREE to people who can't afford to pay for treatment for their pets. Without the help of the PDSA lots of children's and old people's pets might die.
So the PDSA needs all the help you can give.

That is why we are asking you to lend a helping paw.

### HOW YOU CAN HELP

Collect your empty SMITHS CRISPS packs. For every ten tokens you send us WE WILL GIVE THE PDSA 2P. ON YOUR BEHALF. For helping, we will send you a super pet badge that you can wear to show you are helping the pets.

*Tokens on all standard Crisps and Salt'n'Shake packs.*

**OUR TARGET IS TO RAISE £15,000 TO EQUIP PDSA TREATMENT CENTRES. REMEMBER THE MORE BADGES YOU SEND FOR THE MORE WE CAN HELP THE PETS.**

I'M HELPING THE PETS

BADGES-ACTUAL SIZE 2¼" DIA.

**TO GET YOUR FREE BADGES SEE THE DETAILS ON SPECIAL 'HELP THE PETS' SMITHS CRISPS PACKS**

**Opposite:** A tug at the heartstrings from Smith's (1977).

**Below:** Don't be fooled by these fey Flutter-byes (circa 1974). Tudor's free gifts were, as a rule, 'reet hard.'

sew-on patches of his pirate alter ego, Jim Lad, among others). Pop-pickers were equally well served by either Discos' 1981 tie-in compilation LP, *It's Disco Time* (on Pushbike Records), or Smiths' flop flexi-disc, 'When It Comes to the Crunch' ('Is it advertising or is it a new pop-hit?' – clue, it's neither). Walkers also did their Herculean bit to kill music with a C90 Agfa cassette for home taping. Yes, a blank cassette: top-drawer giftage in anyone's book.

Freebies were all well and good but they didn't keep the kids coming back for more. Crispi Crisps' solution aped the modus operandi of Green Shield Stamps, exchanging tokens for gifts from a catalogue, as did Smiths with Trader Smith's Bounty Box (an unconvincingly tanned Melvyn Hayes lookalike in white suit and panama hat wafting 'doubloon vouchers' at a bevy of dusky maidens). Tudor, however, always the first with more experimental ideas, pioneered the instant in-packet item collection, flinging out memorable telly ads and copious promotions from the basic giveaways of ornate plastic 'Flutter-byes', 'Wear-'Em-Scare-'Em' monster masks and footie rosettes, to the infamous 1972 'Munch Olympics'. Bunging a greaseproof plastic sachet into the bags allowed crisps and snacks to mirror what sweet cigarettes had been up to for years. Pretty soon sealed picture cards appeared inside packs of Golden Wonder: 'Have you sent for your All Stars album yet?' teased the blurb; '16 pages packed full of interesting soccer facts and figures, together with spaces to take your card collection.' The 1978 World Cup in Argentina

**Below:** Hula Hoops improve their formula circa 1980.

**Opposite:** Brush up your Wogan with Walkers' Pocket Trivia booklets (1986).

afforded a new set of international football faces and, when the sporting legends ran dry, 'TV All Stars' of the Rossiter/Corbett/Grayson calibre took over. Panini-sticker-style trading was positively encouraged and soon the playground cry, 'I'll swap you Basil Brush for Martin Shaw and Michel Platini,' was commonplace.

Of course, fatty old crisps had long since courted the world of sport. In 1968 Golden Wonder sponsored the British team at the Mexico Olympics and their later 'Go For Gold' competition offered £10,000 worth of prizes courtesy of a medal-wearing cartoon spud. Not to be outdone, Smiths gave away free 'Sport For All' badges to help raise £15,000 'to train our future Olympic champions' (which must be why Britain is now so lauded for its athletic achievement on the world stage). Hula Hoops also dished out the sporting medals, but for display purposes only. No false promises there, then: no unattainable goals or unrealistic expectations, just cheap plastic crap in a cardboard folder.

Other, more worthy, *Blue Peter*-esque fundraisers flourished. Crisp-gorging bloaters could feel better about themselves by sending empty packets to 'Help the Pets' (Smiths' appeal to subsidise animal treatment centres for the PDSA), though at a whopping 2p for every ten bags returned, they needed to scare up 7.5 million wrappers to hit the £15,000 target. Such palsied corporate social responsibility also motivated Golden Wonder's Operation Survival, marking the twentieth anniversary of the World Wildlife Fund in 1981 with the distribution of 450,000 endangered species badges, before switching beneficiaries a few years later to the RSPCA.

WALKERS CRISPS
Pocket Trivia
CHILDREN'S

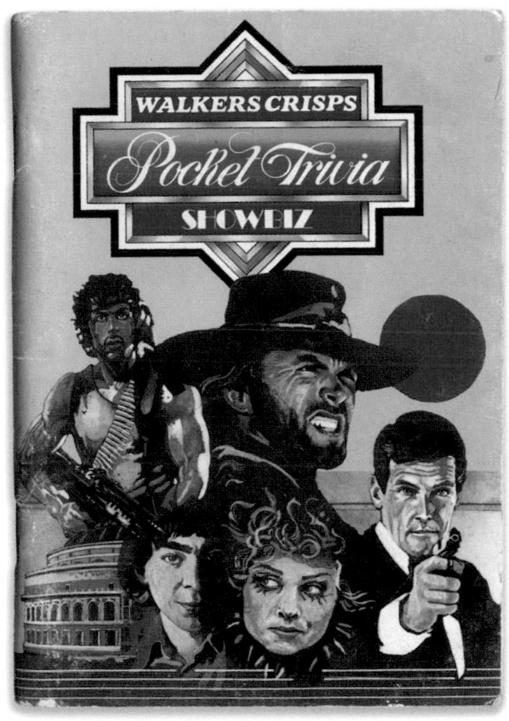
WALKERS CRISPS
Pocket Trivia
SHOWBIZ

WALKERS CRISPS
Pocket Trivia
TV&RADIO
THE QUEEN
Q

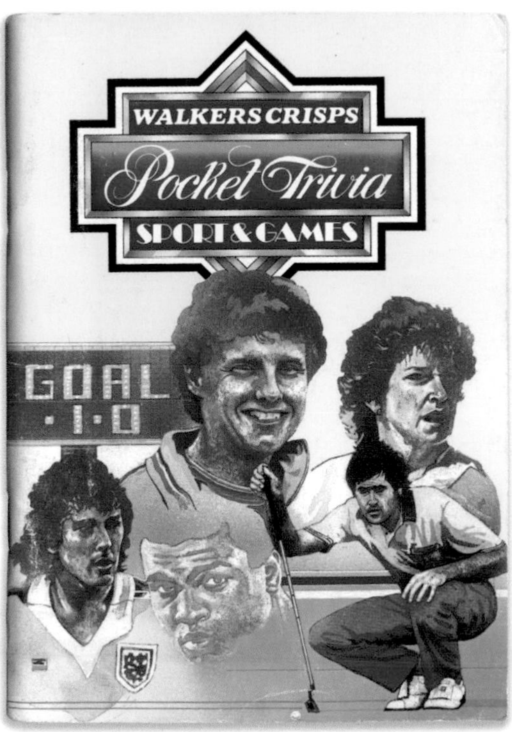
WALKERS CRISPS
Pocket Trivia
SPORT&GAMES
GOAL
1-0

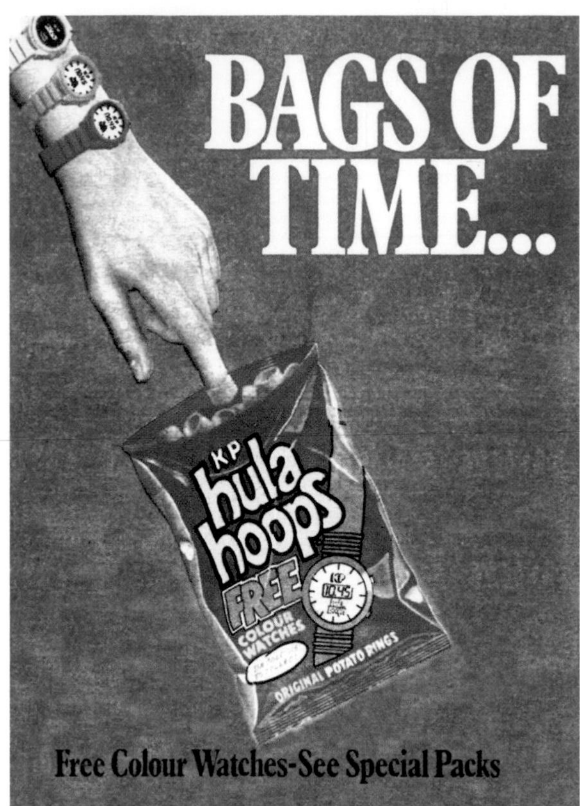


Mostly, though, crisp companies said, 'Sod the carbon footprint, let's all go on holiday somewhere hot.' Smiths' Chipitos did the honours in the '70s, with a 'spot the bandito' competition and top prize of a Mexican vacation, followed by something called 'Football Free-for-all' ('a jet trip to a top international, plus £20 spending money') which boasted a strikingly familiar pre-Fantasy Football pick-a-team entry dynamic. In 1981 an avant-garde tie-up with box-office blockbuster *Clash of the Titans*, saw all the Smiths snacks join forces for a £10,000 holiday promotion (well, it was either that or *On Golden Pond*) but none could beat the marriage of Charles and Di for utter flag-waving extravagance. 'Win a £1,000 Sovereign holiday for two in the resort of your choice, plus 5 prizes of Super FERGUSON video cassette recorders (and a special souvenir cassette of the Royal Wedding).

KP preached knowledge in place of avarice, launching their Crinkles with a tenuous 'educational broadsheet giving interesting facts about 'crinkly phenomena' in everyday life, such as forked lightning, waves, ploughed fields and the treads of tyres'. Furthermore, Wotsits' 'Wonders of the Countryside' wall chart was an environmental competition in disguise: 'Foxes, field mice, wild flowers – colour them as they really are and you could win a big prize.' Points would be deducted for adding discarded packs of Wotsits strewn through the grass verges. All good Keep Britain Tidy nonsense, even so.

**Opposite:** Two very 'of their time' offers – big chunky digital watches from Hula Hoops (1986) and free Kodak film with Chipitos circa 1975.

**Below:** Send a postal order for 35p to a galaxy far, far away... post-Lucas space fun from Outer Spacers (1978) and Atom Smashers (1979).

And 250 runners-up prizes of Royal Wedding souvenir books.' What a lot of booty! It was almost enough to make you believe in princesses, fairytale marriages and happily-ever-afters.

For those whose wanderlust stretched no further than the back field, more modest flying apparatus was obtainable. Indeed, Golden Wonder's exclusive Laker Airways DC-10 model aircraft offer was more modest than most (although, even at only 90p, ultimately worth more than the Skytrain itself). Similarly jinxed, 4,000 Stingray-shaped lifebelts given away by Golden Wonder in 1965 were recalled amid safety experts' claims they could 'turn turtle' in deep water. More traditionally, though equally destined for a calamitous descent, Kung Fuey's high-flying dragon kite was a cotton and bamboo affair, on a single line (as was KP Outer Spacers' *Star Wars* X-wing fighter). For the two-line stunter version, prospective pilots needed to develop an unhealthy appetite for Cheese Wings.

Games and toys like these were naturally the most effective promotions for junior consumers, and it was an area Horror Bags excelled in. Iron-on transfers, flick-a-card games, identi-kits, skull-shaped clips or *Serpents & Stairs* (a board game) – you name it, the 'snacks that go crunch in the night' could brand it up and mail it out c/o Dracula's Dungeon, PO Box 3, Faversham. If the kids wanted bigger presents, like digital watches (courtesy of Hula Hoops) and skateboards (Quavers), or smaller ones, like playing cards

**Below:** Noble brow, clear gaze, firm mouth, stamps to cover postage – Golden Wonder's 1986 comics came not a moment too soon. Crispi Globetrotters, very much from the Troughton era, circa 1968.

**Opposite:** Horror Bags, with a sort of *Crimewatch* for goths (1976).

(Wotsits) and fibre-tipped pens (Snaps), then every demand could be anticipated and met. Who cared, as long as those avaricious tendencies were being nurtured, and the buying habits of adulthood consolidated? None of it really came for free, after all. Every pack simply encouraged further outlay.

As the years passed and the prize coffers emptied, the crisp packet promoters opted for route one: cold, hard cash and the old lucky dip trick. Notes were stuffed inside envelopes and smuggled into random packets. No need to collect the wrappers or read the small print now. Just munch your way through one bag, then another, and another in remorseless pursuit of that elusive fiver. The trinkets, the tat and the cute, classic collectables finally gave way to what the marketing managers understood better than anything else: naked greed. Because the real story behind these giveaways isn't some well-meant attempt to brighten children's lives with gifts and goodies. It's a dull one, full of loss leaders, brand loyalty and prime shelf-space contracts with retail outlets. Never peek behind the curtain – now that really is a giveaway.

> 'Just munch your way through one bag, then another, and another in remorseless pursuit of that elusive fiver.'

SMITHS
HORROR BAGS
IDENTI-KIT
PLUS
OFFER
FREE GHASTLY GIFTS
The gruesome game for 2-4 players.
Can you discover the identity
of the entombed horrors?
See these special Horror Bags for details.
BONES
SALT & VINEGAR FLAVOUR CORN & POTATO SNACK
CLAWS
BACON FLAVOUR CORN & POTATO SNACK
FANGS
It's worth 75p
Yours for 30p
when you buy Horror Bags

## ✻ RINGOS

Of all the ex-Beatles to name a crisp after! Golden Wonder's hoop-with-a-hole corn snacks first hit shops in 1973, the same year as their namesake's eponymous album, though both parties shunned the all too obvious tie-in opportunity. Ringos favoured instead the patronage of a cartoon caveman Professor character in beard and glasses – yeah, more like Lennon, really – and his prehistoric pal, Harry. Telly adverts

**Opposite:** Ringos were our first love, and they will be our last. Ringos of the future (1986) and Ringos of the past (1977).

featured the pair, in a variety of slapstick Stone Age situations, and the invention of assorted objects fashioned from Ringos (which, naturally, were munched to bits at the end). A *Flintstones*-style block of rock logo sealed the deal for anyone who'd missed the subtle allusions.

To promote the launch of salt and vinegar flavour in 1975, the Professor cropped up on packs and in comics, encouraging the inventive urges of kid consumers in return for a £200 shopping spree in Hamleys, the first of many Ringos prize giveaways. A year later, he was forced to share page real estate with Wotsits' panto horse underwriter, Wilbur, in a caption competition. The priggish rules ('We're looking for humour here, so make it as amusing as you can') and an increased £250 toy shop raid reward distracted from Ringos' reworked formula (now including potato) and new savoury chicken flavour. On TV, Wilbur, Harry and the Professor exchanged 'Crazy Caps' and pointed towards on-pack promotions for details of how to obtain your own.

A relaunch in 1977 heralded further changes. Fifty-three per cent more rings in the bag! A crunchier texture! Audrey the Dinosaur! The snack's fun-meets-facts tone, however, lingered like the uniquely powdery, pungent flavourings inside each bag. Tokens could now be collected in return for a *Giggle & Think* paperback, the Professor's final punctilious campaign before the primordial PR conceit was laid to rest for good. Ringos consequently entered the '80s with yet another new recipe – the addition of wheatflour necessitating a change in labelling to 'cereal and potato rings' – and an unpopular beef flavour.

Bombastic, big-movie-voiced adverts made much of the explosive might and naked power of the new flavours before ending on the bathetic question, 'Why journey to the centre of the Ringo, if the Ringo can journey to the centre of you?'

The answer came courtesy of Dalgety (owners of Spillers Winalot) who, in 1986, swallowed Golden Wonder whole in an acquisition from Imperial Tobacco – from dog ends to dog food in a single bound. A new pack design for Ringos coincided with the pan-brand multi-pack giveaway of miniature Marvel *Doctor Who* adventure comics starring Colin Baker (the one incarnation of the Time Lord who genuinely appeared to subsist primarily on a diet of crisps). Ultimately, the decade ended with a whimper, not a bang for Ringos, under the television stewardship of a singing cowboy in the mode of Gene Autry (by chance, also Ringo Starr's first musical influence) and the prophetic tagline 'No ring goes like a Ringo goes'. Sure enough, they were withdrawn from sale shortly afterwards. Attempted revivals by successive owners resulted only in disappointment and a resounding failure to recapture the Palaeolithic taste of the originals. After all, you can't reinvent the wheel.

**'Why journey to the centre of the Ringo, if the Ringo can journey to the centre of you?'**

## * FOOTBALL CRAZY

Crisps and football – wasn't it ever thus? Long before Gary Lineker returned from Nagoya Grampus to the strains of Peters and Lee and started encouraging British kids to munch fatty food from the touchline (as part of a balanced diet, of course), celebrity endorsements were widespread. Who was that flogging 'Superstar Tracksuits' on Smiths' salt 'n' vinegar flavour in 1977? Why, none other than poodle-permed,

**Opposite:** The meat pie's days are numbered – the terrace-friendly Football Crazy (1977).

serial walk-out merchant Kevin Keegan, taking time off from M25 lay-by beatings to earn a few quid. And was that really Ray Clemence encouraging us to send in a 7p stamp in return for a Golden Wonder All Stars wallchart? Or was it Ray Wilkins? Or both? Hard to tell.

Into this pre-Premiership scramble for the hearts, minds and piggy banks of the nation's children stepped Football Crazy, unconvincing ball-shaped nuggets of smoky bacon flavoured maize and potato named after a nineteenth-century Scottish folk song. The snack scored an early hat trick: first, it was priced at an accessible 4½p per bag; second, free promotional samples were handed out by leggy lovelies at footy grounds on match day; third, if you saved enough wrappers, you could send away and join the Football Crazy Club, qualifying for a tin badge, a rub-down transfer of your favourite team, and the regular club newspaper. Sadly, the contents of the latter are not on file at the British Library, but it's probably a safe bet that they included cartoons, jokes and (clean) terrace chants, much as had Chipsticks' *Football Fans Funbook* in 1974.

Recycling of material aside, Smiths' marketing muscle was not only flexed, it was pulled taut like a hamstring. Full-page ads appeared in the comics, illustrated by Paul Sample in his trademark Tom Sharpe *Wilt* novel-cover style, depicting a selection of fascinating facts about football, from the longest FA Cup tie to the heaviest goalkeeper (too many crisps, perhaps?). Such was the snack's success that questions were raised in the House of Commons when the mailing list of Football Crazy Club members was mistakenly sold on, in possibly the UK's earliest breach of computerised Data Protection policy. Smiths also missed a sitter by not launching a Chas & Dave-sponsored Snooker Loopy spin-off product to cash in on the '80s matchroom mania.

Nowadays, chances are you'll see your favourite soccer star appear on a Milan catwalk long before a packet of corn puffs, but in the '70s football players were lumpen Saturday workhorses. Hooliganism, racism and sexism, by and large, occurred off the pitch. How times change. In truth, most kids' sharp-end experience of the beautiful game wasn't the cheery rosettes and rattles of the Football Crazy Club. It was more like the mud-spattered brutality featured in Ken Loach's *Kes*, all lost-property-office-sourced kit, ritual last-to-be-picked humiliation and a clip round the ear from the spineless gym teacher in the bright red tracksuit. Crazy? You had to be.

## GOTTA MAKE WAY FOR THE POTATO SUPERIOR

When is a crisp not quite a crisp? When it's a disc-shaped savoury snack made from reconstituted potato flour, of course. Such an unappetising classification is inevitable when snack scientists seek to remould potatoes into more uniform shapes than their irregular, buckled natural state. It's a never-ending quest for comestible perfection.

When these eerily smooth clones first emerged, a little misdirection was called for to ease a sceptical public into acceptance. Pop music was key. KP launched Discos in 1978, playing on the snack's super-flat similarity to a platter of hit parade funk. The TV ads, sadly, plumped for the less funky device of dressing a chorus line-up as giant crisps, hopefully chanting 'We're Discos! We're Discos! We're KP Discos and we taste as different as we look, look, look!' Uncool visuals notwithstanding, Discos saw off their main rival, Golden Wonder's shell-like Rock 'N' Rollers, despite the latter's indisputably cooler front-of-bag cartoon rock hero.

Americans already had an even more highly evolved crisp, in the hyperbolic paraboloidal shape of the Pringle, but that most featureless of crisps was slow to catch on over here. Cadbury acquired the licence to make them on these shores from soap giant Procter and Gamble in 1978, renamed them Stackers, and test-marketed them to little approval. They weren't properly

**Opposite:** Old school swing with Golden Wonder Rock 'n' Rollers – this is why pickled onion punk had to happen (1976).

**Below:** King Cut Groovers – the perfect accompaniment to a Pookiesnackenburger or two (1986).

launched until 1983, and even then they came and went in short order, before P&G stepped in and rolled them out under their international title, Gilbert Harding lookalike mascot and all.

Another migrant oddity had better British success. Irish snack makers Adams Biscuits debuted Sam Spudz in 1977, a thick slice of reconstituted spud ('more filling than ordinary crisps') with a distinctive crimped shape and a yet more distinctive, though never satisfactorily explained, Bogart-esque private detective theme. Our eponymous gumshoe hero peered out of the packs from under his fedora, while on the back, comic strip intrigue was afoot. 'Quit stalling, Spudz. Make with the thicker crimped crisps or Fingers drills the broad!' 'Not a chance, Spatz! She may be a tasty dish, but that don't make her a great big beautiful mouthful of potato!' *Bugsy Malone* was never like this.

The crime capers may have confused the kids, but the crimped crisps caught on. Rival firms, however, avoided accusations of plagiarism by cunningly varying their adjectives. When KP entered the fray in 1980, their efforts were not crimped, but crinkled. Golden Wonder's variant of '84 sought to trump that with the grandiosely titled Royale Crinkle, but others showed greater originality. In '86 Rowntree offshoot Sooner Snacks launched Groovers, which were, obviously, grooved. They were later renamed Rowntree's Groovers, causing much sweet/savoury confusion, before settling down as King Cut Groovers, which sounded like a rockabilly revival act in the Stray Cats mould. What was it with crinkle crisps and American posturing? KP took the Yankophilia one step further in '87, calling their Real McCoys 'chips', the first time a crisp had been deliberately marketed under that US alias. McCoys, incidentally, were officially described as 'ridged', presumably to evoke those blue mountains of Virginia and the rugged types who chopped lumber therein.

Three years after McCoys, KP expanded yet further by importing Ripplins, 'a rippled crisp lookalike' made by their American sister company, Keebler. Something about that name, however, was deemed too effeminate for the British market. Alternatives were tried out, among them Crispins, Merits and Stripes, before KP finally settled on that manliest of names, Frisps. This was all a pre-emptive strike in a product war that commenced later in the year, when the newly Pepsico-aligned Walkers unleashed their entry in the corrugated canon, Ruffles. Which were, you've guessed it, ruffled. Not all these wavy crisps prospered, but they did wonders for thesaurus sales.

Frisps and their ilk also played on another '80s obsession – low fat. This was an area pioneered, again, by KP, who invented a process whereby superheated steam blasted the freshly fried crisps, removing excess oil from the surface and reducing the overall fat by around 15 per cent. Their first Lower Fat Crisps, launched in 1986 in a naked appeal to women, enlisted Hot Chocolate to soundtrack an ad campaign of sophisticated romancing with the elegant 'It Started with a Crisp'.

While some crisps shed their fat, other healthy snacks took on extra roughage. Golden Wonder's Country Crunch, a shell-like delicacy from 1979, contained wholemeal wheat and, came the ominous claim, 'other good country things'. Eight years later, the same company's Harvesters just went with the wholemeal flour. In between came 100s and 1000s, a kind of bagged savoury Rice Krispie in bacon and beef varieties, though such a fiddly snack didn't last far beyond its 1981 launch date.

**Opposite:** Frisps? Ruffles? (Both 1990.) Which is the more effeminate? There's only one way to find out. Hair pulling!

**Below:** Crisps were a guilty pleasure, until low fat arrived (1986), followed by roughage (1987). Out went the word 'guilty.' And, indeed, the word 'pleasure.'

KP injected bran into Britain's kids in 1982 via their Good 'N' Crunchy Crisps, reconstituted potatoid discs with added 'golden bran' for 'a unique extra bite'. Sadly the results turned out to be either tooth-shatteringly dense or off-puttingly soggy, and despite two increasingly desperate relaunches in as many years, the TV ad's grammatically confused insistence that 'nothing ever like them ever happened before' was swiftly answered by the populace's insistence that nothing ever like them ever happen again.

Ever cautious in the novelty stakes, Walkers restricted their crunchy competition to 1983's short-lived Tuckers, 'the super-crispy potato snack', but no one was immune from the health craze. Even the staid old grandees at Smiths donned leg-warmers, metaphorically at least, with Smiths Jackets, retaining a little brown crust of potato skin in order to 'taste more potatoey', according to the anthropomorphised spuds who skipped merrily en masse to their mechanical demise, gleefully accompanying their sacrifice with a falsetto rendition of Susan Maughan's 'Bobby's Girl', disturbingly reworded as a tuberous mass suicide anthem.

A new decade brought a new level of class to the thicker crisp. KP's Brannigans, packed in a pretend brown paper bag and allegedly named after 'a slightly roguish Irish American who ran a New York deli in the 1920s', actually achieved what its ancestors had been faking, being a genuine slice of virgin potato that just happened to be thicker than normal (for the record, 90/1000ths of an inch on average, compared to the ordinary crisp's paltry 60). KP were also behind Roysters, a British reworking of the American O'Boisies crisps, which based their publicity around dysfunctional backwoods couple Ma and Pa Royster and their wacky brood: 'the Oxo family on drugs' as KP put it. Suddenly the days of the giant dancing crisps seemed rather appealing.

## * RANCHEROS

Not the Mexican breakfast dish of huevos 'n' salsa, but the British school-kid's breakfast of faux bacon potato fries. The evocatively titled packs were adorned with three shady-looking characters (literally, in an early example of chiaroscuro crisp-bag art), their horseback-riding outlines calling to mind the cinematic adventures of... well, nobody in particular. Clint Eastwood territory it was not – in part

**Opposite:** More gringos than Ringos – KP Rancheros (1974).

because 'ranchero' translates as 'herdsman or peasant', as opposed to the presumably intended 'gunslinger or cowboy' – although most likely because the marketing budget didn't stretch to a fistful of Hollywood dollars.

KP, in aiming for the visceral majesty of *The Good, The Bad and The Ugly*, ended up hitting the flatulent horseplay of *Blazing Saddles* (never more so than when they added a pork 'n' beans variety in 1976). Still, there was the tagline: 'They sure taste like bacon'. An indisputable fact, except when they tasted like hamburger, the third flavour in the range.

Rancheros were but the salty tip of the iceberg. United Biscuits also supplied Marks & Spencer with their 'own label' snacks, hence St Michael's Rodeos, which were indistinguishable from the sizzlin' originals. Thrifty shoplifting mums could also help themselves to a family-sized bag of St Michael's Prawn Cocktail Snacks (Skips) or Potato Rings (Hula Hoops) along with the bairns' school uniforms.

The fun didn't stop there, either. In 1980 the KP-sponsored Adventure Express rolled out of Marylebone station to visit twenty-one cities and seaside towns over the summer hols with four themed carriages coupled behind. Snack lovers could board the NASA space centre (Outer Spacers), air chute (Sky Divers), disco (er, Discos) or Western stagecoach (Rancheros) – and, if kids turned up with enough empty KP packets they could get in free. Far better, though, was an earlier TV tie-in with *It's A Knockout* to give away board games and tickets to the 1976 final. Who needs three unshaven desperados when the faces of Stuart Hall and Eddie Waring are guaranteed to get your snacks flying off the shelves?

## * CRACK POP

Poor old popcorn, it hasn't travelled well. In the United States they devour huge volumes of the stuff – 17 billion 'quarts', apparently. Although, given that Americans are undecided on what a billion actually is, it's probably safe to round up a little. Elsewhere across the globe, it's just so much hot air. Sure, popcorn livens up trips to the pictures by the bucketload (especially for those with the cojones to play the 'hole in

**Opposite:** Not to be confused with that LP the Happy Mondays did in Barbados – Matlow's Crack Pop circa 1978.

**Below:** From hard drugs to sexual harassment (nice and light, this entry, eh?) Pascall's Hanky Panky (1979).

the bottom of the carton' trick) but somehow, someway, the pre-boxed, candy-coated kind got lost in translation. Cracker Jack, Fiddle Faddle, Poppycock: the snack-time stadium favourites of mid-West baseball fans just couldn't find a niche among the bike-riding louts of West Midlands recreation grounds.

Maybe it was the 'old-time' straw boater, sleeve garter charm of caramel popcorn with nuts and a prize that failed to resonate. Or maybe it was because nearly every American confectioner laboured under an ungainly Dixieland name. Orville Redenbacher, Otis Spunkmeyer, Wilbur Fartwanker – all equally likely to have dripped from the pen of a jaded satirist on a late-night BBC 3 comedy show (particularly the latter, who doesn't exist). Or maybe the British just preferred the modest taste of fried potato to brash, hot buttered corn.

Consequently, attempts to launch bagged toffee popcorn in the UK involved a profusion of *Carry On*-style innuendo and some good old Anglo-Saxon bluster. For the Cadbury-owned Pascall company, that meant a never-more-pompous Arthur Lowe donning bowler hat and pinstripes to offer a maiden aunt some Hanky Panky on a park bench. Much double-entendry later, he emerged from repeated handbag batterings to protest, 'You never know how good it is until you try it' – whack!

Bumbling businessmen aside, Hanky Panky tried to hide its popcorn parentage – 'Peanuts with puffs of corn in toffee coated clusters', apologised the pack front – and roped in self-confessed 'biggest puff in the business' Kenneth Williams on voice-over duty.

Matlow's effort suffered its own identity crisis, alternately launched as Crack Pop (not so much eaten as freebased) and Crunchy Buttered Popcorn (does what it says on the tin), also in chocolate flavour. Craven Keiller, suppliers of cinema-popped Butterkist ('Ra-ra-ra!') since 1938, introduced an evil-looking mint popcorn in 1970 and a take-home tub to tap into the '80s video rental boom. Paul Newman had a stab at it, and even KFC tried something called Popcorn Chicken (the kernel's recipe, perhaps?). But it took the widespread adoption of microwave ovens to make 'gourmet' popcorn an acceptable output of the British kitchen. As with TV dinners, we've never gone a bundle for tinfoil-sealed, heat 'n' cat food from the hob. It just tastes scorched. Did you not see what happened to Drew Barrymore in *Scream*?

## TWO PINTS OF LAGER AND A PACKET OF CRISPS, PLEASE

Pubs weren't always the high-windowed, dazzlingly lit palaces of pleasure they are nowadays, you know. Before Sky Sports and fake Irish decor, the atmosphere down your friendly local was more often an intimidating mixture of stale cigarettes, mouldering carpet and imminent violence. For most, the first glimpse inside was from a perch atop Daddy's shoulders, through the shutters of the off-licence at the side of the pub. As his takeaway bottles of black 'n' tan were handed over, gloomy figures beyond retreated into Lowry-esque huddles around an open fire, soberly dressed yet slovenly drunk. A scary vision of the future; but a trip worth it for the reward, a small plastic pack containing some crackers, a cheese triangle and a tiny, pickled silverskin onion.

Landlords have always kept a variety of snacks behind the bar. It makes perfect sense. Most booze is high in carbohydrates, which sends a customer's blood sugar up and kick-starts the pancreas's secretion of insulin. Too much of this combined with alcohol's tendency to inhibit the production of anti-diuretic hormones leads to hunger. Bingo! The licensee can now flog a nice packet of salted peanuts (which, by an amazing coincidence, also leaves the punter more thirsty and in need of another beer). That's all the basic biochemistry they teach at brewer's school, which is why there is no cure for a hangover other than hair of the dog.

Sealed bags of nuts were where it was at for a long time. KP (manufacturers Kenyon Produce, the adopted branding for all United Biscuits' snack products from the mid-'70s onward) were undisputedly

**Opposite:** The universally loved KP nuts (1953) and their not-so-universally loved dry roasted cousins (1980).

**Below:** Finger-coating good: Bombay Spiced peanuts circa 1982.

number one in the field, something they celebrated with the launch of the immodest 'No. 1' range in 1953 and relentless advertising thereafter. New wave singer, and Noel Fielding lookalike, Lene Lovich must have been surprised to see her top ten hit 'Lucky Number' seconded to promotional duties and performed by a spiky-haired, KP-fixated wide boy on telly. By the time pretend punk Billy Idol's 'Rebel Yell' spiced up the honey roasted adverts, the message was clear: these were peanuts that recognised no boundaries of class, age, gender or taste.

KP's competitors sought out niche markets. Golden Wonder's nuts were 'jungle fresh' or 'big and juicy', according to the lion-wrestling, elephant-taming Tarzan-o-gram in their adverts. Rowntree Sunchasers, clearly the Club Med of legumes, were 'toasted' not roasted peanuts, whereas American interlopers Planters were aimed squarely at the toff market, or so the monocle, top hat, white spats and ebony cane ensemble of their Mr Peanut character would seem to indicate. What Planters did bring to the cocktail party, in 1978, was the UK's first dry roasted peanut, liberating the packet of nuts from under the horse-brasses of the local hostelry and into the stainless-steel serving bowls of swanky downtown wine bars.

Smiths quickly followed suit, as did Golden Wonder with the unsubtly monikered Chasers, though KP were typically vain in claiming their own 'seductively spicy and very different' dry roasted peanuts to be 'the greatest bite since Cleopatra's Asp'. Sales peaked in 1981, though just three short years later had declined enough for KP to respond with alternative salt 'n' vinegar and smoky bacon flavours. The market struggled to sustain such diversity, however, leading professional curmudgeon Michael Parkinson to grumble in his *Daily Mirror* column about the shortfall of plain peanuts available on a business-class flight to Manchester.

Already unpopular with anaphylactics, the savoury bowl-based peanut suddenly didn't seem so appetising to anyone but the finest connoisseur of other people's trace urine samples (unless that's yet another urban myth).

Who were these adults kidding anyway? They'd happily offer an array of juvenile snacks and crisps at their grown-up soirées, leaving the kids to watch from the top of the stairs as guests munched their way through the cheese balls. But, in a blind taste test, would they know the difference between a Tudor Roll and a Smiths Buff? Not on your nelly. In the early '70s, no Christmas do could begin without the car keys in a dish on the table and a carton of Twiglets to pass around. The famously knobbly snacks were created in 1929 by a French chef, experimenting with crispbread dough and yeast extract in the Peek Frean company's Bermondsey kitchens. For years they (and their dairy-heavy counterparts, Cheeselets) were the only genuinely adult-oriented party snack out there. But in 1982, that all changed.

Roger McKechnie and Ray McGhee, a couple of ex-Newcastle university chums, got together to bemoan the state of the snack industry. There was, they reasoned, a gap in the market for 'aspirational AB' nibbles.

**Opposite:** KP make with the topical Denis Healey gags (1978).

McKechnie, the former general manager at Tudor, had an idea that the more sophisticated barflies and Bellini drinkers could handle an exotic product. McGhee, European vice-president for an ad agency, figured that expensive-looking, oddly designed packaging would attract the attention of first-time buyers. So they formed Derwent Valley Foods to produce an initial range of 'first class snacks from around the world', named them after Jules Verne's eccentric gentleman explorer, Phileas Fogg, and broke nearly every rule in the book in the process.

**Below:** A more antiquated approach from Phileas Fogg (1982).

Far from inexpensive, these snacks featured unusual ingredients, even more unusual names (Californian Corn Chips, Punjab Puri and Mignons Morceaux, to name but three), and the unlikely literary figurehead demanding we 'Pay attention!' on the pack. TV ads featuring top *Hi-De-Hi* snobs Barry and Yvonne Stuart-Hargreaves added to the elitist feel: you couldn't just buy these snacks, you also had to buy into them.

Being light on sales but flush with product, Phileas Fogg struggled at first, but a strong showing at the International Food and Drink Exhibition in London broke the ice. Unfortunately, it also earned the attention of a few future adversaries. Smiths began secretly testing a new range of breadcrumbed pillow-shaped snacks with weird and wonderful flavourings. Though the sweet and sour pork variety failed to catch on, Scampi Flavour Fries became an instant pub sensation upon their 1985 debut. Bacon Flavour Fries (surely just Frazzles in a posh frock?) also went down a storm. Less imaginatively, KP tried to shoot down Fogg's Montgolfier-inspired balloon by moving directly into the 'World Snacks' space in 1987. Their Mexican chips and garlic croutons were carbon copies of Derwent Valley's original recipes but even new spicy poppadoms, pizza biscuits and Hong Kong crackers were packaged in the same quality gravure-printed, metallised polypropylene packs. Twiglets got in on the act too, acquiring a new heavy-duty foil bag illustrated with the

**Opposite:** Twiglets – gathering in a small mound on the edge of a paper plate near you since 1929.

**Below:** Scampi Flavour Fries – daring you to describe their aroma in family-friendly terms since 1985.

constituent ingredients of a Bloody Mary, though that was soon dropped in favour of a more with-it geometric pattern to accompany the spoof 'Dare you enter the Twiglet zone?' ads. In a self-preservatory move, Derwent Valley branched out into cheaper snack production, adopting a one-adjective, one-shape naming policy for their crunchy sticks, pizza scoops, cheese curls and potato rackets. This helped them see out the rest of the decade before landing an exclusive deal to distribute the newly arrived Kettle Chips in the UK.

Pub favourites, like the MSG-saturated Mr Porky pork scratchings, changed hands over time and diversified. New owners Tayto introduced Porky Prime Cuts (apparently in tribute to record cutting engineer George 'Porky' Peckham, a man responsible for the master copies of many a vinyl pressing down the years). More processed meat in the shape of Peperami ('People go barmy over Peperami,' assured a young John Sessions) hung from plastic strips next to the optics and the IPA pumps. Bombay mix – wherever that came from – brought the taste of a fried curried lentil and chickpea pot pourri to the inebriated hoi polloi. No longer was the drunken wage earner limited to a strict

**'Smiths began secretly testing a new range of breadcrumbed pillow-shaped snacks with weird and wonderful flavourings.'**

dietary choice between a pickled egg or one of those little mint cakes at the bottom of the gents toilets.

Where salt and spice succeeded, so too did soft cheese. In the midst of a new product bonanza late in 1971, Cadbury dispatched their first savoury line: Husky, a cream cheese-stuffed wafer topped with malted wheat. The Belgian TUC invasion came shortly after, with Ritz cheese sandwiches blurring the cracker/crisp boundary still further in 1983. KP's Cheese Dip was a variation on their choc/toffee snack (developed by Meiji Seika Kaisha, United Biscuits' trading associate in Japan), and purported that 'dipping a stick

**Opposite:** Walker's French Fries beermats (1977), with handy tips on how to clear a crowded bar.

**Below:** Golden Wonder's 'jungle fresh' circa 1979, versus KP's 'jockstrap stale' (1980).

in is gripping'. But it took the full force of the Smiths development team to come up with Savoury Moments, triangular wheat pockets with a cheesy core. Funnily enough, Michael Parkinson was less petulant when it came to accepting money to star in an advert alongside his old oppos, Rod Hull and Emu, despite the latter's track record of assault on his goolies. Gotta credit the old bird with trying to finish the job, though.

Typically, any product aimed at the alehouse would ultimately find its way into the lunchboxes of children. Walkers' French Fries were conceived as a snappy little bite for seasoned tipplers, an intention reinforced by a series of pub-centric adverts and near-ubiquitous beermat promotion. However, some time in 1982 an executive took the decision to drop the 'stacks in a pack' strapline and instead chase the non-metric pennies with a schoolboy, his ruler, and a reminder that the bags contained 'six and a half feet' of fry.

Modern-day crisp-mongers like Pipers prefer their products to be exclusive to the inn (thus preventing any Tom, Dick or Harry from nipping down to Lidl and buying them at a third of the cost) and toss geographic descriptors willy-nilly at the flavours ('Anglesey sea salt' and 'Somerset cider vinegar', as if anyone cared). That's the price you pay for a family-friendly pub. The children are all allowed indoors but, if you're lucky, you can occasionally glimpse the old punters through the shutters – gloomy figures outside in the rain, huddled around a single cigarette, soaking wet and slovenly drunk. Still, it gets them out of the house, eh? *

## ✻ FISH 'N' CHIPS

There's a whole sub-genre of the savoury snack that owes its existence to the taxman. When VAT was introduced in 1973, potato crisps and processed nuts were classed as luxury items, and had the necessary duty slapped on them at the tills. Prices accordingly rose. Biscuits, however, were somehow considered a staple – so long as they didn't have chocolate on them – and therefore exempt.

**Opposite:** Britain's tastiest tax dodge – Burton's Fish 'n' Chips circa 1977.

**Below:** Another vote winner from those chancellors of the ex-cheddar, Crawford's (1984).

KP were the first company to get to grips with the loophole, understandably wary of their market-dominating nuts being hit by chancellor Anthony Barber's 10 per cent takeaway tax. Their pre-emptive strike was the Wigwam, a rounded triangular savoury biscuit that effortlessly bridged the gap between cracker and nut, while cocking an elegant snook at the Treasury.

A nifty bit of pioneering, but not the most memorable biscuit to nose its way into the snack bag. Burton's were another firm whose leading product – the Wagon Wheel, dressed from top to toe in Sunday best – sat well within the VAT-man's purview. In a flash of cross-comestible inspiration that must have had executives giddy with excitement, a VAT spoiler snack was proposed: little oblong biscuits nestling next to others of a piscatorial silhouette in a bag decorated with mock newsprint, doused in salt and vinegar.

Retailing at a pocket-friendly single figure penny sum, Fish 'n' Chips had the virtue of not only tempting those kids for whom crisps were now jacked up out of their price range, it also enticed folk who fancied a proper bag of chippy chips, but found them similarly beyond their means (takeaway food was also dripping with hot VAT). It was a double whammy unique in snacking, and Burton's name was toasted countrywide.

The true all-conquering snack biscuit, however, renounced fancy shapes. In 1984 Crawfords hit upon the bright idea of scaling down their popular cheesy biscuit range, popping them in snack bags and launching them, initially in Scotland and the north, accompanied by a dainty Richard Williams' animated ad featuring pink ballet-dancing mice. The Mini Cheddar swept all before it, despite being something of a slouch in the value for money stakes – they cost twice the price per gram of their tube packed bigger brothers. We'd come to an end of that brief but joyous time when a little bag of wacky biscuits was, literally, cheaper than chips.

**'A VAT spoiler snack was proposed: little oblong biscuits nestling next to others of a piscatorial silhouette.'**

## ✻ BIG D PEANUTS

Salted peanuts, by and large, are a pretty dull sort of snack. So when Smiths stepped into the market in 1967, installing their Big Diamond whole nut range in pubs across London, it was with some trepidation. Why switch from KP, or even new upstart Golden Wonder? It's a risky business if you can't stand out from the crowd. The solution came a few years later. It was so simple that it was

**Opposite:** A Smiths Big D card circa 1977, exhibiting classic 'half-time' bag formation. NB – 'cheeky' requests for a specific packet will be roundly ignored.

surprising no one had thought of it before. Come to think of it, it was amazing anyone thought of it at all.

Some bright spark in Smiths' marketing department had been mulling over how to get Cheezers, their new cheese-filled biscuit snacks, more attention in pubs. Using his adman's brain, he probed the environment. What do you find in pubs? Blokes. Hundreds of 'em. What, in 1970 at least, don't you find? Women, save the odd barmaid. A quick thumb through the works of Sigmund Freud, and the sales pitch of the decade was written. 'Hidden behind the packs is a large picture of a scantily clad girl, and she becomes more exposed every time a purchase is made.' When Smiths transferred the technique over to their nut range in 1971, 'Big D' took on a rather different meaning.

Turning the purchase of fried nuts into a sexual lottery for randy young men takes a special kind of genius. But spare a thought for the randy young man of 1970. Not for him the endless tide of 'leisure material' pumped into the home of today's lad. He had to make do with Page Three, the Richard Shops catalogue, the Sunday night foreign film, and the slim possibility of copping the charms of Miss Vivien Neves, gamely grinning in a diaphanous nightie in front of a potted palm.

Vivien was the original Big D Girl. But for true aficionados (and we hope that's the correct change they're fumbling for down there), Big D means the lovely Beverley Pilkington of Southend. She took over posing duties in '75 with no small promotional fanfare ('Guess the weight of Bev and win her weight in 10p pieces!') and stayed for over a decade.

Then, in the latter half of the '80s, the ready-salted rudery died out. Not through political pressure: Page Three might have been a hot topic in the Commons, but no questions were raised about Smiths' little racket (possibly because MPs didn't go into those sorts of pubs). The memory never went away, however, and when Smiths flogged the Big D brand off to Liverpool's Trigon Snacks in 2001, laddish culture was deemed just right for a revival, and back they came, albeit in smaller numbers than before. No doubt the lad of 1970 would approve. Although if he found himself in today's world, he'd probably explode.

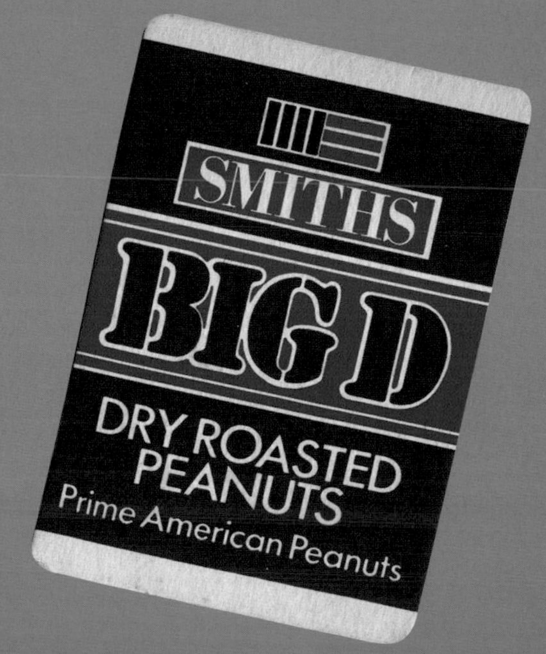

# WEIGH OUTS

It is a dance as old as time. The rituals surrounding the ancient transaction between sweet shop owner and snotty little Herbert are numerous and arcane. This Weigh Out Top Trumps set helps make learning easy and fun. Simply cut out the cards overleaf, paste onto card or stout paper, and shout random numbers at an opponent. (To make the full set of cards, we advise purchase of no fewer than two copies of *The Great British Tuck Shop*. Plus a third to keep for 'best.')

**Spotter's guide to sweet shop artifacts and customs**
Award yourself one point for each of these common over-the-counter sights:

- rusting scale pan of dubious hygienic standard
- brass ounce weights augmented at shopkeeper's whim with rogue pennies
- mysterious unlabelled jar that appears to be half-full of brick dust
- jar of 'olde Englishe working man's bronchial twists' unopened since Suez
- jar of loose salted peanuts that quite frankly has no business being there at all
- old cast iron till with the '½p' symbol stuck permanently up

## Pink Shrimps

**Seafood-shaped sweetmeats immortalised in crumbly sugar fossil form.**

0% Authentic Billingsgate tang
46% Cavity wall insulation texture
20% Pick 'n' mix 'share of bag'
8% Cocktail sauce compatibility

## Sweet Bananas

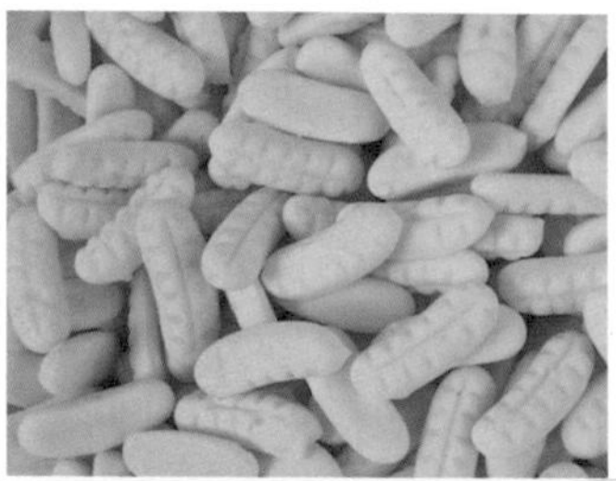

**Squidgy, styrofoam-textured monkey favourite in convenient non-peelable pocket size.**

87% EU 'bentness' uniformity
84% Stomach bloat factor
12% Slaptick skin-slip liability
0% Pyjamas

## Dolly Mixtures

**Fey, pastel-hued, sugar paste mini selection box.**

59% Goon Show references
71% Latent art deco tendency
26% Ironic indie wistfulness
12% Survival rate north of Watford

## Milk Gums

**Sugar-dusted, udder-derived chewy bottles for unweaned sweet-tooths.**

8% Returned empties
40% Lactose intolerance
33% Glint in delivery man's eye
2% UHT aftertaste

## Apple Whips/Cola Whips

**Lengthy, sado-masochistic extrusions of liquorice-like cable.**

19% RS232 interface
28% Stephen Milligan endorsement
67% Ophidiophobia
3% Speaker of the House Of Commons

## Foam Mushrooms

**Spongy, fruit-flavoured fungi of severely limited culinary application.**

50% Wild fungal likeness
50% Human nipple likeness
6% Junior Syd Barrett hijinks
1% Makings of a warming winter soup

- proprietor giving you that 'you've been nicking Mojos while I got that jar of bootlaces down off the shelf you little get' look
- teenage assistant who looks mightily bored despite clearly having the best job in the world
- sudden penny price hikes explained away as 'inflation, son'
- forbidding 'Ark of the Covenant' air of mystery surrounding ancient jar with illegibly sun faded label
- pleasing 'ponk!' sound made by removal of stopper from old-style glass jar
- gradual replacement of glass jars with plastic giving punter first ever pangs of 'time passing' melancholy

## Midget Gems

**Highly-perfumed, fiddly fruit gums, not accepted by Cash Converters.**

84% Satisying in-bag bulk
50% Cubic Zirconium
29% Cacharel pour l'homme
8% Up in value after US debt warning

## Pear Drops

**Bell-bottomed tablets of unmistakable chemical hoy.**

53% Art room fixative
46% Silvikrin firm hold/nail varnish remover
9% Showroom-fresh upholstery
0% Orchard produce verisimilitude

## Sherbet Lemons

**Disappointingly meagre boiled-sweet-encased fizz burst in token citrus fruit guise.**

45% Impatient sucking
67% Frustrated crunching
9% Shrove Tuesday
13% Grandmother's sitting room

## Sweet Peanuts

**Glossy peanut-mimicking sweets wastefully reconstituted from pulverised peanut particles.**

30% Charles Schulz royalties
72% Monkey wages
6% Golf ball dimplage
98% Discarded shells

## Toasted Coconut Teacakes

**Compressed, bronze-faced discs of fairground shy-bothering, hairy nut innards.**

9% Palm tree/gravity incidents
89% Dessication
22% Cream tea affinity
50% North/south bun divide arguments

## Liquorice Root

**Odd-man-out, unadulterated twigs surprisingly infused with taste of Bertie Bassett… for about thirty seconds.**

52% Health food shop smugness
75% Oral splinter removal
65% Absent-minded HB gnawing
5% Regurgitated pulp

- mysterious collecting tin on counter labelled 'Old Ben'*
- determinedly old-school vendor augmenting imperial weights and measures with demand for 'five bob'
- superhuman feat of willpower to resist eating any of purchase until out of shop
- snort of amused condescension in response to question 'how much is the whole jar, mister?'
- smaller boy 'falling' into freezer cabinet to provide distraction for co-ordinated raid on Panini stickers
- deft flicking of stray Fruit Salad chews up past elasticated wristband and into sleeve of red Adidas tracksuit top
- 'maximum three kids' rule

## Bonbons

**Sugar-cased toffee balls with heady tang of assorted fruit.**

61% Fancy continental pretensions
91% Unplanned amateur dentistry
22% Tell-tale facial sugar residue
4% Furtive dust-hoovering

## Cherry Lips

**Translucent 'trout pout' crescents of highly fragrant gum.**

3% Mae West/Salvador Dali sofa
35% Tiny ventriloquist fun
50% Wax polish
1% The Rimmel look

## False Teeth

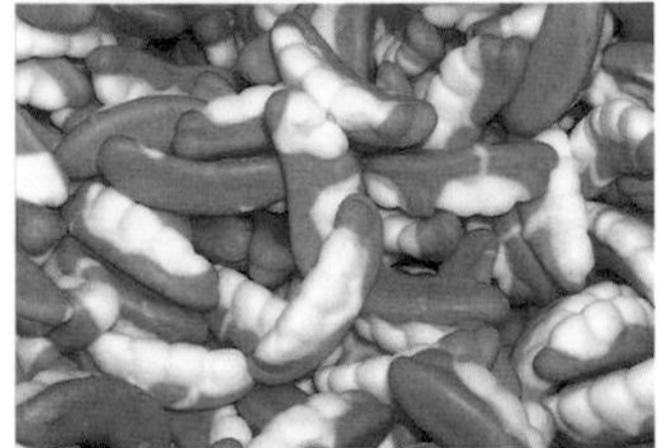

**Ironic, denture-apeing (and, ultimately, denture-necessitating) lumps of gelatinous sugar.**

78% Ken Dodd impression
79% Esther Rantzen impression
28% Post-incineration identification
12% Gingivitis

## Fizz Bombs

**Blackpool-Rock-like pellets with mouth-tingling outer layer.**

49% Rabies-alerting gob froth
25% Metal Mickey's Atomic Thunderbusters
18% Lily-of-the-valley bath salts
6% Airport security alert

## Sherbet Pips

**Pint-size pellets of compacted effervescence.**

50% Actual size
42% Back-of-sofa migration
12% Gladys Knight backing vocals
3% Greenwich time signal sponsorship

## Flying Saucers

**Extra-terrestrial-themed rice-paper mule for oral sherbet delivery.**

93% Roof of mouth adherence
83% 1950s B-movie prop department
10% Mouse frisbee
46% Holy communion wafer

flouted by bundling through doorway with alarming ferocity in rugby scrum formation
- old buffer queuing impatiently for four ounces of ready-rubbed and some pipe cleaners behind long line of indecisive kids
- absence of 'first choice' sweets lending oddly bitter psychological after-taste to 'consolation' assortment
- pious refusal of shopkeeper to sell two ounces of loose sherbet in bottom of bonbons jar for tuppence
- acute moral dilemma posed by assistant leaving counter unattended to visit store room
- acute panic on hearing 'swish' of plastic strip curtain being swept

## Chelsea Whoppers

**Unaccountably well-remembered cocoa-sprinkled slabs of marshmallow-esque fudge.**

- 65% 1960s dollybird chic
- 21% Mockney innuendo
- 43% Brown trout
- 37% Roman Abramovich buy-out

## Chewing Nuts

**Squirrel-fooling nuggets of toffee coated in artificial chocolate.**

- 67% Unexpected toughness
- 43% Rabbit hutch floor deposits
- 98% Clumping probability
- 0% Verified goober content

## Pint Pots

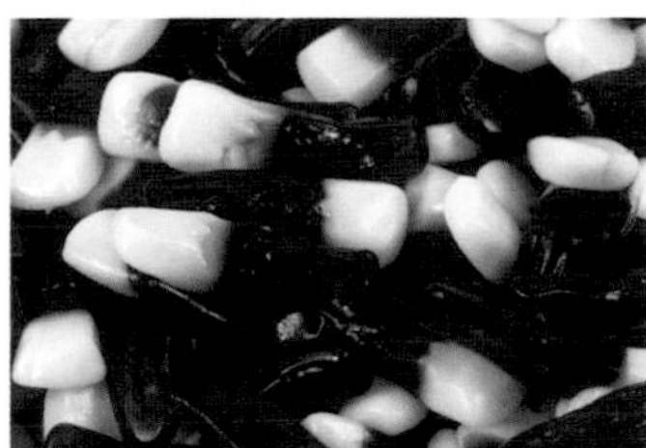

**Sweet shandy gums masquerading as foam-headed bevvy for preternatural alcoholics.**

- 67% Pavlovian saliva rush
- 31% "Big Man" playground kudos
- 25% Billy Connolly advocacy
- 2% Alcohol by volume

## Jelly Beans

**'Iconic' American rainbow-flavoured faux-haricot assortment.**

- 50% Aromatic innovation
- 40% Pledges of allegiance
- 25% Lunchtime for Reagan
- 18% Humanitarian intervention at the scales

## Rainbow Belts

**Colourfully sour lengths of highly masticatable jelly.**

- 53% Glam rock kudos
- 70% Meteorological correctness
- 5% Sartorial practicality
- 26% Robin Williams costume

## Rainbow Millions

**Awkwardly diminutive chewy nuggets of spectrum-straddling hue.**

- 20% Scales-to-bag spillage
- 23% Bag-to-hand spillage
- 18% Hand-to-mouth spillage
- 6% Geoffrey Hayes' lottery winnings

aside by assistant returning from store room

- rising panic on realisation stolen booty hurriedly crammed into mouth was half a dozen sour balls
- intriguingly colourful poster for exotic-sounding sweet range that's either sold out or was never in stock in the first place
- especially weedy kid tucking pack of Action Man sweet cigarettes under sleeve of T-shirt like he's Ray Winstone or something
- stupid sense of pride engendered in being able to dismount from Grifter, lob Grifter aside on tarmac and hop through shop door without stopping
- increasingly harassed proprietor imposing statute of limitations

## ABC Alphabet Letters

**Characters of indeterminate font hewn from sugary substrate.**

22% Government literacy initiative

41% Edible obscenity

0% Italic option

10% Pondering over missing holes in the 'O's

## Kola Kubes

**Cautiously-spelt sugar-coated hexahedra flavoured with non-trademark-infringing fizzy beverage.**

65% Disappointed corporate lawyers

52% Mouth-lacerating sugar shards

11% Two-for-one fusion incidents

0% The Real Thing

## Pineapple Chunks

**Rectilinerar reimaginations of tropical gammon garnish.**

95% Recommended Daily Amount (of sugar)

22% Distant bong of steel drums

0% Heavy syrup

5% Man in white Panama hat nodding smugly

## Rhubarb and Custard

**'Quintessentially British' wartime pudding in two-tone lozenge configuration.**

28% Rose-tinted school nostalgia

53% 'Dig for Victory' propaganda

38% Mr Blobby-approved colour scheme

3% Richard Briers voiceover

## Acid Drops

**Sophisticated balls of low-pH citric assault.**

67% Waspish Kenneth Williams put-downs

25% Sucking-induced Kenneth Williams faces

23% Astringency-induced Kenneth Williams noises

1% Visits to Matron

## Aniseed Balls

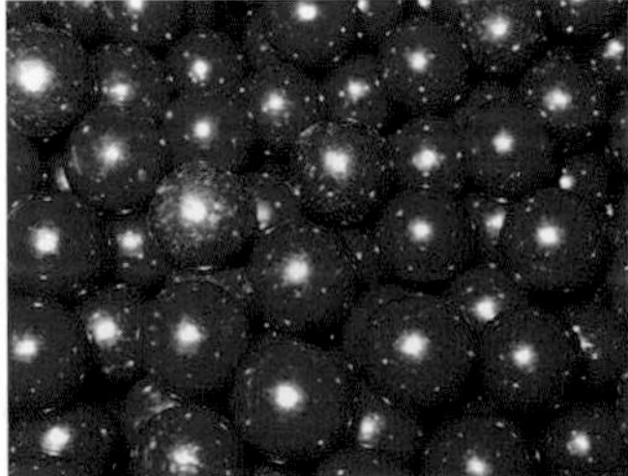

**Liquorice-scented gobstoppers of Beano-alleged canine appeal.**

72% All-encompassing brownness

53% Hilarious consequences

29% Lingering taste for rest of day

4% Gateway to Sambuca addiction

on number of different ingredients allowed in ¼lb 'cocktail'
- sheer unadulterated joy when inseparable coagulation of sherbet lemons results in a 'half ounce over' on the house (rare)
- grumpy adolescent paper-boy loading up a fluorescent orange satchel at 5.30am

*it was the news vendors' benevolent fund, in case you were still wondering.

## White Mice

**Historically inexplicable edible rodents.**

- 12% 1950s housewives screaming on chairs
- 27% Standby piece for Ideal board game
- 0% Warfarin
- 5% Liberation by short-sighted PETA militia

## White Chocolate Fish and Chips

**Dripping-saturated proletarian supper rendered in equally fatty low-cocoa medium.**

- 91% Caledonian frying potential
- 14% Catholic dietary restriction
- 5% Pensioners' special
- 1% Free scraps

## Brown/White Gems

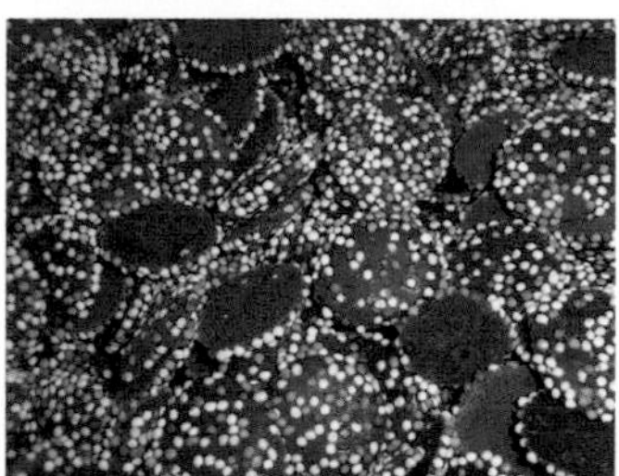

**Outsize chocolate buttons in sugar-bobble battledress.**

- 59% Sweetshop militarisation
- 81% Pre-school snack pimping
- 33% Old-school cupcakery
- 7% Collateral damage

## Chocolate Footballs

**Pleasingly foil-wrapped homages to the beautiful game.**

- 18% Flick-to-kick opportunities
- 31% Frantic transfer window
- 23% Paper-bag-to-mouth running commentary
- 5% Training aid for rodent Ian Rush's

## Cinder Toffee

**Dismembered remains of Crunchies who've seen their last Friday.**

- 14% Bonfire aroma
- 33% Warning from history
- 25% Chemistry in action
- 81% Dentistry in turmoil

## Mojos

**Wax-wrappered chew interlopers curiously dominating the weigh-out glass jar shelf.**

- 17% Pocket lint collector
- 55% Faux British 1960s spy libido
- 30% Spearmint flavoured Pacer surrogate
- 10% Wizardy spell thing

# Jawbreakers.
## The ones that zap all the others.

Because multi-flavoured JAWBREAKERS – REGULAR, SUPERSOUR or FIREBALL – outlast, out-taste and out-value any other gum.

Three in a pack. Half-an-hours sucking for 10p. Layer after layer of rock-hard candy flavours right through to the gum in the middle. And then all that chewing.

Compared with JAW BREAKERS, other gums are kids stuff.

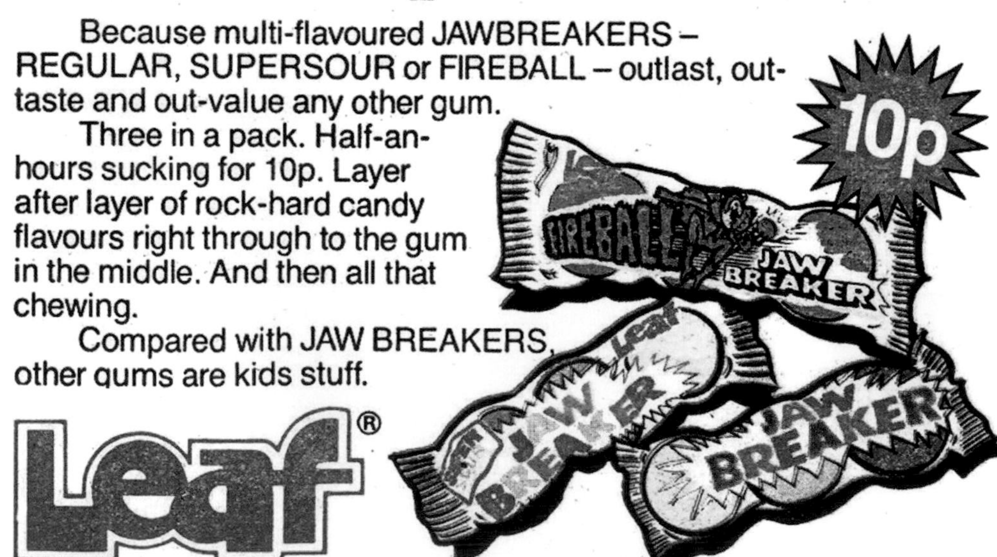


Leaf (UK) Limited. Middle Way. Chinnor. OXON.

# SWEETS

**Opposite:** "LOAD "JAWBREAKERS" SCREEN$." Leaf International appeals to the Atari generation circa 1985, and avoids a play on the word 'byte.'

**'Nauty Pauty Jack-a-Dandy
Stole a Piece of Sugar-Candy
From the Grocer's Shoppy-shop,
And away did Hoppy-hop.'**

What sounds like a simple eighteenth-century children's song may actually be a surreptitious satire, sticking a tongue out at the upper-middle classes. The 'dandies' of London society – parasitical, aspirant aristos basking in the reflected glory of a true blue-blood's lineage – were considered fops and deserving of ridicule to the commoner's eye. Simple rhymes such as this often concealed heavy words, lightly thrown. Candy, rather than the modern homogenised alternative word for sweets, is possessed of ancient Sanskrit and Persian heritage, so, used here, it could hide a double meaning.

Similarly, the word confectionery is derived from the Latin *confectio*, meaning 'made up' or 'prepared'. Small wonder, therefore, that the fundamentals of the confectionery arts were fostered in the kitchens of pharmacists, who added sugar to their potions to cover the nasty taste of the medicine; yes, it seems Mary Poppins wasn't just some crazy flying nanny, after all. The tablet or lozenge shape most sweets take in the present is a lingering echo of the sixteenth-century alchemist's craft. Liquorice

and marshmallow too began life as both tincture and tonic (which is worth remembering if you're ever caught stuffing your face with Barratt Flumps after throwing a sickie).

Sugar itself has left an altogether more bitter legacy. Britain developed its sweet tooth while exploiting a vast empire of trade routes and colonies, importing sugar cane from the slave-stocked plantations of the Caribbean, and exporting architecture, cricket and Christianity in its place. The world may have needed a great big melting pot, but small skillets were already being warmed up at home. Thus candies became high-status, luxury novelties for a privileged elite – and, whereas the Greeks used an abundance of natural by-products like honey and almonds to fashion their sweetmeats, British confectionery's forefathers coerced boiled sugar into altogether unrecognisable and aberrant forms. A further mishmash of Commonwealth influences furnished traditional goodies with foreign-sounding names: jujube, nougat, fondant, comfit.

None of this seems to stop the British closely linking confectionery to their sense of identity. According to polls, more people want to see the reinstatement of the Opal Fruits brand name than red

**Opposite:** This'll put lead in your pencil case. Sketchy merchandise for mini multi-taskers, circa 1980.

**Below:** The Pub Landlord's favourite mints (1944), and Beyonce's favourite lucky bag circa 1982.

telephone boxes, steam trains or local bank managers. Where sugar is concerned, we do seem to enjoy living in the past.

Nostalgia – a word inherited from the Greek side of our patchwork language – not only means a sentimental longing, but also an acute medical pain. As early as 1971, Spangles were poking that tender spot with adverts that recalled the Olde English days of Barley Sugars and Acid Drops. As a confused adult, it's tempting to wallow in the comforting tastes and smells of youth. Thankfully, Dr Confectionery is always more than happy to write out a prescription.

The story of sweets is also one of innovation and imagination. Sugar behaves differently at different temperatures; witness the fibrous clouds of candyfloss versus the sticky morass of bonfire toffee, both of which taste equally good out of doors. It can be mixed with other ingredients – butter, milk, starch, egg white, fruit acid, gelatine – to create endless new permutations.

Pulled sugar, the like of which is used to create Blackpool Rock, lends itself to experimentation and ingenuity. The skill is in knowing what to do with the end product - and how to work with it before it sets into a stodgy, useless mess all down your arm.

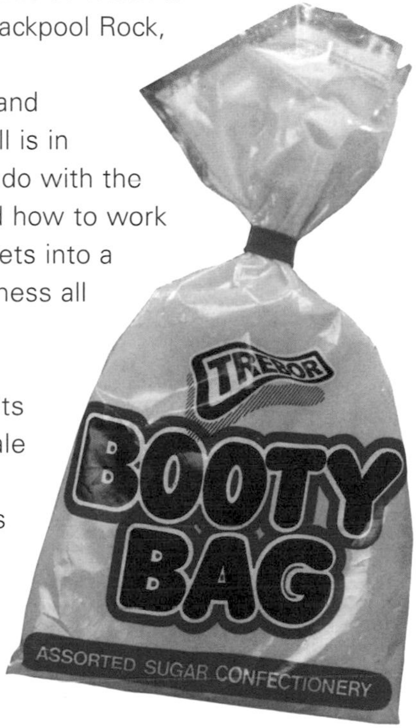

Hence, the sweets and toffees on sale in the grocer's were as varied as the British manufacturers who supplied them. Barker and Dobson, a husband and wife team, founded a Liverpool company justly famous for their zebra-striped Everton mints (assisted by Goodison Park's world-renowned 'toffee lady'). Pascall, a London company of Huguenot descent, had to overcome arson attack before becoming celebrated for their powdered toffee bonbons and honeycomb fruity pops. And Rainbow Drops, from Matlow's of Derbyshire, are a sugar-sprayed puffed rice delicacy that would surely be marketed as a breakfast cereal had they not been invented in a pre-war era.

**Below:** Richard Of York Gave Battle In Grain – Matlow's Rainbow Drops, circa 1978. Paul Roberts, the 1980 great Trebor robber, hits the *Jackpot*.

**Opposite:** There's whimsy in the jar. Mars pushes alle ye same olde buttons in a late attempt to resurrect the fortunes of Spangles, circa 1973.

We are a nation of shopkeepers, and the bond between confectioner, tobacconist and newsagent is well established. Neither sugar, cigarettes nor the press are tolerable in anything but the most stringent of doses, yet they are available on every street corner, as freely as meow meow or crack. Given the option, the British have traditionally chosen to self-medicate, but moderation is not our watchword. We get over-excited – not without reason do we say 'like a kid in a sweet shop'. Comic characters in the 1970s, suddenly flush with a 10p piece, always rewarded themselves by loading up on sugary treats. The same comics often featured competitions to win a trolley dash in a sweet factory for 'one lucky reader'.

These days, much of our sugar comes from European beet, rather than cane, which has made it seem cheap and commonplace. Fine spun sculptures may still grace the dining tables of the rich and famous, but they don't taste much better than a handful of common-or-garden penny chews. Food historian Laura Mason put it most elegantly when she said, 'Sweets have descended to trivia. Like nursery rhymes, they were once full of significance for adults but are now bits of nonsense for children.' But then again, there's no point in being grown-up if you can't be childish sometimes.

# Three favourite Spangles– a taste of the good old days!

Spangles

Spangles

OLD ENGLISH

Spangles

DROP

Barley

Old English... Acid Drop... Barley Sugar...

three favourites from the Spangles range of nine big-value packs. Always in flavour, always good value.

## THE CHEW CHEW TRADE

As Britain wrenched itself mechanically into the steam-powered 1900s, the view wasn't solely one of chimney sweeps, pea-soupers and dark, satanic mills. Some of the air, at least, hung heavy with the smell of gently caramelising sugar. From Calderdale to Crumpsall, tiny villages and towns across the land rattled to the boiling brass pots and pans of the local toffee factory. Ask your granddad. If he didn't work in one of the kitchens, he undoubtedly kept a tiny hammer in the sideboard – for smashing up trays of their brown, brittle output – and had precious few of his own teeth to show for it.

What Britain now knows as toffee it owes to John Mackintosh – or, to be more accurate, his missus. Violet Mackintosh, former confectioner's assistant, is credited with developing the special 'Celebrated' recipe in their Halifax home. A pleasantly chewy mixture of stiff British butterscotch and smooth American caramel, it provided the benchmark for all future filling-looseners. John, however, went on to turn the brand into a household name, taking out advertising space in newspapers, running competitions and, in 1905, sending a tin to every single member of the House of Commons. Enclosed was a plea to dissolve not parliament but a simple mouthful of toffee in order to 'become famous for sweet discourse'. Arguably, this gave MPs an appetite for free stuff and led to some unfortunate expenses irregularities further down the line but no one can say Mackintosh's eye for a quick PR win wasn't dead on.

Soon, anyone with the wealth and the wherewithal to do so was selling slabs of 'traditional' toffee, off the back of a cart or out of local bakeries and grocery stores. In order that his wares might stand out from the ever-expanding crowd, one Edward Sharp of Maidstone enlisted an advertising agency to come up with a mascot. The result was a shifty-looking cartoon toff who went by the unfortunate name of 'Sir Kreemy Knut'. With short cropped ginger hair, a tailored suit and pencilled-in moustache, Sir Kreemy appeared every inch the mannish lesbian plucked from the streets of Berlin in the midst of a roaring '20s jazz festival. Nevertheless, fag in hand, he (or she) did well for Sharps, helping boost sales of

**Opposite:** Sweet bird of youth. Blue Bird toffee (1898).

**Below:** Chewing the cud. McCowan's sacred ruminant, in pineapple flavour circa 1980.

their Super Toffee well into the 1970s before he (or she) was finally kicked in the Knut.

North of the border, an altogether more robust breed of toffee was expected. No mere slab was muscular enough for the customers of McCowan's. They demanded something far less puny: a substantial sweet – brawny, medicinal even – which is why the Scots still serve their toffee as 'tablet'. However, it was founder Andrew McCowan who spotted the market for small chews and individual bars aimed at kids, to supplement the income generated by the highly decorated toffee tins and boxes destined for the adults' mantelpieces.

McCowan's maintained that, up to the age of seven, children were convinced only by quality, not quantity. It took a particularly Caledonian mind, therefore, to roll out the bars as thin and as wide as possible, to give the best impression of size with the most frugal amount of toffee.

With similar economy, the company ensured that each of their children's products was a 'one-coin purchase', a practice that stood them in good stead until the end of the century. Whether it was a Toffee Daintee, Fizzy Lizzy or Robot Chew, all were priced for a straightforward transaction with a single denomination coin. Even their most successful '80s line, the Wham bar, remained at an affordable 10p for over a decade before leaping unceremoniously to 20p in 1994. The adoption of the euro in Ireland in 1998 caused no end of problems, however, as McCowan's lacked the machinery to recalibrate their products for the new currency.

After the soldiers returned from war with the Kaiser in 1918, other confectioners began to experiment with toffee. Keiller's of Dundee excelled in marmalade production, and so took the natural next step into sweets. Walter's of Acton created a sandwich layered bar containing weird and wonderful flavours, including banana split, and called it Palm Toffee. Harry Vincent built what was to become the Blue Bird factory on the outskirts of Birmingham and, in the seaside resort-cum-retirement village of Southport, Arthur Holland's factory began turning out tins labelled 'Best on Earth'. Over time, each small-scale operation would be bought out or acquired by one of the others, although the products and labels might remain the same.

Another European war resulted in the rationing of sweets (and many of the ingredients required to make them) until 1953.

In the interim, the confectionery industry started to employ chemists, inventors and innovators in their kitchens, hothousing new recipes for an era of austerity and stretching ingredients as far as possible. Vegetable oil, corn syrup and skimmed milk replaced butter, with starch and fruit juices instead of sugar. The roots of the modern-day chew were already taking hold as manufacturers fought their own war of attrition.

Family company Matlow Bros., evacuated to New Mills, Derbyshire, from Blitz-battered London, launched a barrage of eponymously named products of various flavours and sizes. New Refreshers (not to be confused with the fizzy roll sweets) concealed an explosive consignment of lemon sherbet in their yellow bellies. The cartoon children depicted on the exterior were rumoured to be none other than members of the relocated Matlow clan itself.

Drumstick lollies were introduced in 1958, although they could only be so named due to the exciting addition of a stick beneath each raspberry and milk flavoured block. One year later, Mars, the dark horse of Slough, came out all guns blazing with an unprecedented packet sweet from their new Liverpool Road factory. The four flavours – strawberry, orange, lemon and lime – inspired the famous 'made to make your mouth water' slogan of the '70s, and were soon joined on the shelves by mint and

**Opposite:** Eeh, what a Swizzel! From tuppenny to timpani via Matlow's New Refreshers (1955), Milk chews (1945), and Drumstick lollies (1958).

**Below:** Saliva gland stimulation. Opal Fruits (1960) and Fruit Tella (1931) engage in a hard struggle for soft chew supremacy.

toffee varieties. The secret ingredient here was glycerol, a humectant (which kept the chews soft and moist).

Advertising positioned Opal Fruits as a means of escape from the traffic-jam mundanity of family holidays and plugged occasional Sunshine Flavours and Summer Fruits editions. A contentious rebrand in the '90s (their original name having been coined by Peter Phillips, a copywriter at Masius Wynne-Williams back in 1959) aligned them with the US version, Starburst, although that confused British readers of the similarly named fantasy film and TV magazine. Rotterdam-based firm Van Melle tried to muscle in on the same fruity territory with packets of their imported uniform-flavour chews, Fruittella – to some acclaim – but the British preferred the ascetic variety of the originals. Opal Fruits were never better than when the punchline to Jimmy Cricket's driving test joke: 'What goes amber, red, green, amber, red?' (More pedantic answer: the Drumstick lolly wrapper – a striped design that saw Swizzels-Matlow safely into the twenty-first century.)

The packet sweets may have been a valuable weapon in the battle for parental attention, but the real conflict happened at a child's eye level. Bad boys knew they could send the poor shopkeeper up a ladder for the high jars of weigh-outs at the back, leaving enough time to steal a good handful of penny chews from the trays down low at the front. Chief victim of such smash and grab thievery was Trebor, coming into their own after having absorbed Sharps in 1961. Bolstered by the Kent confectioners, they found themselves excellently placed to capitalise on a rush of late '70s sci-fi fever: *Star Wars* chews were the first bit of Lucas-endorsed sweet merchandising to hit British streets.

Trebor's range of products reads like a list of children's obsessions. Monster chews unearthed the fossils of dinosaurs, while spooky two-penny Phantom chews joined the decidedly less-than-supernatural likes of Banana Splits, Fruit Salad and Black Jacks. If the golliwog-flaunting wrapper of the latter didn't make life uncomfortable enough in multicultural metropolitan classrooms, there was an added racist frisson to be had from the ching-chong-Chinaman caricature adorning Fumunchews. Trebor Strawbrees, Fruties and Spearminto, on the other hand, were oblong Opal Fruit clones for a younger audience with some pocket money left over. All were variations on a simple theme, essentially the same product with a different flavour or colour and a new wrapper.

Slapping 'new' on the pack generated a bit of excitement for retailers and customers alike, especially if there was a TV tie-in. Fans of the Lou Ferrigno-starring *Incredible Hulk* series might have been foxed by Trebor's cheeky green liquorice and lime Hunk of Chew in 1978. Marvel Comics' lawyers certainly were. Geeks consulting their back issues of *Starburst* were not. IPC, by contrast, were more than happy to hand over the intellectual property of their Captain Hurricane character in return for some quite frankly bizarrely flavoured publicity.

In 1980 McCowan's made it big with Wham (a full two years before George Michael's shuttlecock-smuggling soul boy duo experienced the same success in the pop charts), prefacing a decade of massive hair, massive shoulder pads, and massive gobfuls of toffee. Both McCowan's and

**Opposite:** Sticky stalwarts of the 10p mix-up from the '30s to the '80s – Trebor's Phantom, Hunk Of Chew, Fruit Salad and Black Jack.

**Below:** Hong Kong chewy. Confucius say: 1970s very unenlightened, probably due to power cuts – Fumunchews (1975). Matlow's are just a 'pop' away from a Kellogg's solicitor's letter – Snap and Crackle, circa 1983.

Like the Wham bar, it had a gritty, picked-up-off-the-pavement texture that edged the tart 'burst of flavour' just the other side of pleasurable for the mature palate. Those of a more masochistic bent could advance to the Howler ('the chew that bites back') and, from 1987, the self-explanatory Stinger (in lemon, raspberry or fruit punch flavours). Predictably, the ever-ready battery of 'sour candies' available these days has rendered even the most caustic of chew bars tame by comparison.

Trebor figured mint was the way to go, issuing chewy bars flavoured with spearmint (the Whopper) and Aberdeen Angus (the Highland) respectively. Rowntree attempted a rare and swift sortie into the market with Splicer, a diagonally striped orange, lemon, lime and raspberry affair which looked and tasted like a pack of Opal Fruits after an incident with a steamroller.

As ever, Matlow's slow and steady approach reaped dividends, as they drafted in the troops from the Swizzels end of their fizzyness business to help create Snap and Crackle.

As chocolate prices dropped, so too did the numbers of different toffees on the market. Needler's of Hull, a 100-year-old company who had concentrated solely on production of their signature chewy caramels and glacé fruit drops since 1976, were acquired (along with Blue Bird) by a meat company. Naturally, all parties tried to paint a rosy and patriotic picture on the merger - trade press ads invoked Vera Lynn and the white cliffs of Dover - but the brands faded quickly from public view and the trademarks too have long since expired. McCowan's survived multiple mergers, management buyouts and changes of ownership before finally entering administration in 2011.

**Below:** Prohibition-era gangsters flog Trebor Fizz Kids circa 1979, while trivia-mad android Zeebor anticipates the Internet's obsession with animals, circa 1972.

**Opposite:** Donner und blitzen! Captain Hurricane strikes a blow for Anglo-German relations circa 1974.

Strangely, one company that has done well in the toffee market didn't follow John Mackintosh's rules at all. When Callard & Bowser's thistle-bedecked Creamline Toffees vanished amid the dismantling of Terry's of York, it created a vacuum.

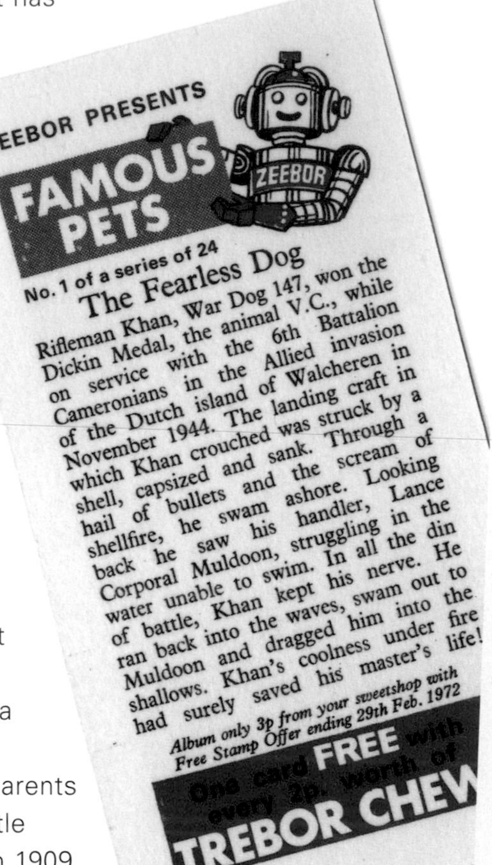

Britain wanted to feel united by a common experience of an uncommonly good butter candy and was willing to accept any offered, even if it was German. So began the systematic brainwashing of a generation, convinced by advertising that their grandparents had shared with them a brittle toffee that was developed in 1909 by Gustav Nebel in the town of Werther, yet which was not marketed internationally until the mid-'90s. Who was it who won the war, again? Ask your granddad.

**'All chews were variations on a simple theme, essentially the same product with a different flavour or colour and a new wrapper.'**

CAPTAIN HURRICANE
CHEW BARS
CAPTAIN HURRICANE AND MAGGOT ARE TRAPPED IN A SHELL HOLE... COMPLETELY SURROUNDED BY THE BEASTLY BOCHE. THE ENEMY IS CLOSING IN. IT LOOKS LIKE THE END FOR OUR HEROES...
PING!!
BETTER GIVE UP THIS TIME, CAP'N. WE'VE HAD IT... PRISON CAMP FOR US!
PTOOM!
CAMP 7
!
THINKS: NO MORE FIGHTING. NO MORE OF OUR COOK'S FOOD. NO MORE OF MY SPECIAL CHEWS!
NO CHEWS! GALLOPING GUN CARRIAGES! THOSE HEARTLESS HUNS HAVE GONE TOO FAR THIS TIME. COME ON MAGGOT, YOU TWERP
ZUNK!
SPLAT!
ACH!
TAKE MORE THAN A REGIMENT AND 50 TANKS TO KEEP THE CAP'N FROM HIS CHEWS... THEY'RE FLIPPING FANTASTIC!
NEW
TREBOR
TREBOR
CAPTAIN HURRICANE
NEW
KOLA, PINEAPPLE, STRAWBERRY & VANILLA, COCONUT & LIQUORICE FLAVOURS.

## * TOFFO

That old-timery 'o' on the end betrays the pre-war origins of Mackintosh's venerable roll of 'Toff-O-Luxe super crème toffees', but after several decades of unfussy plain flavouring, those squat little cylinders which pleasingly moulded themselves to the creases of their individual wrappers underwent a bit of a renaissance. Or they were endlessly mucked about with, depending on

**Opposite:** Toffo (1939), the earliest recorded instance of 'checking what colour the next one is before offering them round' behaviour.

**Below:** There's a new deputy in town. Mackintosh recruits a toffee posse, circa 1976.

your level of curmudgeonly attachment to confectionery tradition.

After a brief and ill-fated dabbling with a patently all wrong blackcurrant variant (doubtless an attempt to replicate the soaraway success of their Fruit Pastilles 'tube with all black ones'), mint and a sophisticated rum and butter flavour joined the originals on the shelves in 1971. But they struck the mother lode five years later with the dark blue assorted roll, wherein old plainy was joined by the instantly popular chocolate flavour, the rather less popular strawberry, and the obligatory pariah flavour, banana with a distinctly chemical tang. As with all variety packs, consumers endlessly complained of a perceived lack of the first of these, and a malicious overabundance of the last.

Perhaps to help police the discontent, TV ads introduced the Toffo sheriff, a super-cool sharpshooter who effortlessly picked absconding bank robbers off a rope bridge without getting up from his lazily tilted chair. 'Go get 'em, Floyd,' he drawled to his wet-behind-the-ears deputy, while the voice-over mused, 'A man's gotta chew what a man's gotta chew,' seemingly oblivious to the brand confusion it was sowing in young viewers' tiny minds by drawing itself uncomfortably close to its rival in Midwest-themed mastication, the Texan bar.

It held its own, though, surviving into the '80s when, in an outbreak of madness at executive level, the sainted chocolate flavour was replaced with... blackcurrant! Another warning from history unheeded, another queasy aftertaste to choke unhappily down. When will people learn?

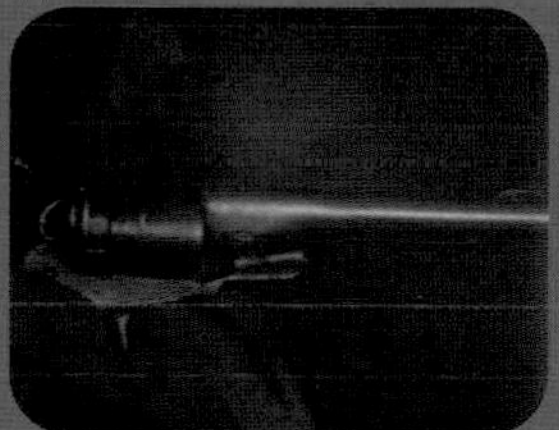

**'The Toffo sheriff was a super-cool sharpshooter who effortlessly picked absconding bank robbers off a rope bridge without getting up.'**

## ✱ CHEWITS

In 1965 corporate financier and asset stripper Jimmy Goldsmith, bored with outrageous takeover bids and fending off bankruptcy, boldly chose to move into the confectionery business. He formed Cavenham Foods, named after the family estate, from an amalgamation of the flagging Carsons & Goodies of Bristol, Parkinsons of Doncaster and Hollands of Southport. This last was at the time best known for its

**Opposite:** Here's looking at chew, kid. Triumphantly post-imperial Chewits (1965).

**Below:** Alternative muncher monster name suggestions: Chew Hefner, Pepe Le Chew, Nerys Chews, Chiouxsie & The Banshees, Chewy Chase.

one penny Arrow bar (advertised in the '70s by a precocious Bonnie Langford, almost certainly giving rise to the phrase 'she can't act for toffee') but a new fondant chew would put the company – not to mention Barrow-in-Furness bus depot – firmly on the map.

Chewits were stickier, more sugary and more solid than their nearest rivals Opal Fruits – so much so that they required special machinery from Germany to manufacture and wrap. A special technique was also necessary to smuggle them into your mouth unseen during double maths lessons. The earliest range offered a choice of strawberry, blackcurrant, orange or banana flavours and were packaged in a mottled camouflage design which made them look a little like military refugees from a particularly effeminate NAAFI. By far their greatest sales boost, however, was delivered in 1976 by the Aardman-animated Godzilla-like star of the 'Muncher' adverts.

In these, a giant Plasticine Pleistocene chewed his way through some b-movie spoofing scenery, before being quelled by the taste of the altogether more satisfying Chewits (wrappers and all), literally off the back of a lorry. Later ads highlighted the creature's claymation capers at a selection of tasty international landmarks (the aforementioned bus terminus, the Taj Mahal and the Empire State Building) and a raucous rampage through wartime London, much to the chagrin of the local ARP warden.

Chewits were popular with pauper and pregnant princess alike. In 1981 an expectant Diana was caught short of cash at a Gloucestershire sweet shop after unexpected cravings for a pack of the strawberry flavour – a story deemed bafflingly headline-worthy by the *Daily Mirror*. Meanwhile, the penniless tearaways of Merseyside knew exactly which bins to raid for misshapen and discarded rejects at the rear of the Chewits factory on Virginia Street. Let them eat cack, you might say.

Jimmy Goldsmith became Sir James in 1976. In the midst of issuing writs for defamation against Richard Ingrams's *Private Eye*, he moved control of his interests to Paris and privatised the confectionery and bakery businesses. Ironically, the Muncher dinosaur (renamed Chewie the Chewitsaurus by new owners Leaf in 1989) lived to fight another day, long after Cavenham and Hollands themselves became extinct.

## ✻ WHAM

Playing the home advantage only gets you so far. For the best part of the twentieth century, Stenhousemuir-based toffee merchants McCowan's chugged along just fine with their none-more-traditional Highland Toffee, save a brief surfing of the Zeitgeist in the form of 1975's Brent-tastic Oil Rig Toffee. All this sporran-tossing homeliness was overshadowed in 1980, however, with the wide-eyed announcement of

**Opposite and below:** Battlestar Ga-lick-tica. Wham wrappers feature suspiciously familiar spacecraft. Glen A. Larson phones his lawyers.

'McCowan's first venture into the space age!'. Woo! The space age had practically ended by this point, but never mind, what exactly was the deal? Only 'the fruity, chewy space age bar that sizzles with sherbet!'. That's what!

Yes, out went meek old brown toffee, and in came the lurid, tangy pink of the tooth-rotting Wham bar, with a tingle on the tongue, a rocket on the wrapper and, indeed, a ker-ching in the tills. An astronomical 2 million 10p bars and utterly out of this world 40 million 2p chews were sold in 1982, possibly because Wham had something for everyone. Adventurous kids got off on the chemical fizz and dental danger. Those of a scientific bent pondered on the way it could warp, like space and time, into an infinitely long raspberry superhighway, where the very laws of confectionery break down. Sci-fi nuts, meanwhile, could get off on the adventures of the good ship *Wham*, as chronicled in a series of 'amusing-dramatic' radio ads.

Matters took an unusual twist in 1983 with the arrival of the Zegazoid, 'the frightening new liquorice and lime chew bar'. Bedecked with green-bonced aliens, who somehow engaged the Wham bar in 'a mid-space struggle for power', the new chew was soon sent packing, despite undercutting its foe by 5p a throw. However, some also remember Gorgo, 'a green monster from the planet Gorg', who lent his name to an alternative version, 'a cosmic green chew bar with fizzy fruit flavour'. Was this the work of a parallel continuum? Or McCowan's hedging their bets? Given that, for either bar, the name 'Gangrene' was seriously considered, it's probably best not to second-guess the motive.

Back on earth, McCowan's struggled to meet that 'difficult second album' challenge. Mumbo Gumbo was a tropical fruit flavoured chew with a fey hippo for a mascot. Dennis the Menace borrowed the *Beano*'s scowling scallywag wholesale for a red and black striped raspberry and blackcurrant bar. Most inevitably, however, an alliance with Barr's Irn-Bru took regional loyalty to its natural conclusion. In 1989 a management buy-out from Nestlé returned the company to Scottish hands, and ambitions once again turned to the stars. Unfortunately, McCowan's chewy cherry cola *MASK* tie-in was yet another dud, but Wham kept the mission ticking over long after the last Saturn V rocket had gone the way of those juvenile choppers.

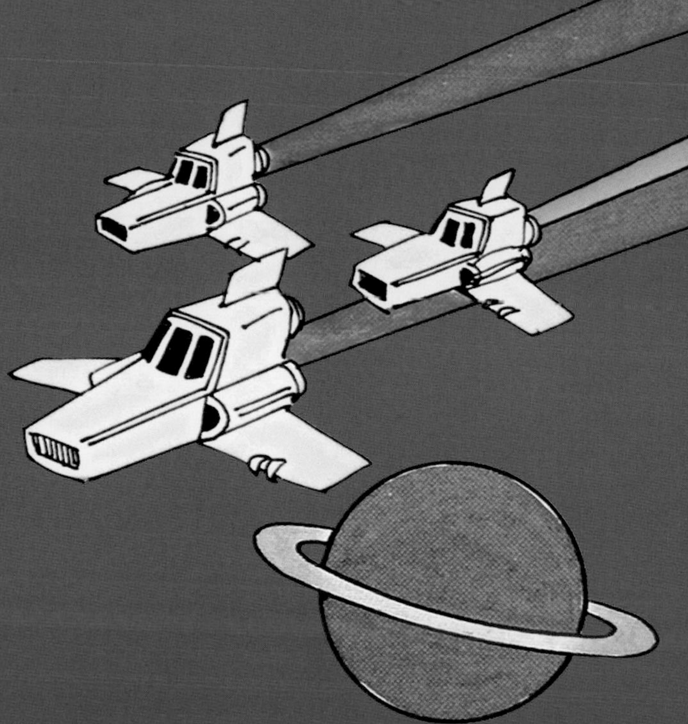

## ✻ PACERS

Why did they used to put so many vending machines in sport and leisure centres? Well, for the cash, obviously, but also 'cos those crafty confectioners wanted to link consumption of their yummy, energy-packed products with an active, healthy lifestyle. In 1975, when doing a few widths of the shallow end, skipping the showers and spending the rest of a Saturday morning stinking of chlorine

**Opposite:** Stripe and pun-ions: the tepid minty tang of those legendary Pacers (1976).

**Below:** Mars paints bars on its stars (1980).

and nicotine in the smokers' gallery put a kid right up there with David Wilkie, liberating a packet of sweets from behind D7 wasn't going to do anyone any harm. The creeping emphysema could be staved off with a sugar rush.

Hence, Pacers: the Adidas of soft minty chews. Originally just plain old Opal Mints, they gained a new name and exciting peppermint stripes around the time Team GB won gold in the 200 metres breast stroke at the Montreal Olympics. The sporty allusions were rife: on TV, perma-grinning ice-dancers, goalkeepers and roller-skaters saw their pristine, Daz-white kit graffitied with a green three-bar motif 'to give a two-mint freshness'. And, as even the spoddiest, drawstring-Day-Glo-pump-bag-carrying dork at the swimming baths knew, stripes seriously improved the coolness factor. It's why Bodie and Doyle ditched their clunky British Leyland cars for go-faster Ford Capris. It's why Signal was more fun to clean your teeth with than Gibbs SR. It's why Pepé Le Pew's girlfriends got some action.

But why add them to Pacers? Was it simply because Mars, suffering a touch of the Steve Austins, discovered that they had the technology? Or was it to bring them in line with the identical American candy of the same name? Prior to stripification, each carefully sealed wax paper wrapper contained a square, emulsified chunk of vegetable fat and glucose the exact colour and consistency of a church candle. Any such religious connotation, sensibly, was disregarded by the marketing bods. No one wanted to see impressionable Catholic kids gnawing on tea-lights during the liturgy. However, in upgrading to an improved two-tone pattern, Mars may have caused a schism amid the football faithful of Glasgow. Celtic supporters could wield a chew kitted out in their home strip, whereas partisan Rangers fans would be less inclined to partake.

It mattered not. Enthusiastically advertised or otherwise, Pacers wheezed asthmatically into the '80s before collapsing in an armchair of obscurity. Their name has passed into history. Optimistic Googlers will find only a list of increasingly provincial running clubs and Indiana-based basketball teams. The health Nazis won: fitness centre vending machines are now full of fruit and Mini Babybels. Now those really do taste like wax.

## BOYS FROM THE BLACK STUFF

Its origins may be exotically Mediterranean, but from the end of the Crusades to round about the release of *Mutiny on the Buses*, the leguminous plant *Glycyrrhiza glabra*, the root of which yields the aromatic substance known as liquorice, was synonymous in the British psyche with one place only: Pontefract. Initially, as with all things sweet, the little discs made from the local crop were entirely medicinal. Then in the eighteenth century, local chemist George Dunhill realised that, with a load of sugar bunged in them, they became something much more fun, and the Pontefract Cake took shape. As the typically down-to-earth Yorkshire publicity had it: 'Very acceptable for smokers. Good for children, too!'

By the twentieth century, the area was a hive of black novelty production. Alongside Dunhill, you had W.R. Wilkinson's, the newly arrived Bellamy's in nearby Castleford, and over a dozen more. But the most famous purveyor was located down the road in Sheffield. In the middle of the nineteenth century orphaned farmer's son George Bassett set up as a confectioner advertising 'funerals supplied with hoods, scarfs, biscuits and wine on the shortest notice'. Once he got wind of the liquorice rush, however, business took a distinctly cheerier turn, and penny novelties, combining the black stuff with cream paste fondant in an array of geometric forms, were soon rolling off his production line, along with liquorice comfits, a secular sugar-coated take on the almond variety so popular at religious celebrations.

Then, around 1899, comes the legend. Charlie Thompson, ace Bassett's salesman, is visiting a confectionery buyer with the company's novelty penny lines, all laid out regimentally on his sample tray. Noises of mild interest issue forth from the customer. At that moment a slightly clumsy shop girl stumbles past, sending the tray flying. As a harassed Thompson exasperatedly rounds up the errant sweets with his foot, our man with the money peers at the heap, and likes what he sees. 'Just supply me with all sorts mixed up together, like that.' And so was born the liquorice allsort.

**Opposite:** George Basset Ltd having a particularly bad spell with Pillo Pak, circa 1972.

**Below:** Albert Bassett Esq in his TV pomp, circa 1980. And pre-assembly (or post-dismemberment) on a box of Allsorts (1968).

Gregory Grimble. This wasn't quite up there with Charlie Thompson in the legend stakes. Better to focus on Bertie himself, now happily endowed with the gift of sight and expression, launched onto the streets in puppet form for a series of ribald *That's Life!*-style interviews with his adoring public, and later getting in some blokey cross-talk with a wilderness years Chris Tarrant.

Well, it's a quaint story. But there's no denying the power of the assortment, and after the war, with cannibalistic mascot Bertie Bassett installed (albeit initially in a slightly disturbing faceless incarnation), Bassett set the gold standard, selling allsorts to sixty countries and, after a bout of cutting-edge factory automation, churning out 2 billion a year by 1967. 'He makes them round, he makes them square! They're the people's favourites – everywhere!'

TV campaigns weird and wonderful appeared. One attempted to establish cults around individual allsorts with the notional Bassett's Swop Shop: Mrs Doris Ankle of Swindon liked the pink ones, apparently, while the blue bobbly variety were idolised by 'Groovy'

**Opposite:** Size isn't everything, Hubert. Stick that in your liquorice pipe and... er, eat it.

**Below:** Bellamy's bugle. Block-booking the back pages, circa 1981.

Bertie's rival mascot was the bowler-hatted Mr Bellamy, forever entertaining purchasers of his liquorice pipes, bootlaces and Catherine wheels with trivia, tricks and the whimsical, and indeed often incoherent, adventures of the Bellamy gang: Hubert Windpipe, Big Brenda and company, getting into and out of hilarious scrapes with the aid of Mr B's threepenny novelties. You name it, Mr Bellamy could turn liquorice into a very approximate shape of it. Sometimes he cheated by using red stuff that wasn't really liquorice at all, but the kids loved this eccentric, moustachioed haunter of comic back pages all the same.

There's an old Lapp proverb, 'If you use liquorice for your bootlaces they will break.' Weird though that may be, those Scandinavians must know something, as the late '70s played host to a veritable Viking liquorice invasion, which proved cheaper than its British rivals. Combined with inflation, regular scare stories about the adverse effect of liquorice on blood pressure and kidneys, and an unseemly foray into video games, Bassett's profits dwindled throughout the 1980s.

When the ads chirped that good old Bertie Bassett was Britain's greatest asset, there was a growing hint of desperation. At one point a takeover from the owners of Robertson's jam was mooted, but Bertie thankfully avoided conceding his place on the packs to that dubious gollywog. Inevitably, Bertie was eventually taken under the wing of old Mr Cadbury. Still, it could have been worse. Pioneers Dunhill only survived the 1990s by going cap in hand to, of all people, gummy German behemoth Haribo. Cold comfit indeed.

Have fun with the amazing
MR BELLAMY
MR BELLAMY'S BOOT LACE KNOT Offer someone a Mr Bellamy Liquorice Boot Lace. Ask him to tie a knot in it – without letting go of the ends. He won't be able to do it. But tell him you can. Fold your arms before you pick up the ends, like the picture, and when you unfold your arms you will have tied a knot!
THE AMAZING SPOT THE LIQUORICE TRICK. With your back to a table, ask someone to put a piece of liquorice anywhere on the table. Get them to hold one arm in the air. After about 1 minute, ask your friend to put his hands on the table and cover the liquorice with the hand he's been holding in the air.
When you turn round you'll know immediately where the liquorice is. It's under the hand that's paler. Do you know why?
AMAZING!!! BUT TRUE Do you know that Mr Bellamy makes the most delicious, most exciting liquorice novelties ever? He makes thin ones, fat ones, wide ones, long ones – whatever takes your fancy. And the most amazing thing of all? You can enjoy a Mr Bellamy Liquorice Novelty for only 3p
HELP!
SOME FACTS TO AMAZE YOUR FRIENDS WITH
Gorillas can't swim!
Poodles don't moult!
Elephants can't jump!
Giraffes have no voice!
MR BELLAMY'S
Amazing Liquorice Novelties

## ✻ SHERBET FOUNTAIN

When Tangerine, the Blackpool-based owners of Sherbet Fountain, updated the sweet's packaging in 2009, they faced a perfect storm of media outrage. 'A step too far,' seethed the *Independent*. 'Killjoys,' moaned the *Daily Mail*. 'Annoying,' fumed the *Guardian*. It was all rather predictable, given Fleet Street's known aversion to change and bloodhound's nose for stories that might rile the proletariat.

**Opposite:** Memoirs of a geyser. Barratt's Sherbet Fountain (1925).

**Below:** Ten BMX bikes! Fifty Firefox F-7 electronic games! A Barratt competition from 1983, as if you needed telling.

'Hygiene' was the self-confessedly anaemic reason Tangerine gave for the plastic makeover, though deaths attributed to virulent liquorice or toxic sherbet had been few and far between over the preceding eighty-odd years.

The new, hermetically sealed Sherbet Fountain genuinely did fix some flaws: it protected the product from moisture, avoided spillage on newsagents' shelves and prevented sabotage. But – from the Just Williams to the Adrian Moles – generations of wilful kids had delighted in its original, eccentric form. Tucked in the back pocket, along with a catapult or a secret diary, that yellow paper tube looked pleasingly like a stick of dynamite or a (potentially name-coining) firework. Unpacked, the useless treacly liquorice 'straw' could be quickly dispatched and full attention directed to the contents within. If the weather was fine, this would most likely result in an explosion of dusty lemon sherbet and a day condemned to walk the streets with a PIERROT-white face. If wet, the porous cardboard would dampen like a tramp's roll-up, causing the sherbet to stick to the sides in claggy lumps and necessitating a lean-back and open-wide manoeuvre. Squeezing and tapping a fully loaded Sherbet Fountain into your mouth carried with it the risk, at the very least, of a full-on coughing fit.

Here's where the modernisers went wrong. You can add as much anti-caking agent as you like, but take away that sense of danger and you subtract from the overall eating experience. Ironing out the wrinkles and streamlining defects might make sense on the factory floor, but what made the Sherbet Fountain so endearing was its essential Britishness: it was tactile, an action sweet, but nothing about it worked as it ought to. Like Morecambe and Wise sharing a big double bed, it sort of looked wrong, but it sort of felt right.

Barratt themselves had previously experimented with the formula, inflicting orange and raspberry varieties on an ungrateful public. In 1995, Monkhill also tried to tempt the nation into supping the Sherbet Fountain in soda drink form. Yet nothing scared the horses like plastic-gate, which was strange, because – in among all the hand-wringing over the less recyclable nature of the new tube – no one spotted that the flavour of the sherbet had also changed. Now, that one really should have had the journalists foaming at the mouth.

## SHERBET LESSONS

In the eternal playground of youth, nothing defined and divided the genders so much as their taste in sweets. Boys were pigeonholed more readily than girls, even though the majority of confectionery industry players were men. As early as the mid-'60s, they were identified by advertisers as mischievous, unsupervised ruffians, scoffing pocketfuls of sticky, lint-flecked toffees between meals. Girls, by contrast, were made of all things nice – sugar (mostly glucose syrup) and spice (permitted flavourings). There were few items in any tuck shop collection that were out of bounds to the fairer sex – the odd chunky chocolate bar, perhaps, or a hard caramel candy. Lads, however, were required to negotiate a social and political minefield with every purchase.

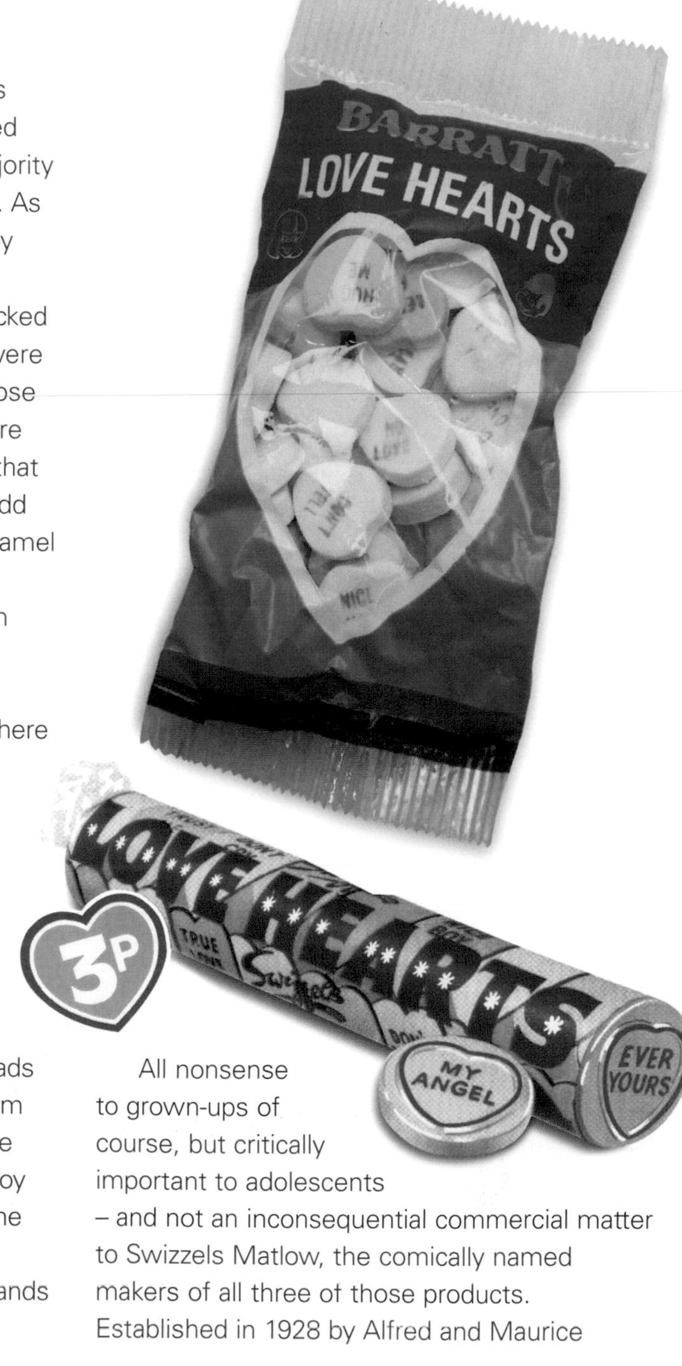


The strict, delineated and oppressive atmosphere of the classroom demanded that a boy's choice of break-time sweets conveyed the requisite disdain for effeminacy. Get it wrong and he would be subjected to homophobic insults for the rest of his academic career. Brandishing a Double Lolly, for example, was the equivalent of affecting a poetic, Byron-esque flamboyance and invited accusations of sissydom. Wearing a Dolly Beads candy necklace was tantamount to singing Tom Robinson hits or admitting to an interest in the works of Virginia Woolf. But woe betide the boy who developed a taste for Love Hearts – for he might as well have just minced into school dressed as Freddie Mercury, doing 'teapot' hands and sucking on a thick stick of pink rock.

All nonsense to grown-ups of course, but critically important to adolescents – and not an inconsequential commercial matter to Swizzels Matlow, the comically named makers of all three of those products. Established in 1928 by Alfred and Maurice

**Opposite:** Aorta not be doing that. Barratt sails close to the trademark winds with its own Love Hearts, circa 1971. And the Swizzels Matlow originals, as seen on sale circa 1974.

**Below:** Swizzels secures the all-important support of the under-sixes – Fizzers – and the over-sixties – Parma Violets, both originally created in the 1930s.

lozenges' to their hearts, the romantic messages inscribed on the surface communicating any love that dare not speak its name. Thus might any gentleman procure the affections of a lady, and perchance a glimpse at the ankle she kept so demurely hidden beneath her crinolines.

Records show evidence of prior brands such as Sweetheart Cachous, Cupid's Whispers and Sugar Kisses, but it was the arrival of Swizzels' Love Hearts in 1954 that turned the idea into a money-spinner. Originally intended as a cracker novelty, their unforeseen but widespread popularity ensured that full-time production and distribution followed only two years later.

Matlow with David Dee, the company initially gained a reputation for producing varieties of French cachous (breath-sweetening tablets traditionally taken by smokers) including the effervescent, fruity Fizzers, and floral Parma Violets. Both of these would continue to turn up down the years in children's lucky bags, along with a cheap toy and a comic, but were originally aimed at the sophisticated inebriate about town. Parma Violets, it was said, were particularly effective at masking the smell of beer after a night's boozing. Shakespeare himself had praised the cachou, having Falstaff 'hail kissing comfits' in *The Merry Wives of Windsor*. And if anyone admired the efficacy of a good a breath-freshener, it was the Elizabethans. In Victorian times, the sexually repressed masses took new 'conversation

Thereafter, 'Refreshers' became the generic name for all Swizzels Matlow's non-Love Heart fizzy fruit tablets. New lines over the years included Wordies (Scrabble-style lexicon lozenges), a tie-in with *Star Trek: the Motion Picture*, a range of *New Shmoo*-recalling Fizzy Faces and the mistimed Hippy Bits ('groovy, with it' sweets intended to cash in on flower power but launched in the infamous wake of Altamont and Charles Manson's 'family' murders).

Wood Green's own George Barratt & Co, since 1966 a subdivision of the confusingly similar-sounding George Bassett Ltd of Sheffield, also produced a fruity, fizzy roll sweet called Refreshers. The name replication was a source of consternation to all parties and each recipe was closely guarded, only divulged to new trainees when they signed on the payroll. (What would the title of that introductory course be? A Refresher course? Most confusing.)

Barratt ran into further titular tribulations in 1984 with Frosties, their junior, button-sized version of sherbet lemons sold in a roll (a kind of children's training sweet, like a bike with stabilisers – well, an acidity regulator, at any rate). Kellogg's slapped an injunction on new owners Trebor that required the brand name never be too far from the 'house mark' on the packet, the legal fallout from which continued well into the late '90s. In truth, Barratt were silly to be so adamant about hard candy when they'd already cornered the market in soft, loose sherbet. It was girls, again, who were the crucial demographic.

What we now know as sherbet, like so much modern confectionery, owes a great debt to the Middle East. Whether sold sealed in multicoloured straws, trapped inside the edible paper disk of a 'flying saucer', or shovelled from a jar marked 'rainbow crystals', it is all directly descended from the flavoured Arabic drink sharbat, beloved of Saladin and the Bedouin sherbet-merchants of Persia. During the early 1800s, British sherbet began a transformation from liquid to powder, catalysed by the invention of a process to create soda water (and its application for fizzy pop). Northern vendors would sell dry lemon alkali (the name betraying the roots of the apothecary's production process), soon shortened to 'kali' by slipshod regional dialects. Though both boys and girls tended to grow out of sherbet by their late teens, one twenty-five-

**Opposite:** Trebor Refreshers (1935), hopping into bed with Obi-Wan Kenobi, not Cheryl Baker and co., obviously.

**Below:** Inflation, tellingly, not included in this 1978 giveaway from Barratt's Sherbet Dip-Dab. Unnecessary flavour variants part 87 – Barratt's Raspberry Sherbet Fountain circa 1970.

year-old Coventry woman was admitted to hospital in 1983 complaining of 'giddy spells and headaches' after overdosing on multiple half-pound bags.

Most kids suffered little more than a back-of-the-jaw tingle, right in the mandibles, rather like the effect of blowing up too many balloons. It wasn't powerful stuff. Both Barratt's Sherbet Fountain and its more flavoursome counterpart, the Sherbet Dip-Dab, were considered too weedy for boys. The Barratt marketing team responded with a forty-two-episode-long advertorial comic strip series, *The Sherbet Gang*, a kind of Famous Five with an obsession for Lemonade Dippers, Jungle Dip and the *Danger Mouse* Lick 'n' Dip. The gang's adventures were usually resolved by the employment of a Big Dipper lolly, Sherbet Fountain liquorice stick, or other such edible 'cutlery', as a weapon. 'May the Fizz be with you' was the expedient catchphrase of the day.

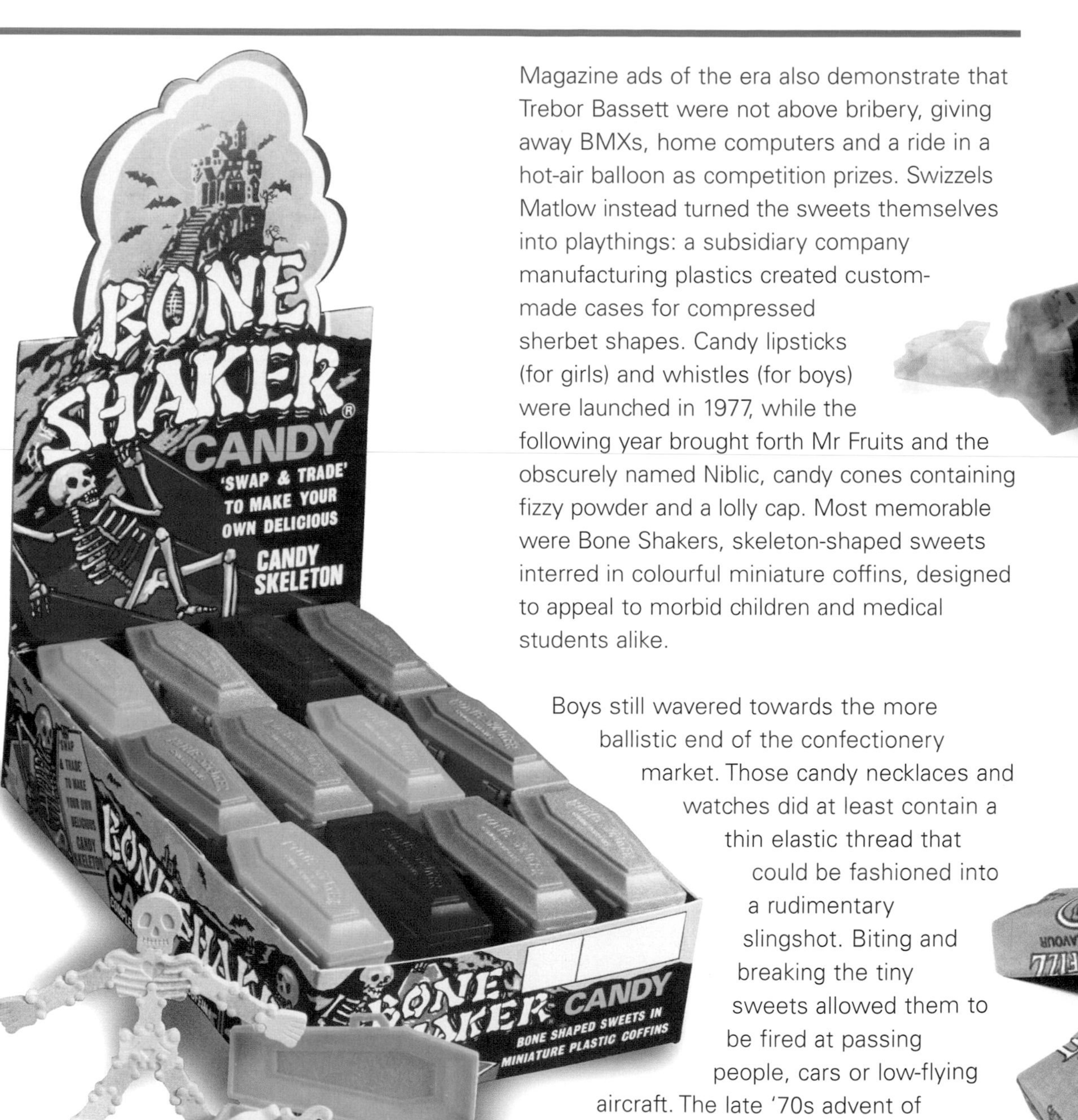


Magazine ads of the era also demonstrate that Trebor Bassett were not above bribery, giving away BMXs, home computers and a ride in a hot-air balloon as competition prizes. Swizzels Matlow instead turned the sweets themselves into playthings: a subsidiary company manufacturing plastics created custom-made cases for compressed sherbet shapes. Candy lipsticks (for girls) and whistles (for boys) were launched in 1977, while the following year brought forth Mr Fruits and the obscurely named Niblic, candy cones containing fizzy powder and a lolly cap. Most memorable were Bone Shakers, skeleton-shaped sweets interred in colourful miniature coffins, designed to appeal to morbid children and medical students alike.

Boys still wavered towards the more ballistic end of the confectionery market. Those candy necklaces and watches did at least contain a thin elastic thread that could be fashioned into a rudimentary slingshot. Biting and breaking the tiny sweets allowed them to be fired at passing people, cars or low-flying aircraft. The late '70s advent of America's Space Dust also proved that research into carbonisation need not be limited to freezing Han Solo at the end of *The Empire Strikes Back* – although a Love Heart carrying the message 'I know' would have been fab.

**Opposite:** The Body In Digestion: Junior Jonathan Millers were happy coffin up for Swizzels' anatomically approximate Bone Shaker (1981).

**Below:** Secret Messages circa 1973, and Jibes (1993), failing to leverage the Love Heart brand equity to extended demographics. 'Lemon flavoured non-medicated effervescent sugar confectionery,' Lemfizz (1974).

Further ideas pinched from the New World included Swizzels' Double Dip (a choice of sherbet flavours and a swizzle stick lolly) and Barratt Fruit Tabs (the British brick equivalent of Pez).

Carter Bond, a former pharmaceutical company tentatively testing the waters in the sweetie trade, came up with their own intensely effervescent paving slabs, Lemfizz. Intended to be plopped into a glass of water for an invigorating drink, they were usually munched whole by brave youngsters chasing a sugar rush.

Despite the name, they came in a wide variety of flavours, including raspberry, pineapple and blackcurrant, and featured occasional horror film-inspired wrappers. One illustration, a dinosaur eating a train carriage, had a sort of thematic congruence but the weird drawing of a vampire's head attached to a bat's body raised more questions than it answered.

Also emerging from the company's Attercliffe Road factory in Sheffield were Secret Messages, a roll of speckled, Love Heart-baiting fruit tablets stamped with yet more lovey-dovey phrases. Well, most of them were, but not all. 'You dope' at the time wasn't considered ghetto-slang for 'you are awesome', it was a straightforward insult. Swizzels Matlow had a crack at releasing a whole panoply of these in the '90s called Jibes but the low-level taunting of 'wally' and 'goon' must have seemed antiquated to four-letter-word-spouting youth even then.

**Below:** You've heard 'Young Hearts Run Free' by Candi Staton? Well, here's, er, 'Happy Hearts 2p' by Candy Brokers. Throw in Trebor Sweeties and let's say, ooh, circa 1972 for the pair?

**Opposite:** Inglorious Colorama: the usually reliable Matlow's slips up by offering that most uninspiring of gifts, the flimsy plastic wallet of dodgy felt tips, with their New Refreshers, circa 1985.

It also appeared that no one in the Matlow family's product team had considered the etymology of the word 'berk'.

Barratt's own Love Hearts – still living dangerously with the trademarks, guys! – were ticker-shaped sugar sweets with messages inked on in food colouring, including a bleak 'No love' and a needy 'Hug me'. While these were possibly aimed at girls who felt they'd already been left on the shelf aged nine, Snipits Happy Hearts spread a little cheer from the decided suburban-sounding 5 Delta Close address of Candy Brokers in Norwich. Trebor, however, played it safer than most with their unisex spin on the compressed sherbet sweet. The unimaginatively named Sweeties were Love Heart-like in appearance, but were imprinted with the Christian names of boys and girls rather than romantic blandishments.

Their function was unclear – at least there could be no ulterior sexual motive inferred by gobbling down a few Glenns, a Paul and a Neil at break time – but in a world populated by Chardonnays, Maddisons and Zachariahs, those tiny sherbet tablets might have to be an inch or two wider now.

**'Sherbet is directly descended from the flavoured Arabic drink sharbat, beloved of Saladin and the Bedouin merchants of Persia.'**

Matlow's
NEW
REFRESHERS
OFFER
SUPER
2p
VALUE
PLUS
FREE
WALLET OF 5
NON TOXIC SUPER QUALITY
FIBRE TIP PENS
ATTACHED TO EVERY 2 x 72 OUTER
LIMITED OFFER WHILE STOCKS LAST
SWIZZELS MATLOW LTD, NEW MILLS, STOCKPORT, CHESHIRE. SK12 3HA
CHEWS WITH A
REFRESHING
CENTRE
Colorama
FIBRE TIPPED PENS
42p
WORTH
AT LEAST
42p
TO YOU

Swizzels
REGD
STAR
REFRE

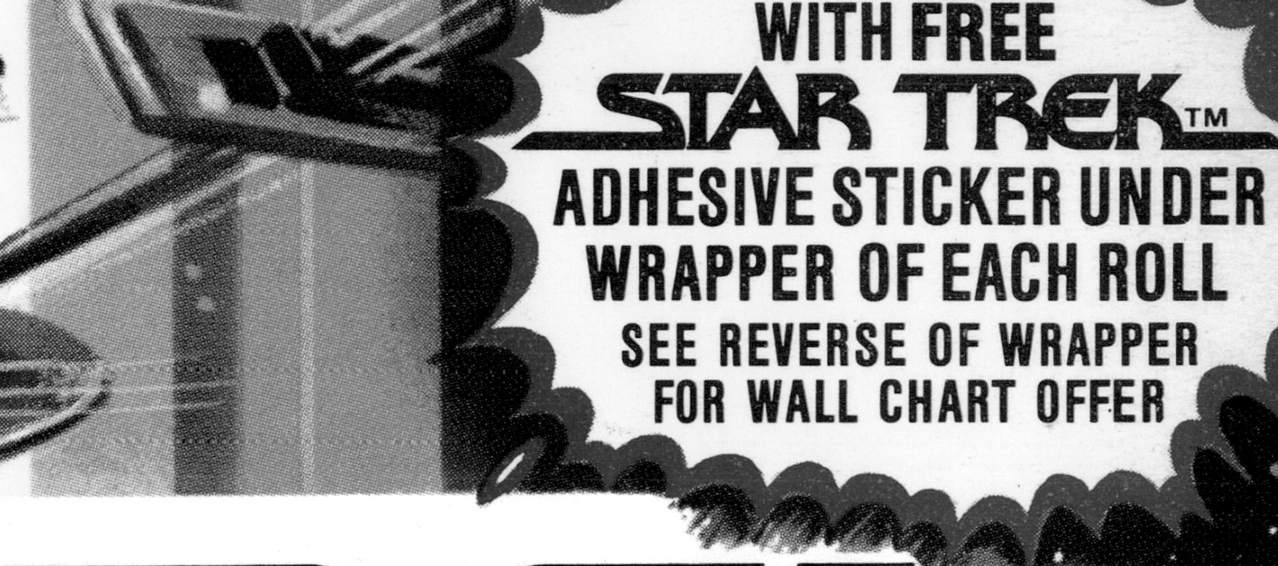


TREK

TM.

SHERS

## * LOVE HEARTS

Far from being a sweet nothing, a Love Heart always carried a fizzy kick in its compressed sugar make-up; a mixture of tartaric acid and bicarbonate of soda that made it a close relative of powdered sherbet. The chemical reaction when the ingredients were mixed with water (or saliva) created sodium citrate and carbon dioxide, hence the froth and tingling in the mouth. A dry production process

**Opposite:** Putting the 'Cor!' into coronary. Swizzels' much-adored Love Hearts in a none-too-subliminal 'Buy me' message shocker (1954).

(known as 'slugging') had to be enforced to prevent the addition of volatile flavourings and binders from setting off a cannonade of sucrose explosions on the factory floor.

Another of Love Hearts' strengths was the simplicity of the design (a trademarked visual image staunchly defended by the parent company) and its flexibility. The old-fashioned messages appearing on early editions – 1950s' 'Hey, Daddio' – would give way over time to more modern sayings, such as 1960s' 'Gay Boy' or the downright futuristic 'Fax Me'. Even so, they were unlikely to find themselves exchanged for a boy's precious dinner money. Possession equalled intent to supply, and that could only mean one thing: giving a Love Heart to – eurgh! – a girl as a token of affection (after having first carefully arranged the order of the pack – boys were nothing if not as underhand as conjurors forcing cards onto stooges from the audience).

No, it was simply unacceptable. Boys had to have their own version, but it wasn't until 1986 that Swizzels came up with an alternative. Soccer Shields were the result of long and complicated negotiations with the – together at last! – dream team of Southern Television, Manchester Polytechnic and the FA. Each 10p roll came with a different club sticker from one of the four football league divisions, and a questionnaire about attitudes to the beautiful game (sample: 'If you were in charge of a football club, what would you do to get more people to turn up?'). England team manager Bobby Robson pitched in to plug the survey: leaflets were printed, cardboard cut-outs delivered to newsagents, and some 'Hey kids!' speech-bubble-friendly quotes sourced, all featuring the white-haired World Cup wizard.

However, Robson bowed out after a single appearance on flagging Saturday morning children's TV show, *Number 73*, and was replaced by last-minute substitution 'Big Ron' Atkinson (who was presumably pleased to note that the packets didn't contain any 'lazy, thick' black ones). The glamorous football associations belied the fact that Soccer Shields, available in either 'mint' or 'refresher' varieties, were a partial reinvention of 1972's Lucky Strike, 'the sweet that won £250,000 on the pools'. Dads were encouraged to use these as counters to help choose the score draws for their Treble Chance each Saturday, although Swizzels also gave away plenty of Lunn Poly holidays and Hillman Avengers via a more traditional 'write a slogan' competition.

Soccer Shields' time in the top flight was brief. On paper, the lads gave 110 per cent but, at the end of the day, it was just end-to-end stuff. Love Hearts continued to lead the field, boosted by the occasional headline (a lorryload of 3 million packs nicked and recovered in 1973) or royal endorsement (a factory visit by Princess Di in 1990). What no one could have predicted was the personalised wedding favours produced for the nation's sweethearts, Wayne and Colleen Rooney, in 2008. Confectionery – it's a funny old game, isn't it?

## ✱ SPACE DUST

Like *Star Wars*, the Sony Walkman, and serial killers, this fizzy sherbet sensation was a huge hit in the States long before the Brits got their tiny mitts on it. US confectionery giant General Foods – that's a company, not a cartoon character – had been sitting on a patent for a process to introduce pressurised gas into candy for nigh on twenty years. It took until 1976 for the manufacturing capability to catch

**Opposite:** Space Dust (1977). Or, as the picture might suggest, Moon Puke. (Wasn't she one of Frank Zappa's kids?)

up with the conjecture, at which point Pop Rocks – the first of their kind – literally exploded onto the market.

Demand, however, quickly outstripped supply. Tiny black envelopes of the stuff changed hands in New York City playgrounds at a higher price by weight than the kind of white lines Grandmaster Flash sang dang diggedy dang di-dang about. Like their street drug counterparts, Pop Rocks also attracted a fair share of newspaper scare stories. Rumours spread that kids who quaffed a can of Coke and chugged three packs at the same time could suffer from what top physicians call 'exploding stomach syndrome', despite daily evidence to the contrary. The urban legend was so tenacious that General Foods felt compelled to send their top food scientist, William A. Mitchell, on a coast-to-coast, myth-busting tour. Even so, consumer resistance coupled with persistent distributor bootlegging did for sales and the company faced a $34 million loss on the product.

Their second attempt was Space Dust, the budgie grit to Pop Rocks' fish tank gravel. Less startling than the original, being more tongue-corroding than tooth-cracking, it sparkled in orange, grape and watermelon flavours for the Yanks, or 'orbiting' orange, 'solar' strawberry and 'lunar' lemon for the Limeys. Nevertheless, the stench of scandal followed, leading Britain's Ministry of Agriculture to investigate unsourced reports that Space Dust gave you cancer (it didn't) and the tabloids to claim that grown-ups were using it to spike their beer (they weren't). General Foods, already spooked, changed the name to Cosmic Candy back home (to avoid further unwanted comparisons with Angel Dust), while the UK launch of Pop Rocks misfired like a mouth-bound blunderbuss. No amount of free 'I'm a Pop Rocker' badges could make it sound less like a stale mid-'70s ITV music show for teens. It was all over. In 1983, Chris Kelly and co. documented the demise of such space-age sweetdom on the Beeb's *Food & Drink* programme.

Not that they ever really went away: by the late '80s Hannah's of Johnstone had already begun importing Peta Zetas popping candy from Spain under the name Fizz Wiz. In the '90s, Dairy Crest introduced a range of crackling Crazy Shakes milk drinks and Duncan's of Scotland were granted exclusive use of the Space Dust trademark to power their Shock-A-Lot choc bar. Yet, despite the fact that a quick Google Shopping search instantly reveals at least half a dozen different brands still on sale, a belief in this sweet's scarcity persists. Consequently, a nostalgia-baiting TV chef can sprinkle a pack on his dessert to wow ingenuous C-list celebrity guests and be declared a retro genius. Oh yeah? Well, knock us up a giant pack of Spangles, Heston, and maybe we can talk.

**'Rumours spread that kids who quaffed a can of Coke and chugged three packs at the same time could explode.'**

## SUCKING SELL

The boiled sweet. Not exactly the most thrilling of foods. Out of the wrapper it pops with a rustle, into the gob for a couple of minutes of aimless sucking and clattering around the inside of the teeth, then, when boredom finally sets in, a couple of crunches and it's gone. A lollipop without the stick, it only really seems exciting in its own right when juxtaposed with something incredibly dull: say, a long car journey to Budleigh Salterton. So how has the dreary fruit drop survived the upheavals of confectionery history? Unsurprisingly, it's not the sweet itself that's important, more the fluff that surrounds it.

Traditional boiled sweets didn't mess about: syrupy in taste, boiled to within an inch of their lives, and woe betide the choppers that come down on them in undue haste. Pascall, curators of the Murray Mint, modulated the tooth-shattering old-school recipe with the softer Fruit Bonbon, an elegant lozenge stamped with their imprimatur, which was kept back from the so-called 'hard crack' stage of boiling, thus yielding in the mouth to reveal an agreeably slushy liquid centre. Variations on a theme were the grand Court Fruit Drops, the inevitable Murray Fruits, and 1970's ambitiously textured Fruity Pops: 'a unique, honeycomb-centred, fruit-flavoured eating sensation'. These elegant delicacies with their cut-above painted wrappings gave the former jar filler a classy new status.

Back in the thick of the mass market, though, Trebor were the boiled confectionery kings. It wasn't that they had a particularly exciting secret recipe or anything like that, but they knew how to hawk what was, to all intents and purposes, a glob of molten sucrose with a bit of flavouring and dye in it. Back in the early '60s you could already see them at work, plugging their Bitter Orange Drops with the fulsome praise of a vivacious 'It' girl. 'What a tantalising taste! Orange, of course, but... bitter orange!' Who could possibly resist?

Image-conscious to a fault, Trebor were as keen to be seen as men of the people as the next Cadbury heir. In 1961 they proudly announced their boiled sweets, unlike most of their rivals', would not be going up in price, as they didn't want

**Opposite:** Drop down menu. A veritable smorgasbord of flavours from Trebor Drops circa 1973.

**Below:** 'The horror... The horror...' Trebor Mummies (1980) and Blobs (1975) go at the kids' market with Hammer and tongues.

'children and old age pensioners to suffer because of chancellor Selwyn Lloyd's 15% lollipop tax'. Keeping the grannies and grandkids on side was canny policy, as was their long campaign, tirelessly waged from the '60s up until 1984, for the abolition of the 'troublesome halfpenny'. Like any self-appointed national institution, they even celebrated their own diamond jubilee in 1967 with special-edition Glitter Mints and Glitter Fruits.

Trebor reached their zenith the following decade, wherein they perfected that most essential of all the confectioner's crafts: the ability to repeatedly flog the same product back to the same kids under slightly different guises. By 1975 they'd perfected the roll-pack fruit drop: a squat, cylindrical boiled sweet with a cavity inside that could be stuffed with sherbet, fruity gloop or anything of your choice. The product was sound, it was popular, it couldn't be improved upon. But with a little bit of marketing nous, this evolutionary dead end could be eked out for a further decade.

First came Blobs. A slightly funkier rival to the new Fizzy Spangles, they featured 'flavours you don't expect to find in a sweet': toffee apple, strawberries and cream, banana and pear, fizzy cider for example. Comics were festooned with ads featuring Patch, a gurning yellow kid in dungarees and a Stone Roses hat who larked about with some stock cartoon monsters, while a new flavour was punted out every six months to keep the brand afloat. That began to run out of steam before long, so a couple of years later they were re-purposed as Double Agents, and the cycle began anew.

Then in 1980 they became Mummies, a horror-themed roll of 'fiendishly black' sherbet-filled sweets in strawberry, lime, orange and blackcurrant – these deemed by

**Below:** Multiple-choice, DIY caption. Trebor Fings (1981):
1. Ain't what they used to be.
2. Can only get better.
3. That make you go hmm.

**Opposite:** One of those 'plane hijack' comic ads that tend not to sit too comfortably post-9/11. Fruity Pops Poppers, circa 1971.

no doubt scrupulous research to be the four most popular boiled sweet flavours. 'The taste of the tomb!' claimed the TV ads. Unfortunately many kids agreed, so after little more than a year they metamorphosed yet again into – and here you can really hear the desperation – Fings. Yep, Space Fings (which came with free UFO-themed stickers tucked inside the outer wrapper) and Crazy Fings (with, er, 'crazy' stickers), later joined by Crawly Fings, which just brought the horror theme back once again.

Away from the tongues of the *Whizzer and Chips* massive (and indeed Trebor brought out a roll featuring that comic's Sweet Tooth character), boiled sweets could be a bit more bracing.

The late '50s saw the heyday of the Lys Bar, a stick-shaped boiled sweet containing cognac and Scotch fillings at much greater strengths (up to 11° proof) than your average chocolate liqueur. Sadly 'the handy way to carry a "small nip" in the pocket' was banned in 1960 on the grounds that a child eating 'a considerable number... might become tipsy'. With licensing laws relaxed, the bars enjoyed a brief revival in 1987.

The '80s health kick inevitably meant diminishing returns in the sugar-spun sector. As the decade drew to a close, the Real Confectionery Company (owned, oddly, by match makers Bryant & May) introduced the Vitafruit, a 'healthier' boiled sweet, retaining all the vitamins usually expunged by the traditional heavy boiling process. They were hardly a hit, but they still proved more durable than Five Fruits Bonbons, the product of Cadbury's tentative move into the boiled sweet market, which gained a little more momentum when they bought out Trebor wholesale in 1989. Even so, the mad marketing wave that had buoyed the glassy sphere through two decades had long since broken. Out of the mouths of babes and sucklings and back into the gobs of aunts and uncles, the boiled sweet ended its brief dalliance with pop stardom and resumed its rightful place – in a rather nasty tailback on the A30 just outside Ottery St Mary.

Introducing
THE FRUITY POPS POPPERS
POP
POP
POP
HENRY SMALL PETE TERRY
THE POPPERS ARE A CRIME-BUSTING GANG WHO LIVE IN GRANTON. THE TWO THINGS THEY LOVE BEST ARE TO SEE A CRIMINAL GO TO GAOL; AND THEIR PACKS OF FRUITY POPS. NOW READ ON....
THE POPPERS WERE ON A PLANE BOUND FOR THEIR HOLIDAYS. SUDDENLY......
THIS IS A HI-JACK. TAKE US TO CUBA.
SLOWLY, HENRY GOT OUT OF HIS SEAT AND WALKED TOWARDS THE MEN.
I'VE GOT AN IDEA. GIVE ME YOUR FRUITY POPS.
WOULD YOU LIKE A FRUITY POP SENORS?
FRUITY POPS POP WITH FLAVOUR
POP
QUICK, GRAB THE GUNS.
POP
THE FRUITY POPS FLAVOUR SENSATION TOOK THE HI-JACKERS COMPLETELY BY SURPRISE. THEIR HATS TIPPED OVER THEIR EYES, THEIR TIES SHOT UP IN THE AIR AND THEIR GUNS SPAN AWAY.
TWO DAYS LATER IN THE CHAIRMAN OF THE AIRLINE'S OFFICE.
YOU SAVED OVER A HUNDRED LIVES WITH YOUR QUICK THINKING. THANKS A LOT POPPERS.
AND GUESS WHAT HE GAVE THEM AS A REWARD. A WHOLE CRATE OF.... FRUITY POPS. FRUITY POPS POP WITH FLAVOUR.
PROVE TO YOUR FRIENDS THAT FRUITY POPS POP WITH FLAVOUR.
EQUIPMENT: ONE BALLOON, ONE ROLL OF ADHESIVE TAPE. ONE DRAWING PIN. ONE PACKET OF FRUITY POPS.
INSTRUCTIONS: BLOW UP THE BALLOON, KNOT IT AND THEN TAPE IT SECURELY TO THE UNDERSIDE OF A TABLE NEXT, PUSH THE DRAWING PIN THROUGH A SMALL PIECE OF TAPE, AND TAPE IT TO THE TIP OF YOUR INDEX FINGER.
NOW CALL YOUR FRIENDS INTO THE ROOM, AND ANNOUNCE YOU CAN PROVE FRUITY POPS POP WITH FLAVOUR. TAKE A FRUITY POP, CRUNCH IT, AND JAB THE BALLOON SHARPLY WITH THE DRAWING PIN. THEN WATCH THEIR SHOCK AS THE BALLOON BURSTS.
Pascall Murray
Fruity POPS
fruit flavoured honeycomb
2½p
2½p
FRUITY POPS REALLY DO POP WITH FLAVOUR.

## * SPANGLES

The year is 1948, and the world is rebuilding itself from the most catastrophic conflict of modern times, filling the void of civilisation with equal amounts of optimism and despair. In the latter camp, George Orwell writes *1984*, a nightmare vision of an omnipotent totalitarian regime. On a lighter note, Mars's Slough factories thrum to the production of new 'luscious assorted crystal fruits':

**Opposite:** The sweet, sweet taste of industrial action – take a trip back in time to the 1970s with Spangles (er, 1948).

Spangles. Little does either party know how culturally ingrained both items would become.

Just as 'It's like *1984*' has become a cliché when talking about institutional repression, 'Remember Spangles?' is the nationally recognised catchphrase of corny nostalgia. Why this particular, innocuous rectangle of boiled sugar, moulded with fingertip-friendly indentations ('the dimple in the Spangle takes your tongue straight to the heart of the flavour!'), should have been singled out is unclear. Two generations of baby boomers happily crunched them without much fuss. They were rather nice boiled sweets, advertised with none-more-whimsical rhymes ('Farmers love Spangles!/Charmers love Spangles!/Nice little boys in pyjamas love Spangles!') and that was that.

The thing is, Spangles were nostalgic even back then. Despite those innovative foil tubes, they harked unashamedly back to the pre-war days of the sweet shop staffed by a cheery man in front of an endless array of big glass jars. 'Enjoy your favourite jar sweets the modern Spangles way!' The '50s and '60s saw a plethora of new varieties: butterscotch, liquorice, glucose barley sugar, golden mint, soft centre ice mint, the infamous herbally infused Old English assortment, and even a 'mystery flavour' with a question-mark-studded wrapper. In 1974, when that lost its shine, modernisation was the thing: a groovy bell-bottomed typeface, 'fizzy' flavours (lemonade, orangeade and cola) and a Day-Glo TV ad in which a juvenile Nicholas Lyndhurst and pals cavorted in a lido with giant berries. ('Suck a Spangle – get happy!')

Ironically, it was this final incarnation that would stick. Never mind the three decades worth of post-war sucking, after Mars discontinued the Spangle (spookily enough, in 1984), their final incarnation joined space hoppers and power cuts in the dressing-up box of default 1970s ephemera. Comedian Richard Digance was rambling wistfully about them on ITV less than three years after their demise, and he was by no means the last to do so.

In 1994 Spangle nostalgia ate itself when Woolworth's assisted in a relaunch of the tangerine, lime, blackcurrant and Old English flavours as a limited edition reminisci-snack, promoted with woolly nostalgia pieces in the popular press, and Honor Blackman draped over the bonnet of an E-Type Jag. The revamp didn't last, but the cliché did. Eventually the passage of time will see off all surviving Spangle-era veterans, and the topic will be confined to the history books. But if you want a vision of the foreseeable future, imagine a human face going 'Spangles? What were all that about?!' forever.

**'Their final incarnation joined space hoppers and power cuts in the dressing-up box of default 1970s ephemera.'**

## * DOUBLE AGENTS

In the post-Spangles cold war of boiled sweet selling, finding a unique hook to excite the kids represented an excellent tactical advantage. Whether it be a new flavour, shape or texture, the trade secrets of the confectionery manufacturers were locked behind massive iron factory gates. Of course industrial espionage went on, but outright Slugworth-style stealing of another company's ideas was frowned upon

**Opposite:** Boiled sweet Burgess. Trebor Double Agents (1977), the spy that came out of a mould.

– though not so, apparently, if you were pinching them from outside the industry.

So it was that Trebor's Double Agents came to be advertised by what can – at best – be called an homage to Antonio Prohías's Spy Vs Spy cartoons, as seen in *Mad* magazine since the early '60s. On TV, exhibiting a spectacular misunderstanding of the meaning of 'secret agent', two animated infiltrators, Boris (aka Black Spy) and Carruthers (aka White Spy), attempted to hijack a shipment of the sweets in broad daylight using an assortment of Acme bombs. While the Concorde-nosed imagery was heavily Prohías-influenced, the action was pure Warner Bros.

The cloak-and-dagger pair also appeared in a series of 'Psst... kids' collect-and-send comic offers hawking such essential intelligence-gathering ephemera as a fingerprint kit, a twelve-cap revolver and an iron-on, glow-in-the-dark transfer. It was all exciting stuff for a budding Anthony Blunt or infant-class Mata Hari. Sadly, the rather more prosaic reality of the sweets themselves was that they were merely the latest in a long line of Trebor's procession of soft-centred tubes, the new packaging adding extra edge to the 'two flavours in one' conceit (chocolate and lime, strawberry and cream, raspberry and sherbet, and so on).

Printed on the underside of the pack were obligatory top-secret 'spy hints' of dubious practical use for actual undercover operations, such as using lemon juice as invisible ink, making a spy-ring stamp out of a potato, or disguising your appearance by stuffing a cushion under your coat. Further messages were hidden inside the individual wax paper wrappers for conspiratorial code-cracking sessions back at base – often a home-made den constructed from two chairs and your mum's spare sheets.

Double Agents appeared at the height of UK spy mania, with James Bond still at the peak of his powers, seducing Barbara Bach and audiences alike to the tune of Carly Simon's 'Nobody Does It Better'. From the Union Jack parachute opening to shark tank battle finale, *The Spy Who Loved Me* is one of the more enjoyable romps of the franchise. It also marked the first appearance of Richard Kiel's steel-toothed henchman, Jaws, a villain who must surely have spent too much time sucking sweets and not enough time visiting the dentist.

**'Messages were hidden inside the individual wax paper wrappers for conspiratorial code-cracking sessions back at base.'**

## LIGHTING-UP TIME

Stand at your average 1970s sweet shop counter. Look to the left of those big bonbon jars. What do you see? The packets, pouches and pipe-cleaners of an altogether more adult form of indulgence. Smoking and sweets have long been linked. Companies producing the former have dabbled in the latter. Folk trying to give up fags have hit the confectionery. But it's the journey made in the opposite direction by sweet-gobbling children that's the most controversial.

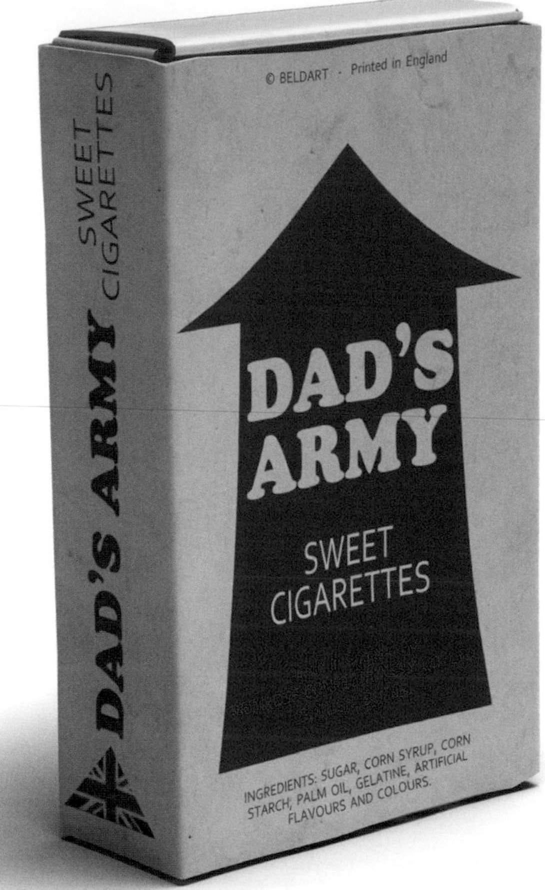


Smoking paraphernalia in sugar form has been around since Benson met Hedges, but post-war innovation produced increasingly mad variations on the theme. Spanish Gold, a little bag of toasted coconut shreds resembling chewing tobacco, delighted kids who'd long fancied themselves as grizzled 1890s prospectors. For the serious smoking wannabe, there were entire selection-box-sized smoking outfits, often adorned with a picture of Sherlock Holmes to add spurious cultural legitimacy. A typical effort by Sharps from 1970 contained edible pipe, chocolate cigars, candy cigarettes and matches, and a foil-wrapped chocolate ashtray. In the same year Candex launched their mini-gum lighters: replica Zippos dispensing tiny nuggets of bubble gum. We'd come a long way from the liquorice pipe.

The biggest seller, though, was the simple packet of sweet cigarettes. Either logs of chocolate 'tobacco' wrapped in sugar paper or solid cylinders of white sugar with a little red dab on the end to symbolise the glowing tip of the real McCoy, they cost nowt to make and sold like mad. The inclusion of themed picture cards, a trick borrowed from their carcinogenic older brothers, meant collectability, which in turn meant sales bonanza. If you were a TV show in the '60s and '70s with even tangential kid appeal, you would have come with a little box of sweet cigarettes attached: *Star Trek*, *Spiderman*, even *Dad's Army* punted out a pack for aspiring Private

**Opposite:** Who do you think you are kindling Mr Hitler? *Dad's Army* provides a Lucifer to light your fag, circa 1968...

**Below:** ... and the Daleks (1964) hide behind the sofa for a crafty smoke.

Walkers. *Doctor Who*'s Dalek-themed tie-in fags contained, according to the pack, 'Skaro', which may have been a playful misprint, and 'hardened receptacle oil', which, frighteningly, wasn't.

Sinisterly named company Trexapalm produced Kojak Sweet Cigars, even though the bald 'tec famously sucked lollipops to wean himself off the dreaded weed. Even lovable cartoon characters got in on the act, like Tom and Jerry and Asterix the Gaul (the latter, mystifyingly, not packaged as Asterix the Gauloise). The music world was hip to the puff too, the glam era being positively tobacco-ridden, what with Barker and Dobson's David Cassidy Candy Sticks and Pop Star cigarettes, the latter featuring picture cards of teenybop favourites. ('Nothing sells as fast to kids as something with a picture of Gary Glitter.')

The big question: were they a gateway drug? A study showed that in the '50s, US tobacco companies treated sweet firms who knocked off their brand designs for candy-selling purposes with rather more leniency than their usual copyright-guarding zeal, suggesting they saw today's Milky Bar kid as tomorrow's Marlboro man. Whether anything of the sort happened in Britain is unknown, but the traditional proximity between sweet and tobacco can only have blurred the distinction.

**'For the serious smoking wannabe, there were entire selection box-sized smoking outfits, often adorned with a picture of Sherlock Holmes.'**

The demise of sweet tobacco was a long one. Sir Keith Joseph mounted the first government investigation when he was social services secretary in 1971, amid calls for bans that would be repeated in the Commons down the decades, but the cylinders of pretend cool have never been officially outlawed in Britain. Instead, corporations have voluntarily cut down, aided by the odd parliamentary nudge.

In 1977 galactic history was made when 20th Century Fox pointedly chose not to add candy fags to their otherwise all-encompassing roster of *Star Wars* merchandise. The following year, amid reports that 60 per cent of dentists approved of the idea of sweet cigarettes carrying a mandatory health warning about tobacco's evils, Trebor Bassett expunged all mention of smoking from their range.

**Opposite:** Another coffin nail. It's 'sweet cigarettes' on Moonbase Alpha circa 1976...

**Below:** ... but 'candy sticks' for Barratt Football by 1987.

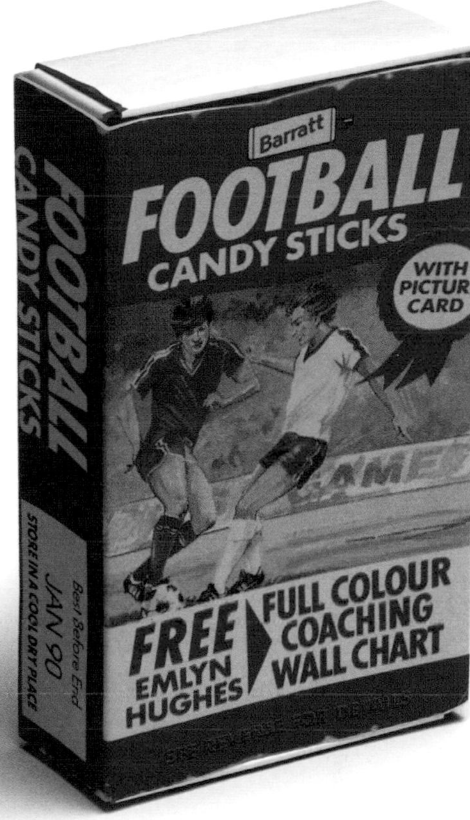


They would, however, trade for a good fifteen years more as neutral 'candy sticks' without that tell-tale red tip, beginning with a rebranded Football range in 1980, about the same time former fag-hawker Superman atoned for his sins with a series of health ads bashing the villainous Nick O'Teen.

Over the next two decades, a slow but sure purge was under way. The big names dropped them one by one, leaving increasingly obscure foreign firms as the only source of sugary gaspers. In 2001 even these fell by the wayside when Poundstretcher declared a moratorium. Finally, on 29 March 2004, the Public Health (Tobacco) (Amendment) Act limited the sale of 'confectioneries normally intended for sale to children, that have been manufactured in such a way as to resemble in appearance a type of tobacco product'. Again, not technically a ban, but by this time it didn't need to be. You try getting hold of twenty David Cassidys at your local newsagent these days.

## * VIMTO LOLLY

Who loves ya, baby? TV's Lieutenant Kojak, that's who – not the only famous lollipop licker of the 1970s, but probably the baldest. The show's writers decided to give the hard-bitten New York detective his trademark Tootsie Pop in a move to appease the anti-smoking brigade. His favourite flavour? Low tar.

**Opposite:** Yes, yes, 'Vimto' is an anagram of 'vomit'. But 'Vimto Lollies' is an anagram of... er... 'Moi loves Lilt.' Vimto lollies circa 1977.

If the sweet makers had their way, though, every telly star from Weatherfield to Walmington-on-Sea would have had a lollipop stick protruding from between their lips. Or any other orifice, for that matter. Big-name backing was a good way to steal a march on the competition. Lollies had been commonplace since the eighteenth century – namechecked in works by Thackeray and Coleridge, no less – so what better way to differentiate than to slap on a celebrity seal of approval?

Nicholas Laboratories chose a circuitous route to success, investing in Whistling Pops. These tuneful toot sweets were a clear homage to Caractacus Potts's cacophonous creations in *Chitty Chitty Bang Bang*, but remained unofficial nonetheless. They also took nearly ten years to perfect, not materialising in shops until long after the film had finished its run at the flicks.

Elsewhere, Liverpool-based Tavener and Rutledge landed a significant number of exclusive deals for the UK, bagging the big screen *Batman* and *Bugsy Malone* for a string of signature lollies, as well as Telly Savalas himself for the obligatory *Kojak* tie-in. Eric 'n' Ernie brought strawberries and cream-shaped sunshine on a stick, while Laurel and Hardy, experiencing an inexplicable mid-1970s revival, also shared the same flavours for Ollie's Lollies.

Blue Bird plumped for another Saturday night light entertainment staple and launched the *It's A Knockout* gobstopper lolly in 1979, though this was quickly eclipsed by 3p Buck Rogers pops – available in five flavours: cosmic traffic light, galactic lemon fizz, terrestrial treacle, draconian lime and meteorite melon.

However, for flavour, and sheer why-didn't-I-think-of-that-first chutzpah, the Vimto lolly outshone them all. Patriotic in a red, white and blue livery, echoing the traditional striped awnings of Olde English market stalls, Vimto was the very model of balance between modernity and nostalgia. Run up on Swizzels Matlow's state-of-the-art lolly-making machinery, yet with a taste reminiscent of Sunday evenings round at Grandma's house, it was that Holy Grail of the confectionery crusades: an instant classic.

And it was almost immediately superseded. The days of one lolly, one flavour ended abruptly with the arrival of Chupa Chups. Literally translated as 'sucky suck', these whorish lollies burst into the UK market like refugees from a Catalonian hen night on the Costa Brava. Flaunting all kinds of exotic, foreign flavours, and a garish Salvador Dalí-designed logo, they spoke nothing of the past and looked set to trample all over the future.

Marketing is all. Those lollipop men would have more luck hooking up with today's selection of big-headed, stick-thin-bodied celebrities for a bit of cross-promotional candy action. As for Chupa Chups' recent 'stop smoking, start sucking' slogan? Well, at least Kojak would have approved.

## A WIBBLY, WOBBLY WORLD OF THEIR OWN

A glutinous relic from Britain's colonial past, gum arabic (mainly produced, logically enough, in Africa) is found in everything from soft drinks to fireworks. Its most toothsome use, however, is in the gum and pastille family: furtive, adaptable rodents descended from their lumbering evolutionary ancestors, the jellies.

Wine gums were the first to emerge, from Maynard's Sheffield factory in 1909. Quite why the consumption of rubbery diamonds and lozenges containing no booze whatsoever but embossed with the words 'claret' and 'port' should prove so popular remains a mystery – the same self-deluding giddy thrill as the sweet cigarette, perhaps, or maybe a temperance aid, an early version of the nicotine patch – but they were all over the country and spawning imitators within a few years.

One such came from the other end of Sheffield, when Bassett celebrated the end of the Great War with their Peace Babies: slightly softer, sugar-dusted gummy homunculi symbolising the country's hopeful repopulation. (The horrific mutilations undergone by these sweets at the jaws of the nation were tastefully glossed over.) After a brief pause for a Greater War, they were reintroduced as the familiar Jelly Babies in 1953, and have scarcely changed since, unless you count an attempt in the '80s to give the various colours different 'personalities'. Presumably the idea was to dispel the inherent creepiness of these gelatinous graven images, but surely that's part of their character? They're most appealing at their weirdest – preferably in a crumpled paper bag inside Tom Baker's coat.

**Opposite:** Apparently, you get a bit more jelly if you buy boy ones. Bassett's Jelly Babies (1918).

**Below:** Those little extras made all the difference. Rowntree's Fruit Pastilles (1881) offered a free shower of loose sugar. More fun was the whole extra sweet (or three) that came away when you were offered an old-school, sticky Fruit Gum (1893).

Less unnerving were the descendants of the medicated throat sweet, the fruit gum and fruit pastille. Their most famous incarnations came from Rowntree, living testimony to the power of direct marketing. Both the hard, jewel-like gums and their softer, sugar-encrusted colleagues had been available for decades, sold loose in paper bagfuls scooped from traditional jars, but in 1938 Rowntree stuck them in handy foil and paper tubes festooned with their corporate livery.

The effect of this move was twofold. First the tubes, being smaller and cheaper than the usual quarter-pound bag, and requiring less kerfuffle with stepladder and scales to purchase, became more of an impulse buy, thus competing with new big-name chocolate products like the Mars bar. In addition, the middleman was removed, the sweets no longer anonymously bagged by your chum the confectioner, but packaged in a permanent advertisement for their manufacturers. Every time you reached for a pastille, there was Rowntree's, bold as brass. Other companies – most notably Needler's – made almost identical sweets, but whose brand would you remember? The one you glimpsed over the grocer's shoulder, or the one that spent all day in your back pocket?

Spin-offs abounded. Butterscotch and liquorice gums were (thankfully) short-stay varieties in 1960, but junior pastille variant Jelly Tots established itself in 1965, and a tube full of the most popular flavour, blackcurrant, did well enough to achieve sitcom immortality when Tony Hancock advised Hugh Lloyd, 'They do a tube with all black ones now, you know.' Elsewhere, paid-for advertising took up the slack. An early ITV campaign in which a snotty kid chanted, 'Don't forget the Fruit Gums, Mum,' gave rise to complaints of copycat irritation.

A decade later, Rowntree re-offended, rewording an old Bing Crosby hit to showcase a 'Pastille Packin' Mama', leading matriarchs to be pestered for chewy treats all over again, this time in full song.

By now Rowntree's gums were jostling for position with numerous rivals. Even toffee firm Mackintosh dipped a toe into gum in 1963, sealing it in a squared-off envelope of crispy sugar and creating the Tooty Frootie. In the '70s it was a matter of repackaging the stuff in different shapes, such as cuboid boxes of fauna Rowntree's Junglies, or practical footwear with Needler's Jelly Wellies. Quick-buck marketing created a rash of topical cash-in varieties, like Barratt's Basil Brush Jelly Babies and the arcade-inspired Space Attackers. There was even a hint of exoticism with American Hard Gums, which on closer inspection turned out to come from Maynard's Sheffield works.

Nor were they that hard, particularly compared to Rowntree's molar-hugging offerings, the oral longevity of which was trumpeted in a new wave of ads, from the Fruit Gum-fuelled antics

**Opposite:** Is it something to do with Tring? Rowntree gives the nation something to chew over with the Fruit Gums Secret, circa 1982.

**Below:** Jelly, that Protean lifeblood of the British toddler, held captive by the unyielding might of sugar for the guzzling pleasure of a nation. Mackintosh Tooty Frooties (1963) and Jelly Tots (1965).

of Sir Lastalot and Ye Knights of Ye Rowntree's Table to a perennially unimpressed child who greeted various feats of skill with the rejoinder, 'Not bad, but I bet you can't put a Rowntree's Fruit Pastille in your mouth without chewing it.' Most elaborate of all was 1982's Fruit Gums Secret – a series of cryptic posters given away in comics providing clues to a postal address which, if worked out and contacted, would garner the lucky winner the unusual prize of a time-share villa. Forget Frisbees and pencil cases, this was aspirational stuff.

These sweets were loved through good times and bad, none more dire than the summer of 1974 which, due to an acute ingredients shortage, saw Fruit Gums disappear from the shelves. Idiosyncrasies were forgiven, even cherished, like the way the gums tended to stick to each other in groups of two or more, giving rise to questions of etiquette on both sides when one person offered another a single gum from their tube, only to part company with several at once.

A late '80s change to a less sticky, more wine-gummy consistency made ergonomic sense, but were Rowntree thanked? Nope, they just got stick for screwing with a classic recipe. When a confectionery product reaches a certain age, it becomes, like an actor, TV presenter or car insurance website mascot, a 'national treasure', and any further tampering is tantamount to treason. The main beneficiary from this disarray in the British ranks was the happy world of Haribo, purveyors of an altogether more rubbery jelly since 1922, who seized the opportunity and flooded UK shelves in the '90s with Gummi Bears and their multifarious cohorts. So swift and decisive was their takeover of the market, they were soon flogging us their own wine gums and jelly babies. So ended a once proud, if rather tacky, empire.

## ✻ IPSO

Confectionery may have started as an offshoot of the apothecary's trade, but that doesn't necessarily mean it remains a two-way relationship. Nicholas Laboratories, inventors of Rennie among other mainstays of the bathroom cabinet, found this to their cost when they embarked on a chemically correct assault on the sweet shop in the late 1970s. Things began well enough, with the

**Opposite:** Calypso lady, shake it down. Ipso (1979).

**Below:** 'British Rail would like to apologise for delays caused by the illusory carnival at Hither Green,' circa 1980.

modest success of Whistling Pops and Sweet Pebbles, irregular gobstoppers bearing an uncanny similarity to ornamental gravel. But to show they meant business they needed a name brand on their books, and for this they looked to the tongue-tingling territory patrolled by the Tic-Tac.

Their carefully formulated riposte, unleashed in orange, mint, raspberry and lemon flavours in 1979, was christened Ipso. Why was never made clear. 'Ipso' is Latin, more or less, for 'itself' (hence the phrase *ipso facto*), a word that's not exactly a harbinger of sugary joy. Perhaps it was coined as a cross-brand bedfellow to Nicholas's Aspro range of headache remedies – but aligning sweets and pills is commercially questionable, to say nothing of potentially dangerous. Equally unfathomable was the choice of packaging: square plastic boxes with bobbles down two adjacent sides which enabled them to join up, LEGO-like, to make various lumpy, two-dimensional shapes in a quaint, yet rather half-arsed, attempt at 'added play value'. Again, the consumer's first question was often: 'Why, exactly?' The packs may have fitted together, but the marketing logic didn't.

Given this blatant appeal to the playful child, it's odd that the TV campaign confused things further, showing the product being scoffed by a businessman, in his suit and tie. Quite rightly avoiding any attempt to represent the Latin tag visually, the ads instead showed a commuter's dull wait for a train enlivened by the refreshing orange sweet, while its idly rattled container sends him into a calypso-based carnival reverie complete with feathered dancers, right there on platform one. Then, just as he starts to loosen up, shed all thoughts of balance sheets and roll his shoulders in classic 'funky duffer' style, he's rudely awoken by a rotund Afro-Caribbean lady (who, one can only surmise, has been tactfully asked by the director to 'be bold' with her ethnicity) with a cheery 'Come on, you'll miss your train!'

Ipsos, it soon transpired, had missed theirs. Maybe it was the cognitive dissonance of the whole enterprise, or maybe the Tic-Tac was just too mighty, but this weird little sweet arrived and departed in a flurry of furrowed young brows and well-meaning racial gaucherie. For the boffins at Nicholas Labs it was back to the stomach pills, their dreams of becoming white-coated Wonkas cruelly crushed.

## MAKING A MINT

Ah, mint, created when the underworld nymph Menthe raised the dander of the goddess Persephone for knocking about with Hades once too often, and was for her sins turned forever into a pungent, sweet-smelling herb. Many centuries later she was united with the god Sucrose, and their offspring became the patron saint of glove boxes and back pockets the world over. If that bit of mythology is questionable, it's in good company. The early, jaw-breaking mints from the Victorian era, from humbugs through Mint Imperials to the Liverpool-born Everton Mints, themselves have origins shrouded in unreliable folklore (the last of these involving the unlikely figure of one Old Mother Noblett).

As ever, it's only when the sweets come out of the jars and into the tubes that records become reliable. Among the first to tube up were the sugar boiling men from Upton Park who created the Trebor Mint in 1935: a flat, hard disc of sugar and peppermint oil which achieved immortality through the jingle 'Trebor Mints are a minty bit stronger'. Notwithstanding the various second lines added to this ditty – all of them unofficial and none medically verified – this humble mint outlasted all manner of more fancy newcomers by dint of being handy, cheap and just plain minty. Assorted promotions helped the old stager keep afloat: free TV licence stamps were the rather quaint giveaway in 1983. Five years later, an equally homely offer of a 'mint condition' pound coin in exchange for wrappers rendered gave rise to an official complaint from one Nottingham resident who, instead of receiving what he assumed would be a shiny new quid, was instead palmed off with a grubby old 1985 Welsh edition. His case, funnily enough, was not upheld.

**Opposite:** A Duke of Edinburgh award to whoever can make this little lot 'last a bit longer.' Trebor Mints (1935).

**Below:** Conquering every corner of the mouth, Trebor Mint Imperials circa 1940.

In 1944, as the guns cooled across Europe, the small sugar firm Murray introduced the altogether more mellow and buttery Murray Mint, an oval lozenge that was more on nodding terms with the whole mint family than a blood relative. Again, an ingratiating jingle clawed at the country's ears as soon as ITV cranked up. 'Murray Mints, Murray Mints, too good to hurry mints!' Not so much too good to hurry as too inconvenient – attempts to do anything other than slowly suck these dense, tacky rugby balls ran the risk of dental Armageddon. So you were forced to sit and slobber it out, the unrelenting presence of the mint strangely appropriate to the length of the situation in which they were most often encountered, those interminable wet Sunday afternoons in an elderly relative's front room.

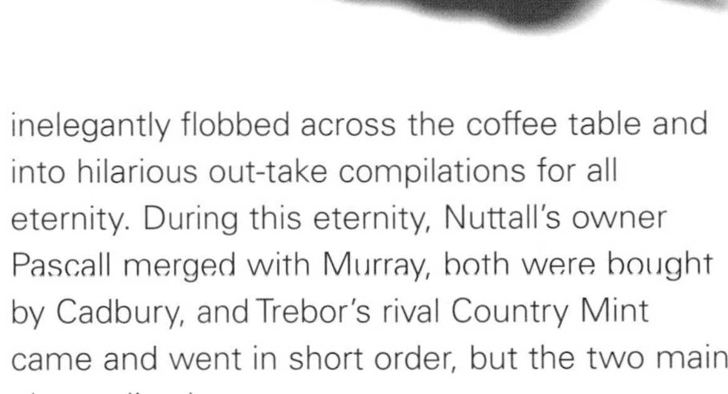


Its partner in soul-eroding crime was William Nuttall of Doncaster's creation, the Mintoe, although this was slightly more glamorous – in the sense that Denis Norden advertised them. Sitting on a swivel chair next to a glass-topped coffee table, Norden pontificated at length on the philosophy of sucking, while twisting the spent mint wrappers into a variety of elegant origami figures. This last happened conveniently off-camera. Inconveniently on-camera, the virtuoso talky-sucky display proved too much for the Norden chops, leading a Mintoe to be inelegantly flobbed across the coffee table and into hilarious out-take compilations for all eternity. During this eternity, Nuttall's owner Pascall merged with Murray, both were bought by Cadbury, and Trebor's rival Country Mint came and went in short order, but the two main players lived on.

All very cosy, but shouldn't mints be zingy, dynamic things? Where's the 'ooh'? Enter Italian confectioners Ferrero, who festooned the nation's points of sale in 1971 with little stacks of their patent Refreshing Mints: 'bean-like delicacies... designed for adults, particularly smokers'.

---

**'Hard-coated chewable mints eschewed the suckworthy longevity of traditional mints for a quick fix of menthylated mastication.'**

---

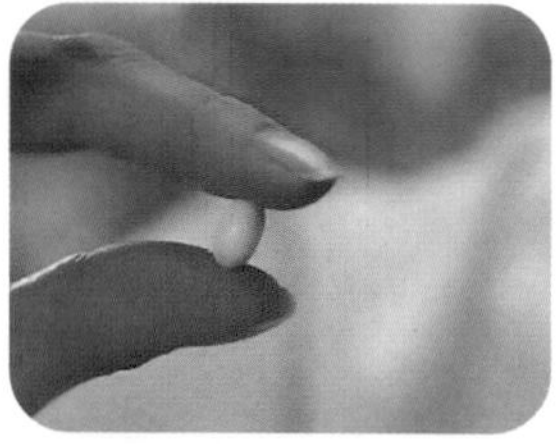

Packaged in little see-through plastic pockets with flip-top lids, these alien micro-organisms were slow to catch on at first, until the following year, when a concerted ad campaign and a change of name to Tic-Tac let the 1½-calorie wonders take root. Such a distinctive product was hard to rival, but Hall's had a go in 1976 with their Dynamints, slightly rounder mini-mints in slightly squatter plastic packs, boasting 'five layers of flavour, each stronger than the last'. Tic-Tac fought back in '78 with partitioned double flavour packs, starting with lime and mandarin.

The weight-conscious '80s led folk to start laying off the sweeties, which clearly wouldn't do. Taking their cue from diet soft drinks (with which, for gaseous reasons, mints should never be mixed), Trebor developed the sugar-free Coolmint in 1983. Its use of Sorbitol as a sweetener caused a mild amount of panic ('excessive consumption can have laxative effects in children and some adults!'). Reports of violent stomach upsets abounded, and shadow health minister Gwyneth Dunwoody called for their segregation in the sweet shop away from the reach of kids. But perhaps the most suspicious thing about them was the way they were shaped like a Polo that had received a filling. They never took off here, nor did the British debut of German company Ragold's world-conquering Velamint. We wanted proper mints, and if our teeth paid the price, so be it.

In 1983 a new front was suddenly opened up when Trebor launched the Softmint. Essentially a Tooty Frootie in mint form, the hard-coated chewable mint eschewed the suckworthy longevity of traditional mints for a quick fix of menthylated mastication. This was nothing new to fans of the venerable Clarnico Mint Creams, but this hi-tech version was crisper, tubular and still something of a gamble. Such brazen innovation in the staid world of the

**Opposite:** Attention posers! Spend ages in front of a mirror practising flicking Tic-Tacs (1971), but pray your bladder's tough enough for Cool Mints (1983).

**Below:** Mentos (1983), one of the lesser known Greek islands. (See also: Asbestos.)

mint required considerable assistance: nearly two years' worth of regional testing and a national ad campaign in which Jimmy 'Whirlwind' White raced through a frame of snooker in order to get his next Softmint. By the end of the year, tubes of chewy delight were flying out of Trebor's swanky new RIBA-prizewinning Colchester factory at a similarly spanking pace.

In the meantime, others had been watching and preparing rival products. Chief among them was Dutch interloper Van Melle, who introduced Mentos Chewy Mints in 1982 for a national roll-out two years later. Their ad campaign - from the director of *Omen III*! - played on the perceived newfangled nature of the product, featuring the boardroom meeting of a wheezy, northern family sweet firm mulling mardily over this chewy foreign intruder. Eventually the chairman, Mr Rockard, loses his nut. 'Chewy mints? Cheeeeeewyyyyy mints?! Has thee all gone soft?' before demolishing the boardroom table to demonstrate the righteous sturdiness of his own product. Cute, but a bit cheeky seeing as Trebor had got there first.

Nevertheless, these mints, soon augmented by Meltis's version and the rebranded Pacers, turned round a declining mint market. In 1987 Trebor added Softfruits to their originals, and plugged both with a memorable telly ad in which a mildly disturbing pillow-headed man (inspired by Swedish pop-art sculptor Claes Oldenburg, art lovers) romped about with an animated pillar box to a reworded version of Steve Harley & Cockney Rebel's 'Mr Soft'. The close-up of the man's misshapen, sightless face in the process of 'chewing' the product proved too much for many younger children, but sales rocketed. Then at the end of the decade, Rowntree turned up late to the party with Minties, a product chiefly distinguishable from the others by their variegated colour. Or as Michael Barrymore explained in the ads: 'They're awright! But they're not awright! Some of 'em are blue!' Sadly, advice on how to make them last a bit longer was not forthcoming.

## ✻ POLO

You always hear about the nylons and the chewing gum. And the first tantalising glimpses of an aspirational, can-do lifestyle hitherto alien to these islands. And shagging round the back of the NAAFI wagon. But what did those American GIs really do for us? They brought us the Polo. It was properly called the Lifesaver, but during the war Rowntree were granted the licence from their manufacturer to

**Opposite:** Tubular sells: the familiar marque o' Polo (1948) and Polo Fruits (1953).

**Below:** Nobody does it better. TV advertising, that is, circa 1986.

make them over here especially for homesick Yanks. After VE Day, a canny bit of tweaking resulted in Rowntree's own version, initially called Pax but soon renamed Polo Digestive Mints. It wasn't an easy start. The 'digestive' moniker was hastily withdrawn when Rowntree were challenged to prove the sweet's medicinal credentials. Then they had to see off a number of copycat rivals like Swizzels' Navy Mints. But by the '50s the Polo had established itself as one of the top 'motoring mints' in town, thanks to its resilient constitution and that hole, which maximised the surface area through which the sucker's tongue could extract mintiness.

When you've got the perfect formula, what else to do but muck about with it? Typically for Americans, Life Savers came in all sorts of cockamamie flavours from violet to malted milk. Things were more restrained over here. Plans were made for barley sugar Polos, and a Glacier Mint-baiting crystal clear variety, but nothing came of them. Polo Fruits, however, did trundle shelfwards in 1953, the familiar foil tube replaced by waxed paper, within which hard, semi-opaque and very, very sticky fruit sweets clung together as if for dear life. Such tactics were futile: if you couldn't prise a group of three apart, you did the honourable thing and downed it in one. (Later variants, like lemon and the short-lived strawberries and cream flavour, stuck to the non-stick format of the originals.)

Despite 'the Mint with the Hole's reputation as a Sunday driver's companion (Rowntree offered free holiday route maps in one giveaway) two-thirds of consumers were women. Predictably, this led to a scare about the mint somehow cancelling out the effects of the Pill. Nothing, though, could sway it from its steady-as-she-goes residency at the top of the minted pops: least of all half-arsed 1981 rival Meltis Mints, a Trebor clone whose centre dissolved faster in the mouth than the rest, turning it into a Polo clone mid-suck. No takers. Meanwhile, a series of wry minimalist ads voiced by Peter Sallis (a pair of sturdy driving gloves in audio form) kept the Polo firmly within the Zeitgeist, and that little well next to the gear stick, without actually changing a thing.

**'When you've got the perfect formula, what else to do but muck about with it?'**

## * FOX'S GLACIER MINTS

'A delicate flavour and smooth in texture' ran the typically informative but dull strapline for this crystal delicacy when Leicester's Fox's Confectionery first trumpeted it in 1918. Its equally dull name, Acme Clear Mint Fingers, was thankfully replaced with the more poetic Glacier Mints, suggestive of cool refreshment, polar romance, those heroic British explorers who had so recently frozen to

**Opposite:** Fox's Glacier Mints (1918), manufactured by the aptly named Big Bear Ltd of Braunstone. Oh yes.

death in the... well, let's just run with the first two for now.

The chilly symbolism worked, though, as the copycat likes of Benson's Arctic Mints attested. But Fox's didn't hang about to be overtaken by the me-too manufacturers. Individual wrappings for the transparent ingots were introduced in 1928, and the brand found a mascot in a moth-eaten stuffed polar bear called Peppy, whose frightening appearance was cleaned up a bit for the labels on the jars.

Peppy was to prove crucial in the mint's '70s resurgence. In June 1972 an unprepossessing series of TV ads was aired, featuring the distinguished, somnolent Peppy (now just called 'Bear') standing proudly on a mint as he had in the logo for so long, while a borderline psychopathic fox ('Fox', if you please) tried various hopeless gambits to dethrone him from his icy perch and reclaim the podium for himself, as was his right, seeing how they were called Fox's mints and that. But, the bear replied in the stately tones of the great Willoughby Goddard, there has to be a bear on the mints because they're 'so cool and clear and min... ty'. This was clearly no kind of answer at all, so Fox kept at it for another twelve years. Then, after a four-year hiatus, he returned, now having gained a voice himself (albeit one suspiciously similar to Bill Oddie's), but Bear (in an all-new Stratford Johns guise) was as immobile as ever.

Various other products played Fox to Fox's, er, Bear. After the early rash of Arctic This and Polar That, Rowntree's strong, mentholated Lyrics surfaced in 1972, square in shape as opposed to the traditional Fox's ingot but recognisably after its market. They tanked, as did Trebor's 1976 circular hopeful, the Clearmint. That was the problem with clear mints: Bear could see the opposition coming.

Peppy left the 1980s 10 per cent mintier, still in pole position. When a glasnost-initiating Gorbachev mentioned to ICI chairman Sir John Harvey-Jones how his granddaughter loved 'those British mints that look like glass', Sir John had no doubt which brand he meant, and sent him a tin. It's tempting to imagine Gorby crunching a couple himself as he drew up plans for his own, slightly more successful, Fox-vs-Bear act.

**'But, the bear replied, there has to be a bear on the mints because they're "so cool and clear and min... ty". This was clearly no kind of answer at all.'**

## ✻ EXTRA STRONG MINTS

There's always been a fine line between mint and medicine. At the extremes of mintiness, indulgent pleasure transforms into a tongue-bashing riot of 'good for what ails you' macho flavour riding. If it's not hurting, it's not working, and all that. Victorian strong mints even sounded medicinal: take two Altoids and see me in the morning. But the titan of twentieth-century confectionery masochism was the Extra Strong Mint.

**Opposite:** National Service for your tastebuds: Sharps Extra Strong Mints (1972).

Made by Sharps of York since 1937, it really took off sixty-five years later, when a national ad campaign asserted, 'You either love them or you hate them!' Throughout the '70s a formerly niche product rose to challenge the Polo itself at the top of the sales tree. TV ads came thick and fast. One proclaimed, 'They'll blow your socks off!' while an assortment of folk had their business interrupted by just such an eruption of the half hose. Later Graham Chapman fed the mints to victims of a medieval witch trial, and a pre-omnipotence Stephen Fry used his mint-heated breath to power a hot-air balloon over the Alps. All over the country folk snapped up the hotter mints for mouth deodorisers, anti-smoking aids and to help 'driving concentration'.

Aside from a strong mint launched by Bassett in 1983, rival firms were slow to take a bite out of the extra strong market, but when they did, it was a deluge. Fisherman's Friend producers Lofthouse were the first to pitch up in 1988, with a minty take on their core product claimed to be hotter than Sharp's by a noticeable margin. Later that same year Rowntree weighed in with XXX, a dead spit for Sharps product in size, shape and even wrapper. Trebor, owner of Sharps, called foul. This was a spoiler, they claimed, to stop their Extra Strongs taking over from Polo as the nation's favourite mint. They forced a change of packaging and barred the new mint from their wholesale chain Moffatt's. Rowntree retaliated with an unprecedented £2 million, five-week ad campaign with an appropriate Cold War theme. Then in 1989 Needler's entered the market with their black-clad ESM, boasting a 'pure white heat' that was 15 per cent hotter than Trebor's. They didn't stay the pace, but Sharps and Rowntree continued to slug it out, and have maintained an uneasy (and, for the unwary shopper, confusing) détente ever since.

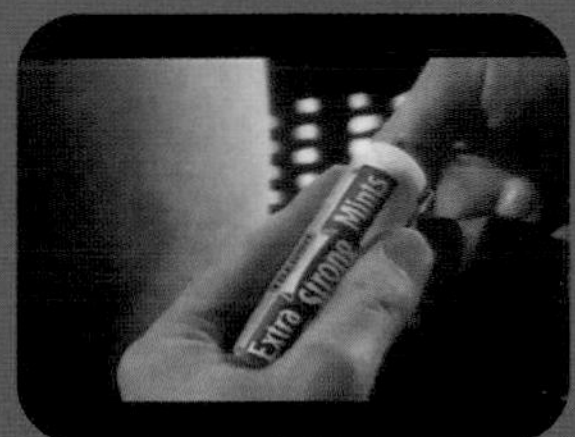

**Below:** Sky high *QI* guy? TV advert, circa 1984.

**'All over the country folk snapped up the hotter mints for mouth deodorisers, anti-smoking aids and to help 'driving concentration'.**

## BIG BUBBLES, NO TROUBLES

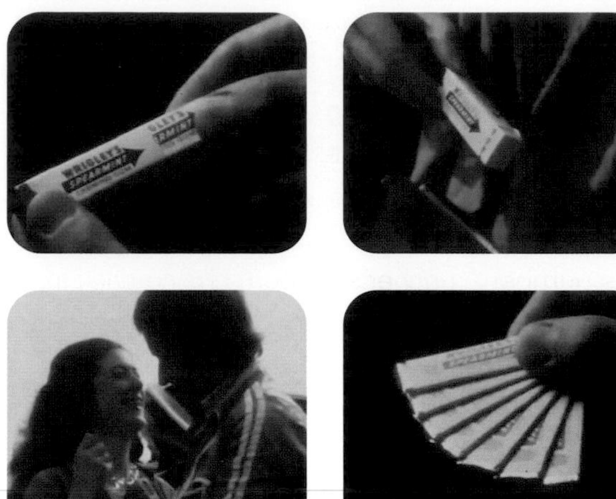


Gum isn't half as simple as it makes out. There's an awful lot of science behind even just one dull, greyish strip of Juicy Fruit. And an unnecessarily tedious history – insolent teenagers, Premier League managers and record-breaking bubble-blowers take note. Two thousand years of tapping tree secretions, sucking out sap, flavouring, refining and adapting have gone into creating your modern-day gum. To cut a very long story short: basically, ever since man developed molars he's been grinding away on some form of tree bark, resin or rubber. It was the mechanised mass processing of chicle gum from the Mexican *Manilkara zapota* tree that led to mainstream mastication in the 1870s. For that, we have Thomas Adams & Sons of New York to thank. Adams' Snapping & Stretching No. 1 was the first chewing gum on the market, followed by the company's successful other lines: Black Jack, Tutti Frutti and Chiclets. Attentive turn-of-the-century businessmen, including plenty of soon-to-be-familiar American names, hitched their caboose to the latex gravy train. William Wrigley Jr introduced Spearmint gum, with its overly literal arrow device (oft-seen on giant packets under surfers' arms or constituting the rear trailer of an articulated lorry), plus two other flavours that stood him in good stead for nearly sixty years. Frank Henry Fleer – or rather, one of his staff – invented a thing we would ultimately all agree to call bubble gum.

**Opposite:** 'Carry it with you! The big fresh flavour!' Wrigley's Spearmint gum (1893). Fact: the original artist behind Bazooka Joe (1953) started out drawing porno comics. Hence the 'pearl necklace' here?

**Below:** Dentyne (1968), for the 'freshest mouth in town.' A fruity United Nations summit for Leaf Rainblo circa 1970.

Walter Diemer is the unsung hero of Dubble Bubble, the first children's blowing gum that didn't stick to everything it touched. An accountant by trade, Diemer formulated the recipe in his spare time, using whatever surplus food colouring was to hand. Legend has it that this number cruncher's random choice back in 1928 is solely responsible for the continuing pink hue of classic bubble gum.

Significant other milestones en route to the present day included: the introduction of Hall Brothers' Dentyne cinnamon gum (the brand name a portmanteau of 'dental hygiene'), somehow convincing the public that a sugary product could prevent tooth decay; the installation of gumball machines outside sweet shops, supermarkets and hardware stores, dispensing brightly coloured pellets into kids' clammy hands like snooker balls from a goldfish bowl; the addition of inner-wrapper comic strips, such as the adventures of 'Bazooka Joe', Topps' eyepatch-afflicted cartoon character with a penchant for cheap giveaway gifts.

Partially blind frontmen aside, Topps led the way in post-war gum innovation. Collectable cards inserted into flat packs soon became more valuable than the gum they were supposed to flog. More than one US TV show plot revolved around the hunt for a rare Mickey Mantle baseball card, which might have perplexed British viewers prior to 1975, when Trebor landed the exclusive distribution rights to Topps products in the UK. Rather than just sports [sic] superstars, the waxed paper packets were also graced by the likes of the Bay City Rollers, *Jaws 3D*, and the cast of top Aussie soap *Home and Away*: 'Awww, not Donald Fisher again. He can rack off.'

The true behemoths of gum card collections were, of course, the 5p *Star Wars* series, issued in multiple, colour-coded sets well ahead of the movie opening in Britain, and Garbage Pail Kids, a bad taste trademark-infringing parody of Coleco's Cabbage Patch Dolls.

**Below:** It's a gum scrum! Bubble Yum (1975), Hubba Bubba (1979) and those all-important, saliva-stimulating 'new' flavours.

**Opposite:** The adventures of Hubba Bubba, mysterious gum for hire, dramatised circa 1980 (before the repeal of the US bubble control act).

Topps were also canny enough to make use of any spare wrapper space to upsell premium 'smooth 'n' juicy' SuperBazooka, another new arrival in British tuck shops, but not the first of its kind.

In 1975 the Philadelphia Gum Company was approached by Life Savers (they of ring-shaped mint fame) to manufacture the world's first soft bubble gum. The new product allegedly enabled the chewer to blow bigger and better bubbles than ever before. Cue many playground attempts at measurement with a custom set of Bubble Yum brand cardboard callipers. The company even licensed a balloon-mouthed Bubble Yum Baby Doll via Mego toys for the Tiny Tears generation, although the soft gum market soon became crowded by a multitude of imitators.

Hubba Bubba, Wrigley's cheekier, chunkier alternative, predicated its appeal on the gum's decidedly un-gumlike abilities. Its bubbles were 'the kind that don't stick to your face' claimed comic-book hero, the Gumfighter, in a seemingly endless series of small-town skirmishes with the Smallbubble gang. The Western theme was no accident, as Hubba Bubba had initially been developed under the codename 'stagecoach'. Bubblicious was Adams' effort, contributing to a 40 per cent growth in the market in just under three years.

Soft bubble gum's year zero was also good news for Rowntree Mackintosh, whose established one penny winner, Anglo Bubbly, benefited from the rejuvenated interest. Initially a product of the Halifax-based Anglo-American Chewing Gum Company, by 1977 Bubbly's sales totalled nearly a quarter of a billion pieces per year. The patriotic kids interviewed for propagandist PR blurb claimed, 'It's got more flavour in it,' although no one was brave enough to address Lonnie Donegan's chart-topping query about losing the flavour on the bedpost overnight. (Steve

THE GUMFIGHTER
HAS A STAGEFIGHT
THE GUMTOWN STAGE NEVER 'PASSED' THROUGH THE SMALLBUBBLE GANG'S TERRITORY – IT RAN!!
SUDDENLY THE GANG ATTACK !!
AARGH!!
NOBODY PANIC!
MEANWHILE ... UP ON A HILL THE GUMFIGHTER SEES ALL.
LETS SEE HOW BRAVE THOSE BANDITS ARE WITH BIG BUBBLES!!
LOOKS LIKE A JOB FOR HUBBA BUBBA!!
Hubba Bubba
THE KIND THAT DON'T STICK TO YOUR FACE
O.K. SMALLBUBBLE – GO FOR YOUR GUM!
HUBBA BUBBA'S SO FAST IT SOON BLOWS MIGHTY BIG BUBBLES–
PUFF PUFF
THAT DON'T STICK TO YOUR FACE!!
SPLAT! SPLAT!
BIG BUBBLES NO TROUBLES
WHO IS THAT HUBBA BUBBA?
NEW Big bubbles No troubles
Hubba Bubba
DUNNO – HE NEVER STICKS ROUND LONG ENOUGH TO FIND OUT.
GET READY FOR YOUR NEXT GUMFIGHT AT YOUR SWEETSHOP NOW!!!

Wright-style 'factoid': the song's original Spearmint-referencing title was changed due to the BBC's then 'no trademarks' restriction.)

Anglo's diverse range of chewing gum swelled through the 1970s. They took over the sales and marketing of Beech-Nut, a 'sugarised' (i.e. candy-coated) product, alongside their own Sportsman brand and Fruit Snips, a colourful variety pack. The XL line offered four different flavours for the price of one, while liquorice flavoured brands Spooky and Black Eye were described as 'a must for the 1p tray'. Another notable newcomer was Magic Cat, a fruit flavoured bubble gum which changed colour on chewing. Cat, chameleon... they're basically the same animal, right?

**'Reports celebrating chewing gum as a boost to short-term memory, were published, disregarded and swiftly forgotten.'**

By now, no one was using chicle as the main ingredient in gum, butadiene-based synthetic rubber being far cheaper. The 'nuisance factor' of improperly disposed-of gum was documented on news reports, or experienced first-hand by school-kids who sat on a freshly spat-out wad during assembly. Scientific reports celebrating chewing gum as an aid to concentration, or a boost to short-term memory, were published, disregarded and swiftly forgotten. Also, scientific reports celebrating chewing gum as an aid to concentration, or a boost to short-term memory, were published, disregarded and swiftly forgotten. Health concerns led to a sudden demand for sugar-free gums such as Wrigley's Orbit ('9 out of 10 British dentists surveyed were all for sugar free gum'). Those who had already lost their teeth demanded a gum that wouldn't stick to their dentures. Freedent was the answer: 'The chewing gum with no ticky-tacky – just the smooth, smooth action that everybody loves.' Shane Macgowan was not chosen as the poster boy.

By the early 1980s, industry-termed functional breath-freshening gums were on the rise. Adams' Freshen-up contained a

**Opposite:** The British bubble gum: plain, sober, none of that 'pneumatic' lettering nonsense. Jolly good. Anglo Snips circa 1977.

**Below:** Tackling inflation with Anglo XL (1956) and halitosis with Adams' Freshen-up (1975).

runny liquid centre which apparently delivered 'more of what you chew gum for' (an abstract notion few other brands thought worthy of addressing), while Warner Lambert helped stave off halitosis with Stimorol and Clorets (containing Actizol, their patented chlorophyll-based active ingredient).

All kids wanted, however, was something bigger and better to gnaw on. PVC drums full of ugly balls and beady eyes peered out from the shopkeeper's counter, sizeable enough at first sight, though all disappointingly hollow. Leaf Jawbreakers, though, were the real deal, large enough to fill even an American maw and rightly worthy of the name gobstopper. At the core of these regular, supersour or fireball flavoured planetoids, some thirty minutes' sucking time away, was a heart of pure gum. Whispered horror stories about in-mouth accidents and fluke explosions only enhanced their reputation. Jawbreakers, after all, had the promise of pain built right into their name and who didn't love a dangerous piece of gum? What else could explain the enduring popularity of that tedious booby-trapped 'snappy gum' practical joke? The moral: never accept a gift from someone with black fingernails and no sense of humour. ✻

## ✻ GOLD RUSH

Of all the shapes, sizes, formats and formulae of gum, Bazooka's Gold Rush had to be unique. In an industry where, by and large, bigger is better, this gum's 'small is beautiful' philosophy stood in proud opposition, evidence that even if your product is clearly broken into a hundred tiny pieces, kids will still buy it if it's packaged correctly.

**Opposite:** Major miner. Topps Gold Rush (1967).

**Below:** Yo! Gold Rush the show. circa 1987.

But what a package! The manufacturing process, such as it was, remained shrouded in secrecy but presumably involved large ingots of gum being pulverised into fragments before being sifted from a river bed by thick-'tached Californian prospectors given to cries of 'Yee haw'. And that was just the women. (Ba-dum-tish!) No doubt the end of each shift at the Bazooka factory was marked by much slapping of hats across thighs, shooting of revolvers into the air, fist-fights in the canteen, and so on. It did not matter because Gold Rush's cargo of precious yellow nuggets shipped in its own custom calico fabric bag.

It's difficult to know which is the greater mystery: that no one had considered selling gum with such a USP in the past, or that the drawstring pouch would live on so well in the memory. In a category stuffed with products of zero nutritional value, Gold Rush offered remarkably slim pickings. Available in an uninspired generic fruit flavour (apart from to the Yanks, who also enjoyed raspberry, grape, cherry and 'scented' flavours), its presence in the mouth could go virtually undetected. Any budding Marmalade Atkins attempting to blow a headmaster-baiting bubble would find herself exasperated by the sheer untenable yield in each bagful. Priced at a premium – a pocket-money-sapping 8p in 1978 – the only people striking it rich from Gold Rush were Topps (the Philadelphia-based gum giant) and Trebor (its UK distributors).

At least the triumphant cloth bag proved useful for children to keep other 'treasures' in – a word deliberately employed by the Bazooka sales team but which generally translated into marbles, coins and other such 24-carat crap. A later waterproof version of the bag was also, as it turned out, both consumer- and nostalgia-proof. Countless imitations of the doughty original can be found today but none has staked its claim quite like Gold Rush.



**'In an industry where, by and large, bigger is better, this gum's "small is beautiful" philosophy stood in proud opposition.'**

# If you haven't tried the latest Mr. Freeze, you've Mr. Lot.

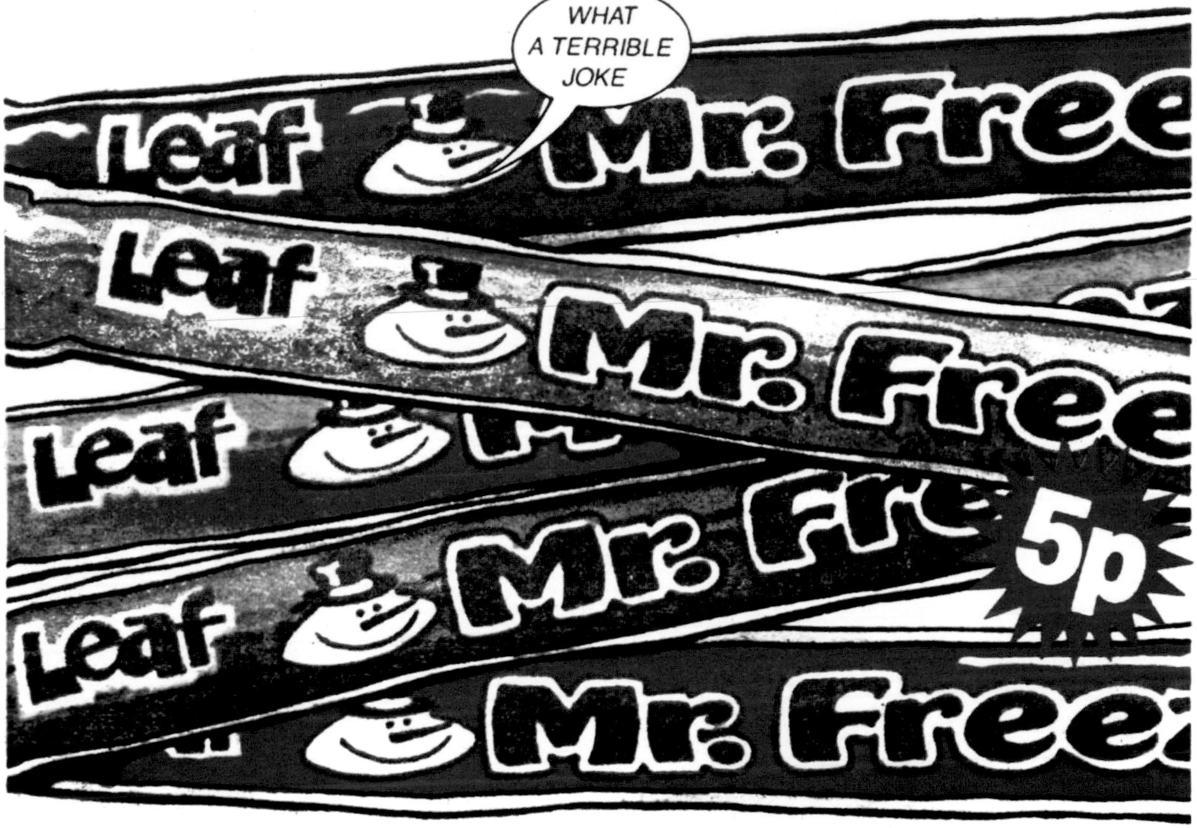

WHAT A TERRIBLE JOKE

5p

You've always loved bigger-tasting bigger-value Mr. Freeze, but wait until you taste new "Blue Razzberry."

It'll knock you sideways.

It's blue-ier and fruitier and completely different. And at 5p, it's the best buy around.

Like our Cola, Orange, Strawberry and Lemon flavours, new Blue Razzberry is stronger-tasting, easier-to-eat and sensational value.

New "Blue Razzberry."

You'll love it. Try it.

Leaf (UK) Limited, Middle Way, Chinnor, OXON.

# DRINKS & ICES

**Opposite:** A chilling scenario – when mascots start vetting their own advertising copy. Mr. Freeze (1961).

**It's all well and good looking after Mr Tumkin, but what happens when Mrs Cottonmouth comes to call? Those sweets, crisps, chocolate and snacks have to be washed down with something: and that means gallons and gallons of squash, juice, cordial and pop.**

Since the invention of the commercial fridge-freezer, full of toxic coolants and gases, retailers have packed their shops with drinks and ice creams, full of toxic additives. Writing in 1978, the consumer affairs journalist Marion Giordan observed that, in Britain, 'We eat the most highly coloured food in Europe.' One glance at the livid identity parade of products in any given newsagents will confirm that little has changed. How we chuckled at the Victorians with their copper-pickled gherkins and red lead cheese rinds but their legacy is Carmoisine, Quinoline, Ponceau 4R and Allura Red – 'vibrant', artificial colours that are still in use 100 years later, despite repeated calls that they be banned.

Amaranth, a red food dye and suspected carcinogen, was still being added to drinks like Ribena until the late 1970s – and this was a product that traded on its wholesomeness. Contemporaneous adverts ploughed a furrow of nostalgia: 'I remember my mother giving it to me,' explained one woman, handing a glass

**Opposite:** Syrup of swigs: Old-style concentrated Ribena, a cordial relation since 1936.

**Below:** AG Barr's more straightforwardly orangey Irn-Bru sidekick, Jusoda (1958). The partially tropical taste of Schweppes' Cariba (1976).

to her own daughter. Yeah, and my father used to beat me to within an inch of my life, but let's not tell social services, okay?

Whatever didn't kill you made you stronger. The line between the poison and the potion was a blur; ice cream was prescribed after a tonsillectomy, Lucozade was considered essential during the influenza epidemic of the 1960s, as was the ascorbic acid trip of C-Vit. Unlike modern-day energy drinks, none of these was considered classy, stylish, or a statement of cool, not by any stretch of the imagination. Before the days of Red Bull (which, rather than a drink, is a meticulous and mathematically calculated marketing campaign for adrenalised living), the most exciting beverage experience would be finding a two-litre bottle of Jusoda in your grandma's pantry. They were more relaxed times, and life ran at a slower pace. Or maybe

that's because everyone was bloated on fizzy pop, and the most stressful part of the day was getting up off the settee.

In an era when wireless meant the radio, not a broadband connection, every regional drinks company had their secret formula, passed down through the ages. From Vimto in Manchester, to Tizer in Leeds, and Irn-Bru in Glasgow, the urban industrial north became a sugary drink Mecca. Meanwhile, in London, Wall's and Lyons Maid established themselves as the Groucho and Harpo of the ice cream world (i.e. like the Marx Brothers, there were plenty of others, but only two were worth watching). Lyons Maid's startling selection of ice lollies left kids spoiled for choice, whereas Wall's ultimately found themselves a prima donna in Cornetto, the menace from Venice.

Big though those brands may have been, they all had to budge up and make room for a bigger name from across the pond. Because that thrumming chiller cabinet at the back of the corner shop was, in actual fact, the home of the brave, the land of the free, and the rightful territory of a drink that was ready to take over the world. Or, at the very least, teach it how to sing...

'From Vimto in Manchester to Tizer in Leeds, the urban industrial north became a sugary drink Mecca.'

**Below:** A panoply of Lyons Maid goodies from the high '70s. Clockwise from top left: Bionic Lolly (1976), Jubilee (1977), Haunted House (1973), Gone Bananas (1977), Coola Bar (1969), Fab (1967), Lolly Gobble Choc Bomb (1974), Dinosaurs (1976).

## EVEN BETTER THAN THE REAL THING

In 1971 a young British governess was stopped on the streets of Rome and asked if she'd like to take part in an advert. Her task was simple: to spend a few hours in a hotel learning a catchy song, then mime along to it while standing on a box at the local pony club. What she didn't know was that she was agreeing to star in one of the marketing industry's biggest ever campaigns. By the following summer, she was one of the most recognisable people on television: the girl who wanted to buy the world a Coke.

It's fair to say that Linda Neary didn't expect to become the face of Coca-Cola. She certainly never met any of the advert's teenage cast, many of whom were strategically and multiculturally arrayed across an Italian hillside. She didn't even warble the famous lyrics – 'I'd like to build the world a home, and furnish it with love' – the New Seekers had recorded the jingle some six months previously, only for it to flop on US radio. She simply stood and lip-synched. Somehow, though, coupled with the pictures of Neary and co., the song began to strike a chord with TV audiences. The Zeitgeisty message of unity and togetherness cut through America's Vietnam-jaded cynicism. Other countries followed suit: the 'hilltop' commercial was one of the first to be shown worldwide (although South Africa's request for a version omitting black people was roundly refused). The song's Coke-light single release (divested of all product references) shot to number one in the UK, knocking Benny Hill's 'Ernie (The Fastest Milkman in the West)' off the top slot.

**Opposite:** A stout, no-frills Coke circa 1976, and the dawn of irksome Yuppie Coke advertising (1986).

**Below:** Pepsi, still using its 'arbitrary hyphenated word' trademark, circa 1980.

Impressive work for a drink that is essentially 99 per cent sugar and water, but then Coca-Cola has always been too ambitious to consider itself just a drink. Founded in 1886 by John Pemberton, a pharmacist operating out of Atlanta, Georgia, Coke was originally sold at soda fountains as a medicinal curative. Six years later, exclusive distribution rights were secured by Asa Candler, who began an aggressive marketing campaign and started licensing the syrup to bottling plants. Despite what the company folklore might now claim, Coca-Cola did indeed contain a tiny amount of cocaine (at least for the first fifteen years of its life), although all trace was removed by 1903. Nevertheless, it is still made from the spent leaves of the coca plant (i.e. those that have had all the cocaine removed for pharmaceutical purpose).

It was the company's expansion during the Second World War that established their factories in over fifty territories. Coke patriotically promised to hydrate the American troops at 5¢ a bottle (with the coincidental kickback that army suppliers were not subject to sugar rationing). When the soldiers returned home, they left behind the foundations and infrastructure for a global business, and the means for Coca-Cola to seize the throat of the world. Science and economics writer Tom Standage has identified Coke as one of the six beverages to have significantly shaped human history, along with beer, wine, spirits, tea and coffee. The space shuttle even had its own Coke dispenser. On earth, it is the most popular branded alternative to water. In some countries, it is more available than water.

Celebrating the drink's centenary in 1986, marketing man Ike Herbert zealously declared that 'People in remote corners of the world who don't even know the names of their own capital cities know the name Coca-Cola.' But there was at least one remote corner of the world that resisted the all-American appeal of a Coke and a smile. At the height of the Cold War, future President Richard Nixon worked at a law firm that represented rival cola Pepsi. Once he was in office, Nixon smoothed the way for Pepsi to be sold behind the Iron Curtain. It was the Soviet Union's first foreign product, attractive to irony-blind communists eager to thumb their noses at the multinational capitalism of Coca-Cola.

In the UK, Pepsi's stock rose after a series of lipsmackinthirstquenchinacetastinmotivatingoodbuzzincooltalkin ads in which wimps were elevated to Lothario status. Mike Grady and Karl Howman were among the many deploying Pepsi in their chat-up spiel from 1973 onward. Keith Chegwin, the archetypal long-haired loser from Liverpool, fantasised about sipping it from a champagne glass on a dollybird-packed yacht. It's unlikely that his later alcohol problems stemmed from this shoot but – as everyone knows – since he went teetotal, Cheggers can't be boozers.

Pepsi further defied the cola hegemony in the 1980s, with the introduction of the Pepsi Challenge, a street-bound blind taste-test fronted by chirpy Cockney rocker Joe Brown. The oft-quoted and unarguable statistic was that most people, given the choice, preferred the taste of Pepsi. Coca-Cola's confidence was shaken enough to lead them to launch a reformulated 'New Coke' along with a redesign of all its packaging. Although 'New Coke' was a disaster in almost every measurable way, Pepsi still failed to overtake it in sales. British loyalties were fragmented among other brands, such as Barr's Strike Cola, boosted by the double innovation of the first ring-pull can ends in 1970 and 'the Strike Force', a hot-pant-clad lady sales team equipped with red, white and blue dune buggies. Tip Top, until then most famous for strange-shaped plastic-bottled products like Twister, Wigwam and Noggin (a 'warming' ginger and orange drink aimed at footie fans), entered the fray late with a weirdly crenellated TNT Cola cup in 1982.

Undaunted by falling market share, Coca-Cola continued to weather a storm of competition, criticism and controversy, emerging stronger year on year. Neither persistent urban myths nor organised boycotts damaged the brand – it definitely wouldn't dissolve a tooth overnight, for one thing – although an Australian poster containing a risqué image smuggled in by a subversive artist was withdrawn from use in 1995. Everyone from the Beatles and Greta Garbo, to Max Headroom and Bill Clinton endorsed Coke at one time or another. It even adversely affected British tea-drinking, with nearly 20

**Opposite:** The SDP of the cola world, Barr's Strike Cola (1970).

**Below:** A can of strong lemon drink: 7-Up (1976) and Sprite (1977).

per cent of the population sacrificing their traditional cuppa over the two decades of the cola wars. Not so much need in those days for the fastest milkman in the West, then.

The ubiquity of the Coca-Cola can opened the door to many a lesser American soft drink. Dr Pepper's UK launch brought a unique 'blend of 23 fruit flavours' – count 'em! – to the reluctant British palate, initially only available in half-litre screw-top bottles. The similarly mystifying lemon-lime flavour of 7 Up materialised in 1976, the same year that the English were finally allowed to share one of Scotland's best kept secrets: Irn-Bru.

For years, national pride prevented Coke from outselling Barr's 'invigorating, refreshing tonic beverage' in its homeland. Since 1901, 'Iron Brew' (as it was known until food labelling regulations required a change to brand names that were not literally true) had been the choice of any self-respecting Jock. Sassenach heid-the-baws in search of a bottle would find it was produced under licence in Sunderland or Bradford, if they were lucky.

Irn-Bru unified their packaging and image with a strong and memorable 'Made in Scotland from girders' campaign throughout the 1970s and 1980s, with every celebrated Scot from Robert Burns to Billy Connolly press-ganged into service. Barr's were also responsible for the relaunched Tizer in 1973, reproduced as faithfully to the original 1950s recipe as possible after a six-month development phase by the company's chemists. Both drinks took advantage of the then modern foam 'Plastishield'-covered bottles which meant that supermarkets could safely stock glass in one-litre sizes, although these were quickly replaced when plastic bottles became commonplace.

Sadly, the long-held belief that Irn-Bru is the number one drink in Scotland, while it may have been the case in the twentieth century, is now no longer tru. In 1999 Coca-Cola sent over a team of marketing hit men to take out the ginger prince and, slowly but surely, Coke closed the gap. Reports dated 2005 claimed that the cola had outsold Irn-Bru for the first time 'some years' before. Coke, in the words of its own marketing and communications team, had succeeded in claiming its 'unfair share' of the market. But then the Coca-Cola company produce over 500 soft drinks brands around the world so, even in countries where Coke isn't the best-selling, it's likely that they own the rival anyway.

**Opposite:** Caledonian carbonation in Barr's Irn-Bru (1901) and Mancunian pick-me-up Tizer (1924).

**Below:** St. Clements cola circa 1986 boasting no artificial additives – a claim conspicuously absent from cans of Cherry Coke (1983).

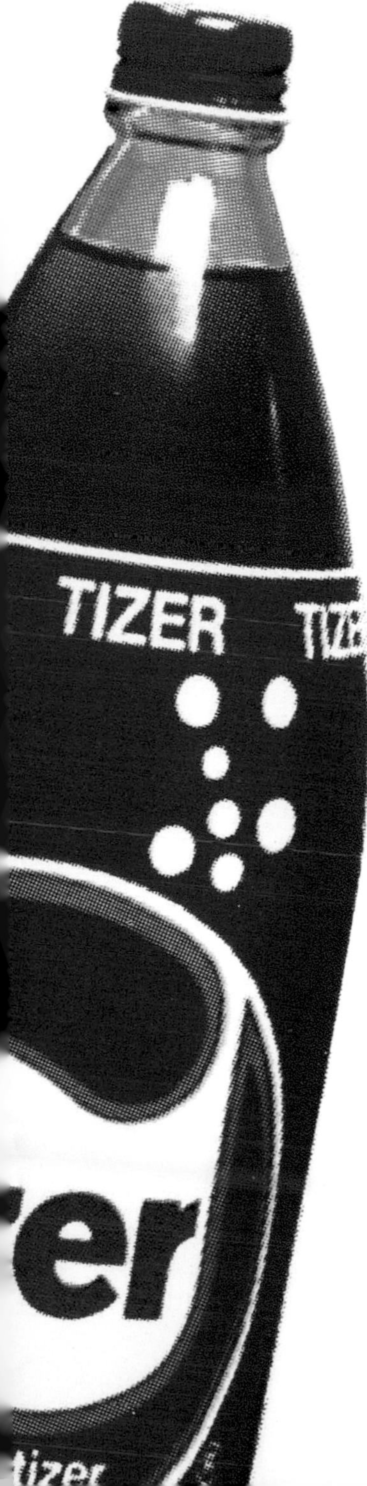

In 1989 ad agency McCann Erickson reunited Linda Neary and the Italian countryside for a new Coca-Cola ad entitled 'Generations', presumably to commemorate twenty years of them neglecting to build or furnish any kind of love-based dwelling. In an ironic final insult, this time even Neary's own speaking voice was overdubbed, to give her an American accent. And, although the cutesy sentiment washed over hardened, post-modern TV viewers, the new ad did at least correct one error in the original. Instead of everyone just singing the praises of Coke while holding the bottle, in this one they actually drank it.

## ✻ FANTA

Don't be misled by the relentless parade of Day-Glo leg-warmers and rolled-up jacket sleeves in those old screen ads. Fanta might have allied itself with 'fresh and fizzy' images of sunny American youth in the '80s – all shopping malls, saxophone solos and spot-free complexions – but forty years earlier it was quite a different story.

**Opposite:** My enemy's enemy is my friend. Fanta (1956).

**Below:** Flip-top shades? Kylie-style top-knots? It can only be appalling Americana in a can, circa 1988.

Second World War rationing had put the industrial squeeze on Coca-Cola supplies, so it fell to an ambitious businessman, Max Keith, and his team of pharmacists to come up with a replacement from raw ingredients. However, Keith and his pals weren't supplying soft drinks to the US or the British as part of the war effort, but to the Germans. After the outbreak of hostilities, an ever-resourceful (or, if you prefer, profiteering) Keith sought to find a way to keep Coke's bottling plants running in the Sudetenland. Yet, as head of the Office of Enemy Property, he was similarly mindful to avoid the wrath of the Third Reich upon a perceived foreign operation.

The answer to all his problems was a new drink, initially a formulation of waste apple fibre, whey and saccharin. By 1943, Coca-Cola GmbH was shifting 3 million units of this syrupy solution, though totally independently of their parent company. Post VE-Day (and a good ten-year hibernation), the brand re-emerged in its more familiar orange crush livery but, far from being a Stateside favourite, the product was pushed mostly to European, African and Latin American markets. Later flavour variants temporarily included coal-tar as a colourant (which maybe inspired the neon 'electric orange' taglines), though rumours of abundant pesticides in the recipe were swiftly quashed.

While the Californian gym bunnies' soda of choice would more likely be Sunkist, British teenagers continued to swallow a peddled ersatz Fanta-sy of Cadillac cruises and beach boulevards. But, in a world where 'now with added vitamin C' was considered a required piece of positive spin for an orange drink, flogging the historical realities of a Düsseldorf-based production facility might be considered less than sparkling.

**'The answer to all his problems was a new drink, initially a formulation of waste apple fibre, whey and saccharin.'**

## * CRESTA

You can't call the chaps at Schweppes predictable. In 1971 two off-the-wall products were launched by the you-know-who drinks giant. There was Sunfresh Funtastic Squash, a wildly ambitious attempt to capture 'the taste of boiled sweets in drink form'. Then there was a slightly creamy, foamy soft drink, five years in the making, 'entirely different from conventional fizzy pops', called Cresta. Guess which one lived to see 1972.

**Opposite:** You couldn't get a more stereotypically '70s drink if you liquidised a space hopper. Cresta (1971).

**Below:** Webster and Williams work their magic on the Zeitgeist.

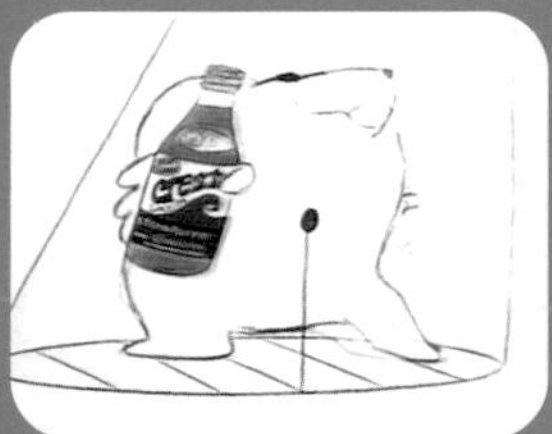

It's questionable as to whether Cresta's survival was down to the drink itself: most people don't recall a fun, frothy drink in five fruity flavours, they tend to inwardly retch at the memory of a sickly, soapy drink in various shades of chemical burn. The bear, though, that's a different matter. Schweppes were canny enough to hire John Webster, ace creative director at ad agency BMP, to do the publicity. Webster had recently seen *Easy Rider*, and loved the scene where alcoholic Jack Nicholson clucked and jerked like a loon after his first sip of morning bourbon. Perhaps it was the, let's say, similarly violent response the body makes to a sip of Cresta that led him to link the two. From there it was a small matter to turn Jack into a burly, husky, displaced polar bear animated by cartoon supremo Richard Williams, given to ice-skating, Elvis impersonations and shouting 'Rimsky Korsakoff!' at the top of his voice in public places, and the campaign trophies flooded in.

Extra publicity came courtesy of some rather blatant product placement in forgotten ITV puppet show *Nuts and Bones*, but Webster and Williams probably deserve the most credit. Incidentally, the drink itself came in those super-sweet 1970s flavours of orange, lemon and lime, blackcurrant, strawberry and pineapple. Let the record show it was frothy, man.

**'People don't recall a fun, frothy drink in five fruity flavours, but a sickly, soapy drink in various shades of chemical burn.'**

## LOCAL LIBATIONS

Of all the drinks that long ago fizzed their last, none lingers as strongly in the memory as the local brews that came to you, not via grocery or supermarket, but literally from off the back of a lorry. The names by themselves are enough to send those of a certain age into nostalgic reverie. Bon Accord of Aberdeen, Dayla of Aylesbury, Bill Co of London, Lowcock's of Hartlepool... wherever you lived, there was a local brew you wouldn't swap for all the Pepsi in Presto's.

The business model was simple and sound. Pop van drivers were hired from the local workforce, reported to the factory, and were duly kitted out with a flatbed Bedford truck (or, for smaller area runs, a Commer van) and a stash of the depot's finest bubbly nectar. The only thing the drivers had to provide themselves was an assistant. Normally a hard lad in flares and a feather cut, the pop van boy noisily unloaded the crates, brandished a bottle in his right hand to clock any predatory dogs lurking behind the front gate, took back the empties from awestruck smaller boys with a surly expression, and hung dangerously off the lorry's tailgate as it scudded down the lane, flicking the Vs at passing cyclists.

Perhaps the most noteworthy of this nationwide band of strapping lads was, er, the young William Hague, great-grandson of the founder of Yorkshire dandelion and burdock manufacturers Charles Hague and Sons, who served a brief tour of bottle-slinging duty before

he decided to hit the Hansard, bought a tiny grey suit, and wowed the Conservative Party conference with malevolent precocity. (This wasn't, it should be noted, the standard career path for a pop van veteran.)

Some pop producers were pub-affiliated. R. Whites was (still is) a subsidiary of Whitbread, while Minster Cola arrived at your doorstep courtesy of Allied Breweries. The dairies were at it too, milk floats rattling with impossible-to-open litre bottles of fizzy delight alongside the gold top and Prize hazelnut yogurts. Larkspur Lemonade came festooned with labels depicting a

**Opposite:** Fizzy exotica from Derbyshire. Mandora (1959).

**Below:** Liquid psychedelia, Essex-style. El-Van circa 1970.

suspiciously Cresta-like polar bear promising 'a billion bubbles a bottle', while Unigate's range was fronted, for reasons known only to some bright spark back at the depot, by a cartoon jazz band. Just to be different, Essex-based El-Van delivered fizzies under the aegis of Clark's, the Butterkist people.

The rugged, earthy titles of regional brewers were often masked by exotic brand names cooked up in pegboard-lined head offices: R. Whites supplemented their humble 'pools winner ticking "no publicity" box' main brand with an exotic alter ego that went under the Italianate moniker of Valento. Elsewhere, Burrows and Sturgess of Derby flogged a superbly sickly strawberry cream soda by the name of Mandora, Malton-based Tate-Smith masqueraded as Sundella, Exley's of Rotherham plumped for the sugary escapism of Suncose, and, let's face it, Diamond Lemonade sounds a tad classier than Gomersall's of Wakefield.

Not that the pop folk were ashamed of their origins. Oh, no. Industrial pride was big: Lawson's of Greenock's labels featured pictures of locally built ocean liners like the *QEII*, implying that the liquid they concealed was a technological achievement on a similar level. Guzzlers of well-loved colas like Barr's Strike and Ben Shaw's Sun Charm claimed they kicked the American conglomerates' arses, saleswise, on their respective patches. Their customers joined in with the regional support to a degree not so far off that enjoyed by the local footie team.

Even today, most former popaholics will solemnly testify that their local brew was unlike anything else. Offset against this blanket respect, tales abounded of dangerous driving as rival vans cut each other up and nicked their enemies' empties, as did horrific rumours that, due to dodgy carbonating practices, local pop bottles were prone to explode at random like faulty hand-grenades. Still, a finger or two was a small price to pay for that sparkling goodness.

The regions loved to get one over on the big names. Carters of Nottingham greeted the challenges of the 1980s with the 'rip cap', a mini bottle that worked out cheaper than a can and incorporated a wide neck for added swiggability. Your lorryload of parochial pop had to be fizzier, sweeter and more intensely coloured than anything available down the Co-op. Ben Shaw's of Huddersfield tinted their lemonade a pleasingly bright yellow, and launched the Apollotastic Space Special – an addictively fruity concoction with a mouth-watering lurid green hue.

**'Alpine's raspberryade and pineappleade were worshipped by generations of kids with no great emotional attachment to their back teeth.'**

**Opposite:** From the tropic of Huddersfield, Sun Charm (1950).

**Below:** Own-brand brews clad in wallpaper off-cuts: Hallmark lager and lime (1974) and Lockwoods cola (1975).

With exemplary recession-era logic, El-Van assumed their products would taste twice as nice if they called them double orangeade, double cherryade, and so on, and decorated the cans with eye-bending Op Art designs.

But the most famous pop van operation was Alpine, whose lorries emerged from Birmingham to conquer the entire country. Their raspberryade and pineappleade were worshipped by generations of kids with no great emotional attachment to their back teeth. The summit of Alpine's hubris came in 1981, when a special commemorative flavour was launched to celebrate the royal wedding – passion fruit. Well, how were they to know?

A number of things brought the van's glory days to an end. Non-returnable glass bottles arrived, followed by two-litre plastic bottles, thus depriving the round of half its unique selling point. Even worse was the rise of the out-of-town weekly shop. The prospect of having to lug huge bottles of pop home from Fine Fare on the bus made doorstep delivery a no brainer, but when driving to Tesco became the norm, such weighty considerations ceased to matter. Now the pop van is as rare as the chimney sweep, with no sign of a phoenix-like return to the streets in prospect. Which is a shame, as, everything else aside, it has to be the most environmentally friendly way to consume fizzy drinks ever devised.

## ✻ CORONA

Born of the South Walian temperance movement and colonising every out-of-town industrial estate from Preston to Portsmouth, the Corona Soft Drinks company cornered the market in clinking, crate-based, bottled pop door-to-door deliveries. They were obviously top of their game, too, because they were the ones with the expensive-looking telly campaign.

**Opposite:** Help me, Rhondda. The Britvic incarnation of Corona (1958).

**Below:** It's that man Williams again (1976).

'Every bubble's passed its fizzical,' claimed a Sergeant Bilko-toned fitness trainer as he put the rest of the knobbly-necked bottle's fat, flat contingent through their paces in the best-remembered of the 1970s animated ads. Canadian-born Richard 'Dick' Williams – hailed by Woody Allen, no less, as 'the new Walt Disney' – was the maestro behind the myriad bubbles. Commercials were his London studio's bread and butter, including the Midland's 'listening bank' and Limara body-spray ads, but Williams's true ambition lay in movies. While he achieved great success with a Michael Horden-voiced retelling of Dickens's *A Christmas Carol*, the *Pink Panther* film titles and *Who Framed Roger Rabbit?* he tragically never completed his masterpiece. Twenty-eight years' work went into *Nasruddin*, a feature-length retelling of the *Arabian Nights* tales, which was ultimately seized by impatient investors and rush-released to an indifferent public.

By contrast, Corona's various flavours were genii in a bottle as far as the punters were concerned. Citric lemonades, limeades and orangeades rattled alongside the richer, fuller, fruitier tastes of cherryade and raspberryade, or an autumnal, sulphurous dandelion and burdock. Corona's USP seemed to be the sheer up-your-nose effervescence of their drinks, which wasn't far from the mark (at least when they were first opened). There was always some risk of carbonated catastrophe in necking a half-litre of American Cream Soda or Ginger Punch straight from the bottle – not least if your mum caught you 'not using a beaker' – but the burps were all the more satisfying for it.
The company encouraged brand loyalty by handing out stickers, T-shirts and other goodies showing the gymnasium-intimidated bubbles sweating their way through extensive weight training and chest expanding routines. Not to mention the fact that you'd get a cash 'deposit' back on each of the empties you returned the following week (as the bold black bottle-cap reminder promised), but only if your dad forgot.

In the 1950s, Corona Soft Drinks also brought us Tango ('the orange pop with real orange in it!'), the perforated-eardrum, playground-craze legacy of which lives on today. Competition and closures led to the franchising out of the pop van routes and, unsurprisingly, Corona themselves were eventually gulped down by Beechams and, later, Britvic, before the bubble finally burst. The name is now more commonly associated with a brand of Mexican beer, equally belch-friendly, but no more fruity than the wedge of lime stuffed ostentatiously into the top.

## THE HARD STUFF

In any child's list of big and clever activities they can't wait to try out, boozing has to come somewhere in the top three. And quite rightly so, because it is demonstrably both those things. But sensory derangement by self-medication with intoxicating fluid was not always as easy as it is in these WKD-fuelled times. In fact, for many young shavers who'd yet to acquire a convincingly tall chum with whom to skulk in the snug of the Prince of Wales, it was pretty much out of the question, Christmas détentes and unguarded bottles of cooking sherry aside. Luckily, you could always pretend. Doubly luckily, brewers, ever with an eye on buttering up their future clientele, were ready to help.

Devonshire cider makers Whiteway's of Whimple created Cydrax in 1905, to cash in on the burgeoning temperance movement. Soon joined by its mellower cousin Peardrax, it became a popular teetotal alternative, 'recommended by Lady Henry Somerset and many of the greatest living abstainers'. By 1963 it was being sold to over seventy countries, although the intense acidic sweetness of the brew, combined with the growing unfashionability of a name that conjured up visions of either a Bond villain or some hastily dumped chemical waste, led sales to decline gradually in favour of rival product Cidona, made by Bulmers since 1955. Eventually owners Allied Breweries threw in the bar towel, and British production halted in 1988. (Although a version of Peardrax still thrives today in, of all places, Trinidad.)

For the serious underage method acting drunk, shandy was the tipple of choice. Not the proper half-and-half mixture served up in pubs, but the ever so faintly beery canned variety, freely available to youthful palates due to the magic words 'not more than 1.2° proof'. Any higher, and it was over-eighteens only.

**Opposite:** The soft drink most likely to say 'So we meet again, Doc-tor.'. Cydrax (1905).

**Below:** It won't get you drunk, but the can design might give you a hangover. Bulmers Cidona (1955). Top Deck circa 1964.

palpable. Dodgy maths was enlisted to prove that, even at 1.2°, it could still get you pissed if you necked fifty cans (probably), and its brown bitter shandy or green lager and lime cans became a vital prop for the wannabe junior tuff. (Although the orange-clad cider variant that turned up in 1972 never achieved the infamy of its hoppy brothers; by this time kids had twigged that non-alcoholic cider was basically just fizzy apple juice with a hard stare.)

There was a cloud on the horizon, though, in the burly form of Shandy Bass, a rival pretend bitter launched in 1970 by Canada Dry UK, soft drink division of Bass Charrington.

(Conversely, any lower than 0.9°, and you couldn't legally call it 'shandy' at all.) R. Whites were among the first to mass-market a ready-mixed shandy in 1953 with their Chandy. 'For shandy, say "Chandy"' went the slogan, but not many people did, and the product's reach was limited to the regional van delivery market.

It would be another decade before a clear national favourite emerged, but when Beecham's Top Deck turned up in grocers' shops, the sense of pre-pubescent joy was

Stout of can and adorned with genuine brewer's livery, it looked harder, albeit less trendy, than Top Deck with its minimalist roundels. The fashions of your peer group thus decided which one you went for: the manly Bass, or the now slightly poncy-looking Deck? It was the nearest thing to a Mods-vs-Rockers schism in the under-twelve universe.

A more serious fight was taking place in the boardroom. Bass was made under licence by Britvic, a company in which the brewer had a sizeable stake. In 1986 Beecham sold Top Deck, along with its other soft drink concerns including Tango and Corona, to Britvic. It didn't take a genius to work out which of the now duplicate shandies would be asked politely to leave the premises. So it was that Top Deck began a slow, inexorable slide to extinction, finally snuffing it for good in 1995.

The nail in Top Deck's cultural coffin came in '91, when the *NME*'s Mary Anne Hobbs visited Nirvana in their dressing room prior to their famous appearance on *The Word*. By way of hospitality Kurt and co. had been provided – in a touch of class typical of producers Planet 24 – with a can each of Top Deck. They mocked this piddling rider with slacker disdain, wondering why anyone would want to make such a product, let alone consume it, before going on air to itemise the charms of Cobain's new lady friend in decidedly unparliamentary language. Someone at Bass no doubt took note, and readied their production lines for the manufacture of the first of the great shandy killers, Hooch.

As Britpop saw off grunge, so the initial generation of fluorescent kiddie-friendly alcopops sent the sludgy 1.2° brigade retreating into the history books at a frightened gallop. If that wasn't enough, those meddling Eurocrats passed a ruling in 1994 lowering the alcohol licence-dodging limit from 1.2° to a piffling 0.5°. Try getting plastered down the recreation ground on that! No longer do young lads have to go through the stage of imagining what it's like to get pissed, thus existentially readying themselves for drunkenness proper. Now they're just pushed into it, completely unprepared. The standards of sprawling unconscious on public transport have plummeted accordingly. Shouldn't there be government pamphlets about this sort of thing?

# 100 cassettes and radios to win from Cydrax!

Get colouring, kids. You can win one of 50 super Prinzsound TR3 Auto Cassette Recorders complete with remote control mike, earphone, cassette and batteries.
For 2nd Prize winners, there are 50 Prinzsound 77 Grand Luxe Transistor Radios (MW/LW/FM - and complete with batteries and earphones) to get crystal-sharp reception of your favourite pop programmes. And there are 400 spend-as-you-like £1 postal orders as runner-up prizes.

Just colour this picture with paints, crayons or felt pens – and send it unfolded with the main label from any size Whiteway's Cydrax, Peardrax or Cyder Shandy bottle to reach Whiteway's by 31st August, 1974. Prizes will be awarded in two age groups – under 10, and 10 to 15 – to the best entries judged in terms of neatness and imagination (age will be taken into consideration).

**Cydrax**

the sparkling apple goodness drink.

The competition is open to UK residents only under the age of 16 years on the closing date, excluding children of the employees of Whiteway's of Whimple Ltd, their associate companies or their agents. Entries must reach us by 31st August 1974 and cannot be returned. A full list of rules is available if you send a stamped addressed envelope, marked RULES, to Whiteway's Hele, Nr. Exeter, Devon. Write us, too, if you have difficulty obtaining Cydrax.

BLOCK LETTERS IN INK PLEASE

Name ..........................................................

Address ..........................................................

..........................................................

Age .............. (in years and months on 31st August 1974)

I certify that this is the unaided work of the above competitor. Signed .............................. (Parent/Guardian)

**Send to: Cydrax Colouring Contest 1974**
**Whiteways, Hele, Nr. Exeter, Devon.**

DON'T FORGET TO ENCLOSE YOUR LABEL

WHO2 Registered in England No. [illegible]

## * TIZER

The archetypal B-list soft drink, Tizer was the brainchild of stout Mancunian Fred Pickup, who moshed together assorted fruity flavours (and no small amount of sugar) to create his patent 'appetiser', which rattled along just fine in its modest way for decades. Come the '70s, a takeover by the sinister-sounding Armour Trust provoked a slew of ambitious spin-offs: the Tom and Jerry-festooned Tizer

**Opposite:** Always the bridesmaid. Tizer (1924).

**Below:** A 'funky' ad campaign that fooled nobody, circa 1991.

Quenchers, Tizer ice lollies, a brave but doomed attempt to introduce Royal Crown Cola to Britain (the USA's third most popular cola after you-know-who and the other one), and even the ethnically targeted 'Shalom' kosher lemonade.

One innovation that did last was the pioneering move from traditional returnable bottles to cans in 1974, after the three-day week led to a pop delivery crisis when glassworks failed to turn out enough new bottles (drinks manufacturers were reduced to putting up posters pleading for consumers to return 3 million unaccounted-for empties). So far, so fair-to-middling, but the enterprise was soon swallowed up by Irn-Bru giants A.G. Barr, who were determined to drag this rather quaint provincial pop into the cool modern world via the miracle of advertising.

First came the Tizers, mischievous little creatures in the shape of the letters T, I, Z, E and R who could be conjured into existence by rubbing a can. Then the diminutive David Rappaport strutted his way round a nightclub boasting that he could 'tell it's Tizer when my eyes're shut'. Most ambitious of all was 'I'se got the Ize', a slightly New Wave-ish song given away as a flexidisc to accompany TV ads wherein a bunch of pseudo-streetwise lads intimidated a pair of security guards by shouting at them in an impenetrable 'L-ize-ingo', by bunging 'ize' on the front of every other word.

**'The diminutive David Rappaport strutted his way round a nightclub boasting that he could "tell it's Tizer when my eyes're shut".'**

Despite these efforts, Tizer stubbornly remained an uncool, slightly comical, steady-as-she-goes 'if wet' second-choice tipple for the pop connoisseur. It's what Fred would have wanted.

## BREW-IT-YOURSELF

It's all a bit too easy, isn't it? Waltz down to the newsagent, hand over your 20p, and walk off with a can of fizzy beverage to enjoy at your leisure. Okay, the ring-pull might snap, necessitating a bit of handiwork with your trusty penknife, but other than that it's a pretty straightforward, toil-free process. If only, thought young consumers with time on their hands, there was a way to make things a bit more frustrating and complicated.

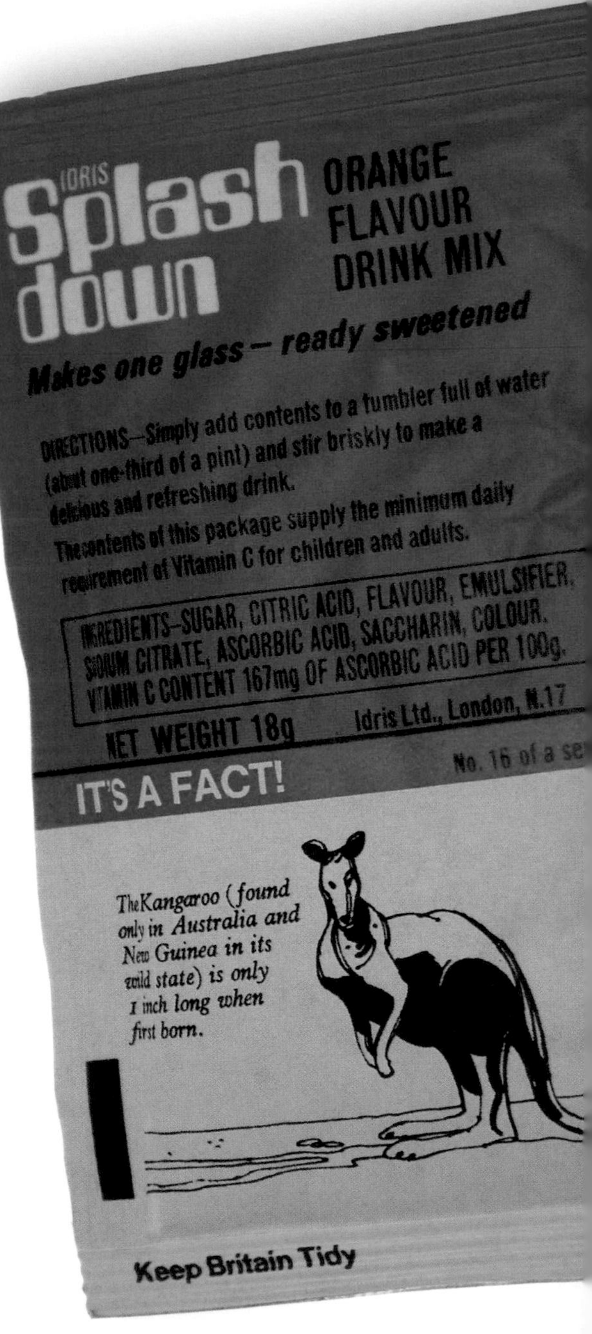

**Opposite:** It's what the spacemen drink, honest! Splashdown circa 1972.

**Below:** Instant fizz for the well-fed child. Swizzade (1981).

Fortunately the soft drinks companies were there to help make life more difficult.

One way of putting back hassle into pop was via the homebrew method. Kids, seeing the head of the household filling the cupboard under the stairs with lethal-looking demijohns full of DIY bitter kits like the Sid James-endorsed Sparklets, sought to emulate this self-sufficiency in their own non-alcoholic way. This they did, thanks to the likes of Lyons' Lyonsade, Swizzels' Swizzade, and Splashdown, a fizzy orange powder from ginger beer giants Idris, which made a virtue of its astronaut-style foil sachets. All these came and went in the space of a few years, but the original powdered fizz lasted decades.

Rowntree's Creamola Foam consisted of Day-Glo crystals packed in baking soda tins which, when added to plain old water, transformed it into something akin to rather flat Cresta, with extra metallic overtones. Rising to prominence during the '50s, its faded 'back of the pantry next to the glacé cherries' glamour lasted until 1998, being especially popular in Scotland, where attempts were later made to revive the brand, despite Nestlé having thoughtlessly obliterated all records of a recipe. Forensic investigations were made into a surviving unopened tin of the stuff found in a remote Highland store, but perhaps it was best left on the shelf.

The second DIY method was altogether more technically adventurous. Since 1903, a small factory in Peterborough had been quietly making a little device that enabled the butlers of well-to-do country houses to keep their masters in freshly aerated soda water for drinks parties. Come the crisis of '73, the factory's owners, Gilbey's Gin, decided to offload the ailing enterprise to a local consortium headed by Anglia Television, for the princely sum of £1. With a bit of marketing muscle behind it, the SodaStream was reborn as the last word in home-made soft drinks technology.

It was, at heart, a simple bit of Edwardian engineering. Clamp a glass bottle full of tap water under a nozzle attached to a canister of

pressurised carbon dioxide, pump it with a couple of doses of gas, and, hey presto! you have some instant fizz to add to your whisky. Or, as was the new plan, to flavour with a variety of gloopy syrups for pennywise pop heaven. The family appeal was across the board. Mums were freed from lugging home huge bottles of pop from the supermarkets, kids loved the extra-curricular mucking about, and dads relished the chance to throw their paternal weight around, taking charge of the cylinder-changing process, which was invested with as much fraught seriousness as the defusing of an unexploded bomb. (And not without reason: before the war, the old model SodaStream was dubbed the 'trench mortar', due to the propensity of cylinders suddenly to shoot through the ceiling.)

The new machine wasn't a roaring success. The business of obtaining the various parts (machine from Curry's, syrup from the supermarket, canisters from specialist outlets) proved too much of a palaver for most families. In 1979 SodaStream remedied this by lumping all three items together as one package, getting it into Boots, and plugging it even more heavily with some funky 'Get busy with the fizzy!' telly ads. This left Kenwood, the makers of the old machine, out in the cold. They hit back with the Kenwood Cascade, a roughly identical machine advertised by a cartoon dragon singing 'I'm Forever Blowing Bubbles', which led to some heavy high court action between the two companies over the next few years. This was suddenly a serious business.

By 1982, SodaStream was worth £16 million, having sold (so they claimed) a machine to every tenth household, becoming the source of over 2 per cent of all fizzy drinks consumed in the UK, and through the first half of the 1980s it was on an unstoppable roll. Vimto and Tizer were big names brought on board among their twenty-five syrupy varieties, which also included

**Opposite and below:** The imperial phase SodaStream (1979).

Caribbean Cocktail, Intergalactic Space Juice and the nauseous Witches' Brew. The SodaStream Carnival, accommodating massive litre bottles, was rolled out, alongside film and TV tie-in syrups like the Gremlins-endorsed Gizmo (pomegranate) and Stripe (bubble gum) flavours, as well as the self-explanatory Mr T's Knockout Punch. Less successful were attempts to break America with the SodaMate, the introduction of healthy fruit juice concentrates (the kids wanted sugar, and nothing but) and the misguided launch of the Mr Frothy Milkstream, an adapted machine which legitimised the dairy-based experimentation every child had tried at some point, with worktop-flooding results. On a more worthy note, old SodaStream canisters were being filled with oxygen and used as cheap, lightweight emergency breathing apparatus by the Draeger Safety Group. Was there nothing it couldn't do?

Now the property of Cadbury-Schweppes and valued at a cool £26 million, the SodaStream embarked on the rest of the decade with more ideas than ever before, though the old sparkle was starting to fade. A grab for the adult home brewing market faltered. Similarly, the SodaStream Alpha, a yuppie-targeted luxury device finished in black ash and brushed aluminium, was short of takers. A former SodaStream executive left the company to launch the rival Fizz-Wizz, which only needed one push of the button to work its gassy magic. Most worrying of all, an exploding bottle scare in 1987 prompted 16,000 complaints and a mass product recall.

The '90s saw a long, slow decline to 'car boot cast-off' status, as SodaStream's management admitted after they bought the company back off Cadbury-Schweppes. An ad campaign starring Lenny Henry's Theophilus P. Wildebeeste, the first of many that were to crop up every few years from then on, didn't really change the situation. SodaStream still refuses to die, but that slightly farty swooshing noise of hand-pumped carbonation will, it seems, never resonate through the kitchens of the nation like it once did. The DIY pop business is long past the point of no deposit, no return.

**'SodaStream canisters were filled with oxygen and used as emergency breathing apparatus. Was there nothing it couldn't do?'**

# THE VIMTO RANGE

Vimto cordial and sparkling Vimto in cans and bottles.
For rapid VIMTO delivery simply give
JOHN NICHOLS or ALAN ISHERWOOD a ring on 061-998 8801.

# VIMTO

*We'll get'cha in the end.*

J. N. Nichols (VIMTO) PLC,
Ledson Road, Wythenshawe, Manchester M23 9NL.

# We've got'cha

## * LUCOZADE

Yet another product from the school of unimaginative brand-name contraction: glucose + lemonade = Glucozade (see also Caramac, Frisps and Pyramint), though perhaps understandably formulaic given its genesis in a pharmaceutical laboratory. A hastily renamed Lucozade spent the best part of sixty years at the bedside of the invalid and infirm, a million autumnal evening sunbeams

**Opposite:** Pile of comics: check. Schools' TV continuity: check... Lucozade (1927).

**Below:** Recovery by the end of *Words and Pictures* guaranteed.

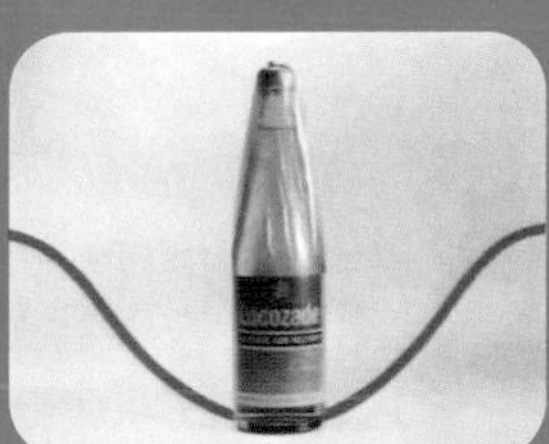

streaming through the window blinds of the ward onto a bottle of the stuff.

The crackling orange cellophane, the chemist's prescription label, the hot-water-bottle bobbles along the neck – they were all familiar sights to the blanched, the bland, the grotty, the snotty and the permanently convalescent. From Zammo Maguire to Roy Figgis, and a thousand skiving youngsters in between, the bittersweet and ironically sickly taste accompanied daytime TV for schools and colleges, feverish naps and a bucket by the side of the bed.

But from the mid-'70s onwards kids just weren't sick enough, often enough any more, leaving grown-ups to finish the bottle when there wasn't any Tizer left in the cupboard. So the 'aids recovery' tagline was binned (along with authoritative-looking magazine advert nurses) and SmithKline Beecham instead targeted stay-at-home mums in search of a sunset-yellow, glucose energy high.

**'From the mid-'70s onwards kids just weren't sick enough, often enough any more.'**

A further 'reposition' in the '80s saw a post-Olympic, pre-ZX Spectrum games Daley Thompson slo-mo his way through a series of sweat-pumping TV spots (and introduced a grateful generation to Iron Maiden's special brand of heavy metal). No longer a 'sickness' drink but a 'health' brand, Lucozade's new, palm-sized bottle, lost its outer wrapper but gained a whole new consumer demographic. Forget the latter-day NRG and Sport editions, every Sunday league footballer worth his monosaccharides knew that Lucozade was the perfect hangover cure. When taken with a full English breakfast, naturally.

## A FRUIT-BASED DRINK FOR THE LADIES

Style. Glamour. Panache. Just three qualities that are forever missing last orders in the British pub. But away from the Carling-bibbing antics of the lads, surely the ladies, perched demurely on chrome stools with little bottles of bitter lemon at their sides, are more of a class act? Not necessarily. British attempts to flog fruit juice with added savoir-faire have a tendency to go down in a blaze of deflating silliness. William Franklyn fronted Schweppes's 'Schhh... you know who' campaign for years with the slightly bemused air of an accountant who'd joined MI6 to look at the books, been mistaken for James Bond, and went uneasily along with it rather than cause a scene.

Schweppes's main rival, the Essex-based British Vitamin Company, had been marketing little bottles of fruit juice since 1949. In 1981 they rebadged their orange, tomato, grapefruit and pineapple juice under the banner Britvic 55. This number signified its content: '55% pure juice – 100% sparkle', as itemised in a series of quaint bar-side TV ads to a retro doo-wop backing. To confuse temporal matters further, they released a tie-in Class of '55 EP on none-more-swish K-Tel Records, featuring rock 'n' roll hits from that year by Bill Haley, Little Richard and the like. Were we supposed to be moving forwards or backwards here?

Unquestionably of-the-moment was a parallel development in the bid for the distaff drinker: diet pop. As so often, the Americans were way ahead of us. Royal Crown created the first low-cal cola, Diet Rite, in 1958. Initially sold by chemists, it really took off when it was moved into grocery stores in 1961. Two years later the big boys at Coke finally unleashed their riposte, a one-calorie can labelled Tab because (tenuous justification ahoy) it enabled the drinker to keep 'tabs' on their weight. (It could have been worse – Coke's computer-generated list of prospective names included Zap and Zorg.) What was a marketing no brainer on Muscle Beach cut little ice on Camber Sands, though, and when Tab

**Opposite:** The drink from over there that never made it over here. Tab (1975).

**Below:** Surprisingly, it didn't go well with crispbread. One-Cal (1976).

finally surfaced here in 1975, it struggled to gain acceptance among a populace who liked their fizz as sugary and as luminous as possible.

Nevertheless, a slimming market was deemed to be there... somewhere. 'The beautiful drink for beautiful people' may not have excited British palates but there was a tide of unsugared rivals coming up behind. Coke brought out Fresca, a four-calorie grapefruit flavour slimming drink in 1976. The same year, crispbread hawkers Energen expanded into soft drinks with One Cal, a whole range of bum-shrinking beverages, including cola, lemonade, limeade, orangeade and bitter lemon. Suddenly, Britain was slimming in earnest. The tills were alive with the sound of muesli, and the population were calorie-controlling, pinching an inch and sporting those belts that looked like tape measures. There was no better time to launch a diet drink.

There was no worse time, either. The first wave of low-calorie drinks was sweetened with saccharin, which was beginning to look exceedingly dodgy. Saccharin in particular was found to cause cancer in rats, a fact triumphantly pointed out by Peter Cook as he ostentatiously swigged from a can of Fresca on the *Russell Harty Show*. Some brands avoided sweeteners altogether, like Beecham's Bitter Sweet, which arrived in 1977 promising nothing but 'the fruit's own sugar' in the can. Other drinks, meanwhile, quietly switched from saccharin to aspartame, advertised on the cans under the brand name NutraSweet. So that was all right, then.

**'Suddenly, Britain was slimming in earnest. The tills were alive with the sound of muesli, and the population were calorie-controlling, pinching an inch and sporting those belts that looked like tape measures.'**

As a new, more conspicuously affluent, era arrived, it was finally time for some genuine continental élan. A pulp-filled sparking orange juice in a stylish 'wine bottle in a basket' bulbous glass container, Orangina was the invention of a Spanish chemist in 1936, which made its way into the pavement cafés of France by 1951. Fresh, stylish and laid back, it was everything the Stringfellows set aspired to but couldn't quite grasp. KP brought it to Britain in 1982, initially renamed Orelia after the US variant, but soon restored to its original moniker.

The UK marketing followed the French lead, with parasols, sunshine and classy dames in broad-brimmed hats, but couldn't resist adding a dash of British whimsy to taste. Orangina's major design flaw was that the pulp would sink to the bottom of the bottle, forming a pool of orange mush that looked a tad gamey to timid Brits reared on diluted squash. Thus the admen penned a cheery entreaty to 'shake the bottle – wake the drink', i.e., disperse that fearsome puddle of pulp and all will be well, as a bottle of the stuff danced a merry jig on the café table through the magic of cotton. Outside the modish Gallic world, cuteness beats poise every time.

In 1983 came the big one. Well, the big two, as both Diet Coke and Diet Pepsi arrived in British shops. Coke swiftly gained the upper hand, after an initial, feeble 'slim 'n' sporty' campaign was nixed in favour of slow-mo sunkissed youth, soft rock power chords and 'just for the taste of it'. The first diet drink with full-fat branding romped

**Opposite:** Poured of the flies – zip up with Diet Pepsi (1983). 'Urgh! It's got bits in!' The UK took time to appreciate Orangina (1982).

**Below:** The perfect accompaniment to a Carla Lane sitcom starring Felicity Kendal. Bitter Sweet (1977).

to commercial victory, bypassing the increasing number of health scares centred around NutraSweet, beginning with a *New England Journal of Medicine* report on its 'mind and mood altering effects' which carried undesirable overtones of Coke's cocaine-addled origins.

So passed ten relatively untroubled, big-haired, backlit years, to the air-punching accompaniment of Robin Beck's Diet Coke-pushing number one anthem 'The First Time'. Then came the most foolhardy innovation of all: clear soda! Crystal Pepsi led the way, but Coke's rival, Tab Clear, was the only one that made it to Britain – but only just. Whether it was the defiantly unfunny mock newsreel TV ads, or just the general pointlessness of the entire venture, the drink failed to last the year. Subsequent sugar-free spin-offs – Pepsi Max, Coke Zero et al. – were reliably brown in hue, and aimed not so much at inscrutable, hard-to-please women of the world, but short-trousered skateboarding goofballs who'll buy the first shiny thing that floats in front of them.

The juice market underwent a similar move away from pencil skirts and into combat trousers. Britvic introduced Citrus Spring in 1986, aiming to do for canned soft drinks what they'd already done for the little bottles behind the bar. Made with spring water and containing more than twice as much natural fruit juice as other cans, and retailing at a corresponding 3p more, it looked set to break the cosmopolitan pop market. Until, that was, they drafted in rubber-faced funnyman Phil Cool and a puppet kangaroo for some over-literal 'spring'-based commercials. 'Pogo sticks could well be a part of the promotional programme,' added a spokesman vaguely. Out for good went fumbling attempts at finesse, and in came the blueprint for ladette-friendly mixers like Britvic's late '90s 55 replacement, the *Little Britain* tour-sponsoring J2O. Good old British marketing – gains admission to the swankiest clubs, and with endearing regularity falls straight through the bar.

## * QUATRO

Pop in the '70s was all froth and fructose. As an altogether more vain era dawned, soft drink merchants looked beyond the ranks of gurning kids to their self-consciously stylish older siblings. How can we sell soda to these moody young trendsetters?

**Opposite:** Gene Hunt's fizzy tipple of choice, perfect with a plate of 'oops. Quatro (1983).

**Below:** There won't be Squirt in Africa this Christmas-time. Or, indeed, in the UK (1983).

First came Squirt. A steady seller in the US since 1938, the tangy grapefruit crush arrived here in May 1983 under the auspices of Coca-Cola bottler CC Soft Drinks, promising to drag the nation's drinking out of the over-sweetened '70s and into a zingy new age. When Paula Yates helpfully waved a can about in the Band Aid video, Squirt seemed set for greatness, but by the time the single hit number one, the drink was dead in the water. 'People were trying to make it happen with grapefruit,' lamented Squirt's marketing manager. 'There was the grapefruit diet, the Grapefruit Marketing Council... but it's not a popular flavour.'

As Squirt hit the buffers, CC's owners Grand Metropolitan set about flogging their dithering offshoot to Coca-Cola. All was not lost, however, as CC already had another new drink on the go. This time they hedged their bets by augmenting the sad old grapefruit flavour with orange, lime and pineapple, slapped some painfully up-to-date graphics on the can, and rather smugly concluded, 'it's a miracle – but we've made it'.

Quatro's TV campaign was a doozy. Directors Rocky Morton and Annabel Jankel, creators of *Max Headroom* and as of-their-time as it was possible to be, created a post-apocalyptic future in which lone youths roamed the neon-lit streets, restless, feral, yet somehow still able to get hold of enough Studio Line to maintain their luxuriant Paul Young-style coiffures. Using every faddish device in the book – scratch video, stabbed synthesiser chords, beams of dusty blue light – it told an everyday tale of a renegade hipster using karate to extract a bespoke can of Quatro from a steam-powered vending machine made of unnecessarily lumpy cast iron. 'MALFUNCTION!' This all made perfect sense at the time.

The adverts certainly made a splash, but Quatro never became the smash the Coke grandees desired. When they pooled their soft drink interests with Schweppes in 1987, the lacklustre crush was rationalised out of existence, securing its place as the first point of call for carbonated nostalgic mockery. Tonight, thank God it's them instead of you.

## * LILT

The tropical fruit crush is possibly the great underachiever of the soft drink family. Folk may love or loathe colas, ginger beers and orangeades of various hues and half-lives, but the slightly citrusy, slightly green combination of grapefruit and pineapple juices never seems to provoke very strong passions for or against. It's just sort of... nice, something you might drink if it's hot, and there's nothing much else on offer.

**Opposite:** No, it ferments of its own accord! Lilt (1973).

**Below:** A rare stereotype-free ad.

When Coca-Cola entered this unglamorous market in 1973, they had their work cut out. With Lilt, they played safe. Palm trees, white beaches and vertically bisected pineapples were the wholly predictable order of the day. Sales were steady enough, but no reason to tap-dance on the boardroom table. Like Mars's Bounty, it combined bland package holiday imagery with uncontroversial flavouring to produce something people consumed in their thousands, but about which nobody seemed terribly enthusiastic – the beverage world's very own *Emmerdale Farm.*

Things bucked up in 1976, when competition appeared in the form of Schweppes's Cariba. Similar flavours, similar tropical overtones, and cans depicting a very similar fruity autopsy. The two crushes shared an uneasy peace for years, until in 1983 Lilt got serious, and began building a self-consciously cool brand image, all laid-back West Indian swagger and lashings of cod reggae, to try to, well, crush the young pretender. A carefree coastal idyll populated by sunkissed catalogue models was created. This Caribbean paradise was serviced by the Lilt Man, a cheery Jamaican equivalent of United Dairies' finest, tootling about the island in a float made from lashed-together driftwood.

It was a campaign dripping with precision-tooled nonchalance. But like a virginal first-year Eng. Lit. student with a wall of Bob Marley posters, Coke were fooling nobody. Lilt itself remained the same unremarkable fizz it had always been, and no amount of well-meaning yet rather patronising racial stereotypes or hip-by-association promotional material (peaking in 1985 with a free 'Totally Tropical Tape' of summery pop hits) was going to change that.

In the end, the matter was settled in a more mundane fashion. Coke joined forces with Schweppes in 1987, with the former company inevitably taking priority. Thus, exit Cariba stage left, leaving Lilt to rule over the grapefruit crush kingdom unchallenged. Which was nice.

**'Like Mars's Bounty, it was something about which nobody seemed terribly enthusiastic – the beverage world's very own *Emmerdale Farm*.'**

## BOTTOM OF THE POPS

Away from the multinational beverages that command the lion's share of the market, there's a whole world of lesser soft drinks fighting for survival. On the surface, it's all searingly bright colours, jolly fat lettering, and cartoon kids smiling with unrestrained delight despite the fact they've been drawn with one eye higher than the other. Underneath, it's a sometimes murky world of iffy trademarks, passing off and brackish aftertastes.

Many small pop houses nurtured grand aspirations of becoming 'a world-class drinks business' which were clearly beyond their parochial means, but the tenacity with which they stuck to them was all the more endearing for that. Who doesn't think the world would be a much better place if, instead of nasty evil Coca-Cola dominating everything, the globe was instead benignly ruled by good old Hendrys Double Top?

The biggest sources of budget soda are the supermarkets. Every chain worth its salt has long produced its own version of the big names of pop, priced them significantly lower and stacked them within slightly easier reach since the 1950s. But, as with so much junk food, the watershed moment for supermarket pop came in the summer of '76, when parched customers, unable to reach a standpipe, were prepared to fork out for bottled fizz rather than collapse from dehydration. Once the big names had gone, they started mainlining the shops' own brands, and store managers were careful to order more of their own cola before placing

**Opposite:** The worlds of snooker and darts collide with Hendrys Double Top Cola (1961). Celebrate your divvy with a Co-op shandy (1979).

**Below:** Twist your tongue round Corona Coola Cola (1963). You might not be too impressed with Presto Orangeade (1981).

requests for an extra batch of Pepsi. Supermarket soft drinks (and, for the first time, supermarket bottled water like Safeway's Isabelle) were finally on the map.

By and large, shop brands opt for straight-up, utilitarian names. You're in the Co-op, you see a can labelled 'Co-op lemonade', it's a fair bet that you're looking at a can of lemonade manufactured and sold under the auspices of the Co-op. But when shops decide to give their pop line a name of its own, things get complicated. Sometimes the names chosen for own-brand ranges gave the lie to the parent store's pretensions. Hence aspirational middle-league grocer Gateway filled their shelves with would-be sophisticated Le Fizz Cola, while salt-of-the-earth Asda conjured up more of a package holiday vibe with their range: Sundorm.

For the most part, these cosmetic differences were all that really separated one own-brand drink from another. The contents were supplied by a handful of specialist manufacturers, the most ubiquitous being Canada's Cott Beverages (slogan: 'It's Cott to be good!'). Nevertheless, some own brands inspired fierce loyalty, and a 1991 taste test in *Which?* magazine rated in-house colas from Sainsbury's and Scottish grocery chain William Low above Pepsi. Perhaps emboldened by this triumph, Sainsbury's went on to challenge the big boys directly three years later, by slapping a label on their Classic Cola featuring distinctly familiar squiggly white-on-red lettering, until Coca-Cola themselves called foul and made them take it off.

Minor pop brands have their own weird naming conventions. Vague adjectives were the order of

**Below:** Two beverages of parental embarrassment. Don't let your friends see you drinking My Mums (1987) or Jolly Pops (1984).

the day at one point, be it for the hopefully titled Jolly Pops, or the notionally fashion-conscious low-budget bottled froth of Pontefract's Trendy Pops. Or you could try a crafty rhyme like quixotic perfume magnate Carlo Dini, who came to Britain to market his additive-free Rola Cola in the early 1980s for a test run that was fleeting, but still long enough for the young Peter Kay to formulate half an hour of nostalgic material around it. (The drink lives on overseas, and comes in packaging of which, the company excitably claims, 'THERE IS NO CAN LIKE IT IN THE WORLD'.)

Grocery chain Happy Shopper attempted to give their own-brand drinks a homely feel with the moniker 'My Mums', the chief selling point of which, for some reason, was its ability to 'send fizzy bubbles up your nose'. Unfortunately, when it came to registering the trademark in 1987, this 'composite mark comprised of laudatory, descriptive and non-distinctive elements' was refused by the Board of Trade on the grounds that it might confuse the populace. 'The expression "My Mums cola", ruled William Aldous QC, 'could be understood to mean the cola mother buys (or even the cola drink she makes). The expression does not tell you which brand mother buys, unless you happen to know that "My Mums" is, or is intended to be, a distinctive element of a trade mark.' This kind of logic-chopping wouldn't have been out of place in a sketch by '90s comedians Lee and Herring, who had to enlist the BBC props department to recreate a bottle of My Mums Lemonade for the purposes of mockery in 1998.

WATCH MY MUMS ROCKET OFF YOUR SHELVES!
My Mums TEA BAGS
My Mums MEATY DOG FOOD
My Mums COLA
Mum Knows Best
My Mums PEELED PLUM TOMATOES
mmmmm! mamma mia
My Mums TABLE SALT
My Mums PURE ORANGE JUICE
My Mums PROCESSED PEAS
My Mums TOILET CLEANSER
OVER 130 QUALITY PRODUCTS AVAILABLE NATIONALLY IN OUR 96 BRANCHES
NEW COLOURFUL PACKAGING GIVES EXTRA THRUST TO My Mums—STOCK My Mums TODAY AND WATCH YOUR SALES ROCKET!
GIVE YOUR PROFITS A BOOST BY STOCKING THE My Mums RANGE OF EVERYDAY QUALITY PRODUCTS—HIGH PROFIT ON RETURN AND LONG TERM LOW, LOW PRICES MEANS My Mums IS THE NO. 1 BRAND FOR INDEPENDENT RETAILERS!
My Mums is out of this world!
LINFOOD CASH & CARRY
Mum Knows Best
The NO.1 Cash & Carry

**Below:** The drink whose sales mimicked the sex life of its mascot. Panda Pops (1975).

One low-rent pop marque stands above (or should that be below?) all others as a nationally recognised signifier of cheap and cheerful cola. Launched by Dorset brewers Hall and Woodhouse in 1975, Panda Pops didn't mess about with those difficult older demographics. They decorated the cans with a cartoon of China's cutest export since Ken Hom and went straight for the under-tens.

And here's where we come to the vexed question every parent asks themselves when tempted to save a few pence on a lesser known cola: what the hell's in this stuff? While no laws or regulations of the time were transgressed, it's still safe to say that Panda Pops' chemical curiosity was on a par with Iggy Pop's. They knew precisely what the little 'uns wanted – muscular flavours, nostril-seeking bubbles and colours above and beyond the visible spectrum – and delivered it by the pint. The usual citrus-based tastes were augmented by a wave of dentally lethal concoctions of Panda's own devising: bubble gum, sherbet lemon, strawberry jelly and ice cream, rhubarb and custard. Colourings paid no heed to internationally agreed conventions: cola was green, raspberryade blue. The only exception was the reliably brown Panda Shandy, made with lashings of Hall and Woodhouse's famous Badger Bitter.

Then, as if somehow to atone for their sins, Panda was revamped in 1987 in more medically acceptable terms, jettisoning artificial ingredients and basing the drink on pure spring water. A more adult line, Arriba, arrived in 1989, quickly renamed Rio Riva after Schweppes complained it was too similar to their Cariba crush. (A rather petty complaint, seeing as the latter was then well on the way to oblivion itself.) The zany flavours kept on coming too, including a Black Lemonade to cash in on 1999's much-hyped solar eclipse.

The millennium itself wasn't so good for Panda. Sales fell, and it was sold off to Vimto supremos Nichols, who tinkered around with it for a few years before finally putting the old beast down in early 2011. The imperial age of the endearingly amateur pop purveyor was long gone. You can, however, still come across the odd can of luridly badged dodgy stuff if you know where to look. Let the unthinking masses have their Coke. You can tell a connoisseur by his can of Pin-Hi.

BIG JOHN'S IN TOWN!
BIG JOHN'S AMERICAN CHOCOLATE SODA POP...
. . . the new soft drink sensation that swept the States is now available in the U.K. but only from J. N. Nichols the VIMTO people.
* BIG 2 LITRE BOTTLE
* BIG P.O.S. BACK UP
* BIG VALUE
* BIG PROFITS
* BIG MISTAKE IF YOU DON'T STOCK IT!
BIG JOHN'S
American
CHOCOLATE
FLAVOUR
SODA POP
BIG JOHN'S
American
CHOCOLATE
FLAVOUR
SODA POP
2 LITRE
A GREAT NEW DRINK FROM VIMTO
J. N. Nichols (VIMTO) p.l.c.,
Ledson Road, Wythenshawe, Manchester, M23 9GL. Tel: 061 998 8801

## *R. WHITES LEMONADE

The 'R' stands for 'Robert'. Along with his wife Mary, he formulated his original lemonade in Camberwell in 1845, distributing it to local grocers and via the reliable fleet of flat-bed lorries travelling up the highways and byways of south London. The operation steadily expanded over the following century, until in 1969 it was subsumed into the brewing chain Whitbread, which meant a pub

**Opposite:** Inspiring furtive pyjama-clad creeping since 1845.

**Below:** It's a-one a-those a-nights. A-gain.

presence to sit on top of the van rounds. Business was booming, but there was still room for improvement.

The brand gained nationwide fame in 1973, thanks to a campaign courtesy of 'jingle king' Rod Allen, also the originator of such entries in the Great British Songbook as 'This is the Age of the Train', 'Milk's Gotta Lotta Bottle' and 'That's the Wonder of Woolies'. The ad employed gangly mime artist Julian Chagrin (previously most famous for playing invisible tennis in swinging London film classic *Blow-Up*) to sneak downstairs to the fridge and croon an Elvis-lite number about pop addiction. Said song was actually delivered in the dulcet tones of Ross MacManus (previously most famous for tootling in the Joe Loss Orchestra, latterly famous as the dad of Elvis Costello, who helped his dad out with backing harmonies on this job). It's a tribute to Allen's ear for a catchy inanity that the secret lemonade drinker more than held his own against the Cresta bear, the Corona bubbles and other mascots of the 'personality pop' boom.

In a subsequent ad, Chagrin's problem drinker graduated to full rock stardom as lead singer of the Thirst, a band that featured MacManus on keyboards and a young E. Costello on guitar and backing vocals, making what looked like a pre-emptive bid for lemonade-themed chart success, which was sadly never released. When the film on that started to wear out, an '80s-friendly sequel was made starring Aylesbury's daft punk one-hit wonder John Otway as the pyjama-clad addict seeking help from the Samaritans. Then in 1984, despite having achieved cultural penetration to the stage where a Secret Lemonade Drinkers Handicap was being run at Lingfield, the ad was cut. Too old-fashioned, you see, with its memorable song, likeably goofy protagonist and other such outdated elements. As the '90s dawned, advertising bible *Campaign* confidently dismissed the jingle as a thing of the past.

They were proved wrong in 1992, as the Chagrin original was revived for some pioneering retro fun, with assorted amusing celebs like Ronnie Corbett, Saint and Greavsie and John McEnroe taking the place of Chagrin's unimpressed wife behind the fridge door. (For McEnroe, the admen flew to Paris and built the kitchen there around him.) Those head-slapping upstarts at Tango were duly reminded who was the daddy of carbonated clowning.

## TOO ORANGEY FOR CROWS

Once upon a time, to everyone below a certain age, advertising had little or no effect. Pre-school responsibilities were slight. The folks did all the worrying and the buying for the house. Days were filled with Plasticine and Play-Doh, and pants were filled with poo. Cats and mice had fights when the cartoons came on TV, then beans and potato waffles materialised at dinner time with a Tupperware beaker of squash. Bath time, story, lights out: the steady routine. And they all lived happily ever after. The end.

Except it wasn't quite the end. Advertisers, past-masters at selling to adults and adolescents, also had their sights set on the ankle-biters, and that meant infiltrating a tricky parent-child dynamic. Sweets and crisps and snacks and pop – the gaudy, glossy, easy wins – were too easily dismissed as 'junk' by Mum and Dad. Good-for-you food wouldn't appeal to kids. Full of vitamins and minerals? Yawn. Where's the fun stuff, man?

The manufacturers had to box clever. Haranguing the breadwinners was out; the regulators put paid to that. No more ads with kids swinging off gates, pleading for sugary gratification. Those plans for a chorus line of screaming toddlers in a hypoglycaemic seizure would have to be shelved. In any case, all the research showed that children took an instant dislike to the other children they saw on television. Precious few options remained.

So a litany of issues faced Schweppes as they tried to revitalise their third-in-its-field fruit

**Opposite:** Hope that dog got his royalties. Kia-Ora (1983).

cordial at the tail end of the 1970s. Kia-Ora – a name pinched from the Maori words for 'good health' – was under threat of being binned by the major stores. Its assorted cup-drink incarnations, glimpsed during Pearl & Dean ads down the local flea-pit, were being pa-pa pa-pa pa-pa pa-pa-pensioned off too. Flamenco, Cascade, Suncrush, Sunfresh – varieties that, ironically, diluted the umbrella brand – were gently scrapped, and the money hoarded until the time was right. Because something else was going down in juice town; something with a straw up the side; something ready to drink.

**Below:** An appropriately bland advert for Quosh (1983).

In 1977 Libby's Orange 'C' became the first fruit squash to appear in single-serve, lunchbox-sized soft foil pouches. (The now more familiar Capri Sun didn't check in until 1983, for some reason calling itself 'the fruit sniffer'.) Hot on its heels, Bradford-based George Barraclough's GeeBee Juice shipped in revolutionary new Swedish Tetra-Briks. Even Robinson's, the enduring archetypal barley water, succumbed and introduced their own stolid ready-to-drink line. The profits stacked up, like the cartons themselves, whose list of unique selling points went on and on. They were innovative, hygienic, portable, convenient, tasty, healthy, simple and cheap. By 1983, Beecham's Quosh and Ribena, relative latecomers, were the market leaders.

In this suddenly crowded space, Kia-Ora looked crushed, but Schweppes were unbowed. Ten years earlier, the Cresta bear had shown the way and they were hopeful that cartoon lightning could strike twice. Luckily, John Webster, the brains behind the original ursine campaign, had learned a lot in the interim, not least about young children. They were, he concluded, 'unclouded by logic', their reference points rooted not in the real world, but in the language of Looney Tunes, Merrie Melodies and Silly Symphonies.

They careered about with heads full of magic – free form, blue sky, noodling ideas where everything was possible, and unquestioningly plausible. Appeal to that, and you wouldn't need to hit them with a sales pitch at all.

Webster returned from a sojourn at the home of ABBA's producer, Michael B. Tretow, in Sweden to find the Kia-Ora brief on his desk. It was the start of an extraordinary campaign. One of Tretow's tracks, 'Fido', recorded under the pseudonym Caramba, was a jaunty little calypso layered heavily with sampled dog barks. Webster wanted to marry this 'wild' new sound with kid-friendly retro animation and tasked Oscar Grillo's Klactoveesedstene studio (itself named after a Charlie Parker jazz number) with visualising it. Grillo, an award-winning commercial artist, pillaged sources far and wide to create a literal parade of authentic characters, from Disney's tar baby, via *Dumbo*'s gang of vexatious crows, to his very own award-winning *Seaside Woman*. He even insisted on animating it all at a Hollywood-faithful twenty-four frames per second, rather than television's more usual twelve.

The resulting tartrazine-tinted ad, with its whimsical, sub-Stooges 'I'll be your dawg' hook, caught kids' imaginations. Letters poured in to Webster's office, demanding a full-length TV show or a single release of the music – a wish granted later in the year, as a full-length version now titled 'Fedora' (all brand names duly excised) peaked at a lowly fifty-six in the charts. Fellow ad exec Martin Lambie-Nairn joined in the back-slapping, calling the campaign 'brilliantly observed', although he and many others seemed unfazed by the indiscriminate importing of racist 1940s stereotypes to the present-day living room. It wasn't even unique – Nabisco's Shreddies were also advertised by a gang of zoot-suited cartoon crows at the time – but, far from being delisted, Kia-Ora saw its distribution rise 20 per cent over the next three years, generating more sales than the commercial alone.

Soon, the other drinks brands were hammering on Oscar Grillo's door. Libby's developed a product in a white Tetra-Pak that passed the shelf test (i.e. it could stand on a shelf for a year without turning mouldy or melting through the laminate) but they didn't have a clue what to do with it. In 1983 it was tossed to the creatives at Leo Burnett over a round of golf as an informal, 'have a go if you like' project, eventually falling into the in-tray of junior copywriter Andy Blackford and art director Andy Hill. The pair toyed with predictable names like 'Jungle Juice'

**Opposite:** Joke sunglasses, backwards cap – someone give that child a slap.

**Below:** 'Looks pretty weird but it tastes just fine!' Not the most inspiring of taglines, that. Moonshine (1985).

until inspiration hit (on a Jubilee line train between Baker Street and Swiss Cottage), and Blackford drafted some lyrics for what would become the 'Um Bongo' song.

Grillo's accompanying film, even in rough cut, generated phenomenal levels of recall in research tests – possibly because the name of the product was repeated several thousand times in thirty seconds – which pleased the bosses back at Nestlé. On the back of their success, Blackford and Hill were invited to come up with an entirely new concept, and so devised a drink that blended ten wild berry fruits with a splash of *The Dukes of Hazzard*. Aimed at six- to twelve-year-olds, Moonshine was launched in 1985, again featuring an Oscar Grillo animation and a Blackford-penned jingle, this time about redneck, bootlegging weasels. Any resemblance between the ad's amphibious antagonist, Sheriff Nathaniel Toad, and members of Paul McCartney's frog chorus was purely coincidental. (Although Grillo had worked with Linda and Paul in the past, he wasn't involved in that particular atrocity.)

While Stanley Stoat and brother Irvine raced for the county line, Libby's took their juices on tour. For one lucky generation, memories of the 1984 Pontin's Um Bongo Hot Wheels BMX competition were eclipsed only by Radio Lollipop's triumphant Um Bongo roadshow three short years later. Moonshine begat a board game and some 117 events at Butlin's Holiday Camps but the ads' influence was felt further afield. Quosh's new campaign featured faux 'interrupted transmissions' from aliens on the dying planet of Zarg, and Unigate Dairies sacked off the Humphries in favour of a new gang of cuddly-looking animals (also available in glove puppet form) for Crazy Milk drinks. (Another milk drink, W.F.L.A., tarted about with the post-modern slogan, 'No tin, no fizz, no lobster'. No sales, either.)

Citra's *Danger Mouse* drinks also tried to ride animation's new wave of popularity but, if anything, the David Jason-voiced Cosgrove Hall cartoon was too clever for its own good. Wittier it may have been, but the simple, short tunes and phrases of Kia-Ora and Um Bongo were easier for kids to mimic; the characters – more like clowns than animals – easier to understand. So, even if their children didn't explicitly ask for the products, mums and dads were in no doubt what to buy. That takes a special kind of persuasive genius. Yet it's the pretentious black and white art-house eyewash of Guinness's surfer ad that routinely wins Greatest Advert awards. Where's the justice, eh?

## ✻ UM BONGO

A frankly cloying tropical mix drink which nevertheless was ingrained on the public consciousness thanks to its ritual, rhythmic advertising jingle. That said, the core refrain, 'Um Bongo, Um Bongo, they drink it in the Congo,' sounds less of an endorsement than it does an indictment when taking into account the years of political and social instability in the area. As the Democratic

**Opposite and below:** Currently being drunkenly recited at an All Bar One near you. Um Bongo (1983).

Republic fought to gain its independence, Libby's PR prudently shied away from images of brutal force, ethnic strife and civil war, which is maybe why they soaked up 10 per cent of the juice box market inside six months.

Instead, cartoon anthropomorphism was the order of the day. Viewers were treated to a lively and inviting animation featuring a 'sunny, funny' jungle-based assembly line dedicated to the sole purpose of sating Britain's thirst for Um Bongo. What a team they were! Whereas the man from Del Monte would walk only briefly among the lower ranks before delivering the all-important yea or nay, and Five Alive seemed to spring full-armoured from the ground, Um Bongo was an altogether more egalitarian outfit. For example, what Westerner would dare claim dominion over the hippo who 'took an apricot, a guava and a mango' (along with sugar and additional flavourings), juggled them, then 'danced a dainty tango'? (Answer: none. The *Hippopotamus amphibius*, though a mostly herbivorous mammal, is rightly considered one of the most aggressive and dangerous animals in Africa, even more so if it is depicted as some sort of demented pink music-hall act.) Truly it is a brave new world with such creatures in it.

Yet, while there is also a name-check for the rhino (brand strategist), parrot (art director) and python (quality control) in the advert's on-screen captions, little mention is made of the Congo's remaining potential animal workforce. Given the area's great biodiversity, it's difficult to imagine that at least one rare or endemic species failed to offer its services as shop steward to the fauna of the rainforest factory floor, although the presence of a troublesome marmoset (presumably illegally imported mandarin-picking labour from the Amazonian basin) might have put paid to the unionisation of Um Bongo's blue-collar (and/or blue-arsed) employees.

Back home, Libby's managerial menagerie launched a London Zoo-hosted promotion to push the tropical tipple to kids. Fifteen gorilla-suited employees were released about the various enclosures and the first to find the lot won a free safari holiday in Africa. History does not record whether all the costumed staffers returned to work later that day or if one took up permanent residence on a tyre-swing, but legend has it that only a lucrative offer of a role in a Cadbury's Dairy Milk advert tempted him back.

**Opposite:** Alan Finch saves the planet with his sixteen-incher.

## ICE WATER FOR BLOOD

Coming in at a respectable fifth place in Channel 4's Top 100 Most Likely To Be Mentioned By Stand-Up Comedians On Archive-ransacking List Shows, it's Jubbly, everyone's favourite tetrahedron-shaped orange nostalgia touchstone. In the days before Del Boy, and way ahead of Austin Powers (by way of a plethora of playground ribaldry), Jubbly was nothing but an innocent drink. Referring to neither bonus nor boobs at the time, 'luvvly jubbly' (or 'jubblies') was the slogan employed by Sunray of New Barnet in the 1950s to flog their otherwise ordinary ochre-tinged offering.

The outstanding innovation was in the packaging, an airtight, four-sided, plastic-coated paperboard affair from Swedish design genius Ruben Rausing and his team. The 200ml Tetra Classic debuted in 1958 for milk and still drinks and was quickly employed to store and transport Sunray's squash to the nation's shopkeepers. Rumour has it that enterprising proprietors then froze the drinks to prolong their life, and sold them on at a penny extra mark-up 'to pay for the electricity'. Snipped at the corner, the triangular blocks of orange ice were sucked and squeezed by little tykes until they turned white.

Revisionists might trace the ancestry of the ice lolly back no further, but the august publication *Ice Cream Topics* noted in 1949 that water ices 'capture the kiddy trade, being cheaper than cones and wafers filled with ice cream'. Undeniably, the snooty bosses at Lyons Maid saw the ice lolly as a poor alternative to proper ice cream, fit only for the penniless and beggarly. Children, conforming all too unhappily to that description, lapped them up, but it wasn't until the 1970s that the market really exploded. It would have taken a brave company spokesman to adopt the phrase 'kiddy trade' in those more enlightened times.

SLUSH PUPPIE

There is anecdotal evidence for an even earlier provenance of the ice lolly, in 1905. This American version, it is claimed, was invented by the then eleven-year-old Frank Epperson, experimenting with drink powders from his local grocery store at the height of San Francisco's 'big freeze'. A wooden stirrer left in a glass of pink lemonade overnight became the stick down the middle of Epperson's Icicle, although the lack of financial and technical support available to a pre-teen boy at the turn of the century hampered its early development. In 1923 Epperson was granted a patent, but never did trademark the name, so it fell to his own son, George, later to christen the lolly in honour of his father: the Popsicle was born.

*ADVERTISEMENT*

# ALAN FINCH alias Super Freeze

ALAN FINCH IS NO ORDINARY SCHOOLBOY....

AS THE BIG HEATWAVE CONTINUES

ZOO

WHITEY THE POLAR BEAR GETS MORE AND MORE UNHAPPY

THIS CALLS FOR DRASTIC ACTION

SWEETSHOP

ONE BITE OF A "MR FREEZE" FREEZE DRINK & ALAN BECOMES

ZOO

WOW! AN ICE BLAST BEAM!

ZAP

ZOO

WHITEY'S IN HIS ELEMENT NOW....

...BUT I THINK THE KANGAROOS ARE HOPPING MAD!

5p MR FREEZE IS AVAILABLE IN 4 TASTE-TINGLING FLAVOURS - COLA, ORANGE, LEMON & STRAWBERRY. NOW YOU CAN MAKE THESE SAME FANTASTIC FLAVOURS LAST OVER 3 TIMES AS LONG WITH NEW 15p GI-NORMOUS MR FREEZE.

WITH GI-NORMOUS MR FREEZE, ICE IS THRICE AS NICE!

ACTUAL SIZE IS OVER 16 INCHES LONG!

Although domestic freezers were commonplace in the US by the 1930s, they didn't achieve the same degree of proliferation across the UK for another forty years. Until then, even the most unexciting of ice pops was seen as a melting miracle spirited from the glacial depths of Jack Frost's very own cool box. In the Swinging Sixties, listeners to pirate Radio London, huddled under the covers with a trannie pressed to their ear, would have heard ads for Glenville Fridge Freeze Ice Pops between the hits of the Troggs and P.J. Proby. Winter or summer, these Wigan-produced ice poles came in four flavours and sizes, heat-sealed in a Melinex polyester laminate courtesy of ICI, and were stocked in supermarkets, cash and carries, and corner shops. The tongue-staining contents often tasted as synthetic as the plastic sleeve, so it was difficult to know where one ended and the other began, but that didn't diminish their popularity. Far from it.

Leaf International, knowing that kids homed in on anything remotely likely to exacerbate their ADHD, launched the 'stronger' flavoured Mr. Freeze brand. Choices included cola, strawberry and razzberry, a long, screenwash-blue ice pop they promised would 'knock you sideways'.

Wells Drinks of Worcestershire, previously better known for Jaffa orange juice and spring water, promoted their more sedate range of Dolphin Freezpops with a send-off coupon for swimmer's inflatable armbands. Glenville remained unassailable as the top of the pops, however, when in 1973 they managed to flog 230,000 to the inhabitants of Greenland, including Eskimos living on the 10,000-foot-thick Arctic ice-cap. (They have over 100 different words for 'irony', you know.)

When Glenville finally retired from the scene to start a new company threading camels through the eyes of needles, the ice pop was superseded by the ice crystal drink, or slushie. Somportex of London, an import and distribution outfit whose holding company's share prices clogged up the business pages of the broadsheets, secured the UK rights to this sector's breakthrough brand. Represented by a bobble-hatted beagle, the Slush Puppie was the brainchild of Ohio-born Will Radcliff, who conceived both the product's vast dispensing machine and unique business model. The first franchised cup was served in 1972 and,

**Opposite:** Your basic fruity ice. Wall's Strawberry Sparkle (1967).

**Below:** D. Trotter unavailable for comment at time of writing. Jubbly (1950).

five years later, British kids were queuing up to chug down a litre or so of frozen cherry or lemon-lime flavour in one sitting. A new phenomenon, brain freeze – or 'the Slush Puppie migraine' – had arrived.

Conscious that they were missing out on what had become a lucrative concern, Lyons Maid dropped their high-and-mighty attitude to the ice lolly business, although they were keen to be seen as 'juicier' than their rivals. Orange Maid ices were heavily plugged in the 1972 Children's Film Foundation film, *Zoo Robbery*, wherein they were used as bait to trap an escaped yeti. Wall's rival Orange Frutie, sadly useless for ensnaring mythical beasts, was another 'drink on a stick', but both companies were equally active at the cheaper end of the Frigidaire. Wall's Lemonade Sparkle vied for attention with the Lyon Maid's Cola Smash and dozens of no-brand Special, Squeeze and Quench lollies. In the end, Wall's sank £400,000 into a single TV campaign to promote the launch of Calippo, a 'child refreshment brand' no more sophisticated than a sorbet in a cardboard chute.

The frozen drinks trade was hotting up. Despite the immortality conferred on it by John Sullivan's perky Peckham trader, and a million misappropriating Moroccan market stallholders after that, 'luvvly jubbly' was discontinued when Sunray Drinks folded in 1984. A disloyal, disaffected and dehydrated kiddy trade immediately found an alternative – frozen Kwenchy cup drinks from Calypso. These corrugated containers were at least as old as Jubbly and came pre-filled and fitted with a thin film lid. A low price point ensured that retailers made money hand over fist, and the short incubation period meant any tuck shop entrepreneur could briskly establish their own fruitful icemongery business.

Still, nothing quite pushed buttons like the prismatic Jubbly and, true enough, a tragic tug of love was just around the corner. Calypso's owners, Cooke Bros of Tattenhall, tried repeatedly to win the rights from Gerber Foods (makers of Libby's fruit drinks), eventually wresting them away after a lamentable TV tie-in with *Gladiators* and a prolonged Patent Office review. In 2005 Jubbly returned to the shelves in its original Tetra-Pak – except, of course, it was considerably smaller than in its 1950s heyday. Even Derek Trotter would have seen through Calypso's slippery PR flim-flam about making it more convenient for junior-sized hands. No amount of retro box-ticking, Chopper bike competition, 'will this do?' promotional activity can excuse it, either. You just can't go around shrinking people's childhood memories – and, for a stone-cold classic like Jubbly, that goes doubly.

## LICKED INTO SHAPE

Of all the goodies in the corner shop, the ice cream has been around the longest – and not just in the 'best before' sense. As a manufactured product, it hails from as far back as biblical times, to King Solomon, whose milk and honey was liable to have been mixed and frozen in ice. In breadth of scope, it has influenced writers as notable as Voltaire, Ralph Waldo Emerson and Raekwon of the Wu-Tang Clan. 'French-vanilla, butter-pecan, chocolate-deluxe – even caramel sundaes is gettin' touched.' Admittedly, the philosophy of the great thinkers isn't as catchy as it used to be.

Make no mistake, though. Ice cream is as much about ideology as it is technology. Modern-day manufacturing, delivery and refrigeration processes may be responsible for putting that Magnum in your hand but, for hundreds of years, ice cream was the privilege of kings, emperors and explorers. Well into the nineteenth century, the bourgeoisie jealously guarded their luxury dairy desserts from highly defended Berkeley Square parlours. Ice cream remained bound up in the rhetoric of class warfare and the mealy-mouthed lip service of politicians. What else can explain the Strawberry Split, the very definition of socialist division, with its red, New Labour skin concealing a militant vanillitant interior?

**Opposite:** A feat of sub-zero engineering. Wall's Strawberry Split (1967).

**Below:** A favourite with David Vine. Wall's Superstar, circa 1975.

In 1917, as the British proletariat fought in the trenches, the Ministry of Food banned dairy ice cream back home. This led to a prolonged period of experimentation led chiefly by Pritchitts of London, makers of Frigidix vegetable oil, to promote ice cream made with vegetable fat. The result – in the US it would be called Mellorine – had a longer shelf life and could be deep-frozen. It became the accepted taste of ice cream to plebeian Britain for over fifty years. The manifesto was hidden in plain sight, written right there on the packet.

'Contains non-milk fat' was a largely ignored four-word warning which masked a multitude of sins: calcium phosphate, sodium phospha stabiliser, glyceryl monostearate, all battling to hold together the artificial sweeteners, colours and flavourings that went into an average ice cream.

Not that 'going organic' was any better in those days. Dairy hygiene was poor – a major 1946 typhoid outbreak was traced to ice creams served in the Welsh seaside town of Aberystwyth, probably the last notable thing to happen there – so anything that could be frozen or dried and later reconstituted at point of sale was a bonus. Proprietary industrial ice cream powders, all apparently inspiration for team-names on *The Apprentice* – Luxona, Ensolac, Apex – flourished. Meanwhile, the manufacturers started to obfuscate in the marketing blurb, as these ellipsis-mad ads from 1960 demonstrate:

> **Lyons Maid Dairy Ice Cream is a poem of pleasure that appeals to every palate... a charming tribute to win the heart of every guest... a *pièce de résistance* no gourmet can resist.**

> **[It] is the 'champagne' of ice creams. Its delicious flavour... creamy-rich smoothness... and 'melt-in-the-mouth' texture gladden the heart of every guest.**

It's disconcerting to note that – while still sold on the 'luxury' ticket – Lyons Maid ice cream's 'melt-in-the-mouth' quality was considered unique enough to warrant a mention. Before domestic fridges were within the financial reach of most households, premature thawing was a significant drawback. In its early days, popular ice cream recipes included cornflour or other binders to prevent it from turning into a sticky puddle en route to your mouth.

However, the invention of both the mechanical hand freezer and milk homogeniser in the late 1800s began an inexorable pushing back of the frontiers of lolly and ice cream technology.

The choc-ice was probably the first major step. Christian Kent Nelson, a Danish immigrant sweet-shop owner in Onawa, Iowa, is credited with inventing the 'I-Scream' bar to satisfy an eight-year-old customer who couldn't choose between chocolate or ice cream. A couple of years later, in 1922, sales of the re-christened 'Eskimo Pie' made Nelson a very wealthy man indeed. Originally made by hand, using a block of ice cream on a stick, choc ices were ultimately constructed by machine; cut, dipped and wrapped inside a procession of sub-zero 'hardening tunnels'. Further advances, including freezing the brickettes inside liquid nitrogen, meant that your mum's Midnight Mint, Rum & Raisin or Golden Vanilla choc bar could be purchased from an usherettes' tray having never been touched by human hands. A particular relief for patrons of Aberystwyth's Commodore cinema, there.

Yet the illusion of natural, homespun, fresh-from-the-farm ice cream pervaded. The J. Lyons company renamed their frozen food wing Lyons Maid in 1955, after top-selling lolly Pola Maid, gaining an added association with buxom, frilly-sleeved dairy maids and other connotations of comforting femininity. New legislation a couple of years later required the industry to differentiate between its 'ice cream' and 'dairy ice cream' products on the label – a subtle distinction that dogged manufacturers into the 1980s, even though lenient EEC regulations allowed 'dairy ice cream' to be sold containing just 5 per cent milk fat.

**Opposite:** The not exactly aerodynamic Red Arrow, and the aptly-sized Mini Milk, both circa 1975.

**Below:** You're meant to take those wrappers off from the bottom, you know. Wall's Chilly Choc (1976).

The *Guardian* railed against such 'rancid over-sweetened air-puffed syntho stuff filled with chemicals with six-syllable names'. Trenchant critics complained of a duopoly holding British ice cream to ransom, and accused Wall's and Lyons Maid of supporting a two-party system that enshrined mediocrity.

Others, mostly kids, rejoiced at a new dawn of creativity and variety. Ice lollies, initially plain (either a 'spade', 'rocket' or 'tube') were being fashioned into ever more interesting shapes. The simple process involved submerging rubber moulds in a rotating brine bath (the added salt lowered the freezing point of the water outside) then feeding syrup in via nozzles. Lightly defrosting the exterior allowed for the removal of the mould, if need be. Or partially frozen syrup could be poured out and the part-lolly shell refilled with ice cream, to create the Mivvi (or the Red Arrow, or the Chilly Choc). The fillings varied, from jelly (Jelly Terror), to toffee (Toffee Crumble) to sherbet (Fizz

Bang). A new, natural stabiliser, carrageenan (made from seaweed), prevented the colours and flavours from 'sucking out', and stopped the whole lot dripping off its stick.

Strange, extremely non-dairy ice creams appeared, with novelty textures the key. The Wall's Super Chew's special centre was described as 'a cross between fudge and chewy fruit sweets... that tastes "warmer" than usual'. Against the odds, Wall's fancied an ice lolly that might sell in winter. Keiller's Captain Cosmic bar was also 'surprisingly like ice cream, amazingly not ice cream', and could be stored unfrozen with a shelf life of up to two years, whipped into milkshakes, turned into hot chocolate, or added as an 'ideal dessert topping'. Cat litter, window putty, stock cube – you name it, the Swiss Army knife of ice cream could do it, although that was the only thing remotely Swiss about it.

The allure of the two-in-one ice lolly was near impossible to resist but adding confectionery-style centres required new formulas and specialist expertise. The chocolate at the heart of a product like Wall's Big Feast (which sold 40 million in the UK in 1984) needed to be soft and firm when passing through the machinery, yet not too brittle to eat after prolonged deep-freezing. Initially, fudge was used as a replacement. As Wall's turned to the food scientists of Birds Eye for answers, Lyons increased their investment in Glacier Foods and Findus. The emergence of ice cream extrusion technology advanced the capability to create patterns, swirls and even faces in a single lolly. Early results were a little too enthusiastic: Wall's Kinky was an explosion of striped psychedelic experimentation, while the Lyons Maid Freak Out was a wild, tie-dyed affair that Sergeant Pepper would have rejected for being too trippy. These were, however, ice cream's Woodstock, laying the foundations for later greats like the Wall's

**'Wall's Kinky was an explosion of striped psychedelic experimentation.'**

**Opposite:** Something to chew over. Wall's Big Dipper circa 1980.

**Below:** Get your plunger round this – Wall's Dalek's Death Ray (1975).

Heart (a chocolate-coated cardiac creation with strawberry ventricles) and the Tongue Twister (a rotating, rope-like coil of fruit sorbet and vanilla ice, later shortened to Twister). Someone at head office clearly took the instruction 'use your creative muscles' literally.

Neither were the other organs any less important. 'Eye appeal' was a key selling factor from day one, when Wall's first SnoFrute ice lolly was made available in a dazzling array of unnaturally vivid colours. In 1987 a new jet-stream extrusion moulding method was, claimed Wall's, motivated by 'the concern to produce products with shapes that were more like the picture on the wrapper'. Shelf space in the newsagent's freezer led to increased visibility, so both Wall's and Lyons Maid began to provide their own ornately decorated chiller cabinets on exclusive, long-loan contracts (with the proviso that no rival products could be displayed inside). However, a Monopolies and Mergers Commission report found this practice to be restrictive and anti-competitive, forcing an end to ice cream's very own cold war.

As hostilities abated, the two superpowers became further polarised. The Milk Marketing Board's Campaign For Real Ice Cream (CAMRIC) attempted to drive in a wedge. 'Lyons Maid does not see a great future in

**Below:** If in doubt, sling a big game hunter in the ad. Wall's Feast (1974).

**Opposite:** Enter the Wall's Kinky competition, circa 1971, and write Men At Work's hits for them!

sales for ice cream with an exceptionally high dairy fat content,' grumbled a spokesman, clearly unaware of the oncoming reign of sumptuous, all-natural, 'premium' ice creams from America. Forever obsessed with profitability, British companies focused on ways to eke out ingredients and increase 'overrun' (the percentage of ice cream expansion when air is pumped in).

Economics, politics and ice cream remained connected long after Lyons Maid called in the receivers and Wall's bowed to the might of Unilever. The likes of Ben & Jerry's are all over the Fairtrade Foundation, guaranteeing a better deal for Third World producers.

Gael Greene, food critic for *New York* magazine, once wrote that 'it's not the least bit excessive to rank the quality ice cream explosion with the sexual revolution, the women's movement and peace for our time.' Capitalism was spoon-fed to us: banana-flavoured, chocolate-coated and dipped in hundreds and thousands. We are all Thatcher's children, after all – each and every one of us spawned from one of her many millions of eggs.

WORK OUT YOUR IDEA OF A SPACE ROBOT FOR A LANDING ON MARS.
Post it to us with a Sky Ray wrapper and *you* could be one of that lucky 100 winners each month who will win two favourite comics free every week for a whole year!
WIN COMICS FOR ONE YEAR!
100 WINNERS EVERY MONTH FOR
Wall's
SKY RAY
SPACE ROBOT DESIGNS!
Wall's
wonderful world of fun!
WIN THE TOP TEN!
WRITE A GROOVY LAST LINE FOR A POP LIMERICK!
Wall's
Kinky
10 SETS OF THE 'TOP TEN' RECORDS TO BE WON EVERY WEEK
You'll find an unfinished Pop Limerick on the wrappers of Wall's Kinky.
Send us an amusing last line and you could soon be playing your own set of the Top Ten Records. This is fun! Don't miss it!
What's your last line for this Wall's Pop Limerick?
An Australian group from down under
Had a sound reminiscent of thunder.
When they started to pound
With their tails on the ground...
Here is an example: The fans fell about, lost in wonder!
All entries to:—
T. WALL & SONS (ICE CREAM) LTD., WALL'S HOUSE, GLOUCESTER.

## ✻ COUNT DRACULA'S DEADLY SECRET

‘Kids today, eh? Addled with filthy music, junk food and daft fashions, and well before they reach their teenage years. Why can't they just grow up naturally, like we used to? I blame these raunchy new pop stars. Like that David Essex. And the Rollers, they're wrong 'uns. And as for that rag *Whizzer and Chips...*’ It's the eternal refrain, but you heard it in the *Daily Mirror* first, when in the early '70s

**Opposite and below:** The original Dracula's Secret, before it was classified 'deadly,' to make it sound more scary and less as if he just had a hidden stash of Pickettywitch records or something (1974).

they identified the 'Weenies', an ominous new, conspicuously consuming, old-before-their-time pre-teen generation. While perusing life-size posters of Kenny, these reprobates subsisted on a diet of Trebor Blobs, spaghetti hoops and 'iced lollipops – especially the "frighteners" like Count Dracula's Deadly Secret'. Horror again! The nation's moral guardians would no doubt have preferred a series of ice lollies themed around the Duke of Edinburgh's Award Scheme or Hard Sums, but it was not to be.

The spine-tingling ice under analysis came from Wall's: 'a creation of "black as night" water ice with a concealed centre of ice cream as bright as the moon when it's full.' Such florid descriptions were part and parcel of the horror genre of course, and someone in the publicity department relished being HP Lovecraft for a day. The design team went that extra mile, too: the following year, the Count was on the receiving end of the industry's first focus-group makeover, after a panel of kids demanded he be made 'even more deadly-looking' with an additional core of strawberry jelly. Food and fanbase in perfect, fiendish harmony.

Children's enthusiasm being the mercurial thing it is, though, the Count only saw a handful of summers before Wall's saw fit to hammer a stick through his heart. You can't keep a good vamp down, though, and he rose again in 1981, this time just as 'Dracula', but in glorious, chiselled 3D. 'The first ever 3D lolly,' in fact, 'complete with protruding fangs and talons and appropriate strawberry colouring.' This masterpiece of the ice moulder's art was cast from a model by one Bob Donaldson, 'who has also been commissioned to sculpt for the Queen'. European aristocracy has connections everywhere, even beyond the grave.

**'The nation's moral guardians would no doubt have preferred a lolly themed around the Duke of Edinburgh's Award Scheme or Hard Sums, but it was not to be.'**

## THE SERIOUS CHIMES SQUAD

Once upon a time there was a van for everything. Butchers, grocers, fish-and-chip fryers and lemonade companies all queued up behind your cheery milkman on a B-road near you, providing regular four-wheel deliveries to, if not your doorstep, then at least that unused sort-of-lay-by bit of brick rubble-strewn waste ground at the end of the road. The more cosmopolitan your environs, the more likely you were to have ready access to one of them super market things, which over the years rendered most of the above Bedford-bound purveyors a spent force. But one van didn't buckle under multinational might, and carried on almost undaunted with its uniquely superfluous sales mission, despite being, at first glance, the most disposable of them all. After all, no one, it's probably safe to say, has ever really, desperately needed the services of an ice cream van. No, you're exaggerating, it just felt like it.



The invention of the modern 'stop me and buy one' machine was the crescendo of a long and varied evolution in ice cream technology. First, the cones. Edible containers for scoops of vanilla, in their modern wafer form at least, probably originated in Manchester, where jobbing Italian migrant Antonio Valvona patented his 'Apparatus for Baking Biscuit Cups for Ice Cream' in 1902. Not a cone, but close. At the St Louis World's Fair two years later, a Syrian waffle vendor helped out his Italian ice cream-selling neighbour when he ran out of dishes by offering his rolled-up product as a makeshift conical container. Or so the legend has it – many salesmen have claimed the invention as theirs. Some even operated at the same World's Fair. The origins of ice cream paraphernalia are packed with such Spartacus situations.

Meanwhile, displaced citizens of Rome had trundled their so-called 'hokey pokey' pushcarts, cooled by huge blocks of dry ice,

**Opposite:** 'When it plays a tune, that means they've run out of ice cream.' Wall's vans – the punchline to many a dad-joke.

**Below:** Back then, 'hundreds and thousands' were still just 'ones and tens'. A pre-inflation Midland Counties blows the promotional budget.

around the streets of New York since the late nineteenth century. These sold ice cream in little reusable glass dishes, emptied by the consumer on site at a penny a lick – undignified and not too hygienic. As soon as the edible container and the mobile transport married up, a trade was born. Things were motorised as soon as possible: *Daily Telegraph* owner Lord Burnham got in an early van-related 'man of the people' photo opportunity when he was pictured dishing out cones to underage hoi-polloi from a steam-powered ice cream lorry at a fair in 1919.

All these early wagons sold scoops taken from factory-made ice cream blocks kept in chunky freezers under the counter. But what about 'soft serve', the gloopy extrusion that fills out the majority of cones? The kudos goes to the Illinois family-founded Dairy Queen chain of ice cream parlours, serving air-whipped frozen treats since 1940.

It took another family, the Irish-born Conways, to take a soft serve machine and nail it into the back of a Chevrolet van in 1956, creating the first ice cream van as we know them today, under the brand name Mister Softee. Soon the vans were making a big enough impact to get Lyons interested in importing Mister Softee to these shores, with the first vans tootling around Kent by 1959. So the often-told tale that the whole soft serve malarkey, with its 50:50 ratio of ice cream to thin air, was the gaff-blowing brainchild of arch-monetarist and former Lyons research chemist Margaret Thatcher, is just so much emulsified fat. Nor can Douglas Hurd's distinctive hairstyle claim any frozen glory. It's all down to the immigrants, Madge.

With soft serve on board, Lyons raced ahead in the kerbside vending stakes. As the cost of the Mister Softee vans (initially an extortionate three grand) started to come down to break-even point, rivals sniffed about. The grandiosely named Ice Cream Alliance had 2,000 members by 1973, but 80 per cent of the total trade was carved up between just two of them: Wall's and Lyons Maid. The latter keenly gobbled up smaller van merchants left, right and centre, notably Midland Counties and Italian-derived Middlesex operation Tonibell. Wall's countered by getting hold of its own soft serve franchise, Mr Whippy. Once again, it was the clash of the Titans.

Every van purchase involved a little ritual. Like cathedral bells, the chimes called the faithful to worship. The impatient queuing, counting one's small change and sizing up the price list – all were potentially daunting on-the-hoof decisions to be made as the line of kids slowly dwindled. Bog-standard cornet or the mysteriously named, Flake-toting 99? Double cone or Dalek-shaped plastic Hi-Ball cup? Wafer sandwich or one of those funny oyster shell things with the blob of marshmallow inside? (Clue: never one of those funny oyster shell things with the blob of marshmallow inside.) Hundreds and thousands? 'You want red on that?' All options to be considered and measured against available pocket money at lightning speed. The ice cream van did wonders for a child's mental agility, even if it was less of a boon to the physical kind.

Kids may have loved the vans, but few adults did. In the early '60s, the makings of the Noise Abatement Society had many a van driver up before the beak on charges of disturbing the peace with clangorous entreaties to get fat on their wares, leading Wall's to lead the way in environmentally friendly chimes, playing at a

**Opposite:** We made our own racial stereotypes in them days. Robertson's Golly Ice Cream Mix (1972).

**Below:** Catchy name, decidedly un-catchy slogans: Cadbury's 99 Flake badges.

reduced volume pleasant five-note mini-symphonies by composer Peter 'Flyaway Fiddles' Yorke. These days, thanks to a copyright crackdown, it's mainly rights-free tunes like 'Greensleeves' and 'Yankee Doodle Dandy'. Street vending is killing music!

If it wasn't the noise, it was the prices: vans at the London tourist traps were castigated in 1972 for charging up to and over 25p for a small cornet. Traders finding it increasingly hard to make a living up against council pitch restrictions were unrepentant. 'When I die,' reckoned one old hand at Kew Gardens, 'they'll find "caveat emptor" engraved on my heart.' Small wonder home-made alternatives were introduced around this time, like Robertson's colonially remorseless Golly Ice Cream Mix, which could serve a family of four with a reasonable facsimile of Mr Whippy for 10½p.

Then things became decidedly sinister. In 1980 the East End's Blundell brothers were charged with using violent intimidation on sellers seeking to muscle in on their unofficial 'patches' in front of Harrods, Madame Tussauds and the big museums. Rival vendors found their vans rammed by furniture lorries, or themselves on the receiving end of a sawn-off shotgun or good old-fashioned headbutt. Unfortunately some of the rivals were plain-clothes coppers and the Blundells went down. A couple of years later a far more ferocious turf war broke out in Glasgow, when gangs using the vans as a front for drug-dealing set fire to the flat of a driver who refused to cooperate, killing six people. Uneasy jokes about acid at the bottom of the Two-Ball Screwballs abounded for years afterwards (and thanks are due to the good people of Glasgow for originally perpetrating the pun that adorns this section). Such high-profile knobblings put the mockers on the innocent days of skipping to the van for a Cornish wafer. This was a harsh business. Never Mind That Child.

The van business was by now in decline anyway, losing sales to a rival for which the two big players only had themselves to blame: their own multiplying freezer cabinets in supermarkets and grocers all over the country, populated by an ever-increasing array of novel-looking alternatives to the cornet. Society's inbuilt heritage valve prevented them going under completely, of course, and those familiar chimes are still heard on seafronts, outside schools and in the abandoned car parks of rain-sodden council estates today, long after their pop, butcher, grocer and fish-and-chip counterparts have dwindled almost to extinction. A stirring testament to the nostalgic power of the ice cream van. Or a savage indictment of the indulgence of a lazy generation who can't even be arsed to cross over the road to get to the corner shop, depending on which side your majestic wafer's buttered.

## * 99

In much the same way that the two-ball screwball smuggled vulgar bubble gum past otherwise tut-tutting parents, the 99 was an ice cream van's Trojan horse for chocolate lovers. The quality, size and shape of the cornet were immaterial, only a Flake jammed in the top made it a 99. In your face, Mum and Dad!

**Opposite:** Stodgy whip, squat cone – that's a proper 99. Just don't ask us why it's called that.

The 99 is also the ice cream most broadsheet journalists invoke to convey an image of the Great British seaside – a, for once, genuinely iconic beacon atop a landscape of donkey rides, deckchairs and dirty beaches. Many column inches have been devoted to debating the correct way to eat one (Flake first, or stuffed down the cone and saved till last?). Yet, for all the syrupy sweetness Fleet Street's finest have slathered over it, neither they, nor the combined energies of the BBC and the OED, have managed to uncover the source of the 99's name.

What is certain is the sheer volume of misinformation out there. There are dozens of second and third-generation immigrant Italians who believe, no doubt in good faith, that their ice cream-vending antecedents were the first to think of sandwiching a scoop of vanilla and a half-sized Flake between two wafers. The earliest documented proof of this practice – a Cadbury's price list, circa 1935 – was uncovered by *This Life* actress Daniela Nardini (herself from a Scottish ice cream-making family) on BBC2's *Balderdash & Piffle*. Soon after, the corporation fielded several calls from irascible grandchildren pointing to their forebears' premises at 99 The High Street, Nowheresville, est. 1930-ish.

Other, less credible 99-naming theories include: an allusion to the elite '99' guard of the King of Italy; a bingo call ('top of the house'); the curling movement required to dispense Mr Whippy ice cream into the cone; pig Latin based on the Roman numerals IC (for 'ice cream'); an Askey's wafer serial number; the length in millimetres of the chocolate itself – unlikely, given the Flake's introduction in the pre-metric 1920s. However, imperial measurement might provide a clue, because Cadbury's boxes used to be labelled in old money – '1 gro[ss] singles 6/6. One price only' – which, read upside down, may or may not be just a coincidence.

Appellative issues aside, the 99 is one of the few childish treats adults can appreciate in an 'of course I'm being ironic' way. You're not fooling anyone, you know, with your bucket and spade, and that 'Kiss Me Quick' hat. If there's one thing the British do well, it's end-of-the-pier-show-style tackiness. To paraphrase the great Ice-T, we got 99 problems but our kitsch ain't one.

## NAUGHTY BUT ICE

It began with one of those forthright, table-thumping boardroom observations of the type Burt Lancaster usually delivers in ancient Hollywood corporate intrigue movies. Granted, it probably didn't have the same jut-jawed glamour coming from a head office in Acton, but nonetheless the cry went out in 1975 from Wall's HQ: 'Grown-ups aren't buying enough ice cream!'

They had a point. Look at Europe, they lamented, where your average French or Italian adult would think nothing of a leisurely slurp on a gelato – in public, yet! – as they went about their sophisticated continental business. But over here, it's all frozen Zooms and bashful cornets. How can we make ice cream classy? Painfully aware of previous misfires on their books, like 1971's Cooltime frozen yogurt lolly ('Calling all yogurt fans!'), the Wall's boffins hit the laboratories.

The following summer, a raft of adult-baiting ice creams was launched. There were the Midnight Mint and Jamaica rum and raisin choc ices. There was Dark Secrets, a selection of five orange and mint-centred mini choc ices in a Black Magic-style box. But most of all, there was an innovative all-in-one ice cream cone ensemble plucked from the product lines of Spica, Wall's Italian Unilever stablemate: the Cornetto.

Ice cream wholesalers had been after a way to replicate the traditional street vendor's cornet for years, but combining wafer and dairy in one product always led to soggy disappointment, until the Italians came up with a way of adding an intermediate layer of protective chocolate. With ready-made cones in freezer cabinets nationwide by May, and just a little help from the longest, hottest summer in living memory, the Cornetto cleaned up.

**Opposite:** You think that song's annoying? Just you wait till they invent insurance comparison websites. Wall's Cornetto (1976).

**Below:** Lyons Maid get classy, with Dark Satin, Cornish Treasure, Nut Cracker and Caramel Gold (all 1972).

The Italians may deserve the technical credit, but the self-consciously wacky publicity overload was all British. This wasn't the first time they'd tried to flog the Cornetto over here: a 1965 campaign promised customers 'a little piece of Italy for only a shilling', but got no takers. This time, though, they got it right. 'Just one Cornetto' was hardly a leap of the creative imagination, but as so often in advertising, the bleeding obvious is exactly what you want. A snappy strapline, a tune everyone sort of knew already and, yes, a certain amount of unreconstructed 'funny foreigner' shtick, and the national consciousness is yours for the infecting.

No small amount of help came from pastiches by everyone from Little and Large to *Private Eye* to a flop single from one Count Giovanni Di Regina, who turned out on closer inspection to share a baseball cap with Jonathan King.

Most famously of all, breathless royal courtiers reported Lady Di trilling the jingle in Clarence House as she hopped into her distinctly ice creamy frock for the Wedding of the Century. (Presumably she didn't sing the popular playground variant: 'Just one Cornetto/Give it to me/Not bloody likely/It's 30p'.) Meanwhile on the ground, Sue Cuff, Derek Batey's able assistant from *Mr and Mrs*, toured the regions in person and cardboard-cut-out form as the Cornetto Girl. As a result, Wall's owned the long hot summer of '76, a summer that sold a record 321 million litres of ice cream.

Clearly, this wouldn't do at all. Wall's main rivals in the freezer wars, Lyons Maid, pored over the new secret weapon all winter, scurried away to their lair and emerged the following spring with the King Cone.

Any suggestion that they'd just copied Wall's was allayed by the entirely different patterning of chocolate sauce and flaked hazelnuts on the top, and the slightly funkier ads, which eschewed cod-Venetian travelogue fluff for a rip-off of Amen Corner's 'Bend Me, Shape Me' ('Lick me, bite me/Any way you like me...'). Besides, the King Cone, taking its name from Lyons Maid's late '60s King Cornet range, was just the centrepiece of a three-pronged assault on the adult ice market, alongside the wafer-encased King Sandwich and Magnum-esque choc ice, the King Stick. 'The latter two are said to be new concepts for the British market,' crowed the PR department. And, indeed, the latter two failed to stay in the British market long past the first summer, possibly because the names could cause confusion. ('I want a King Sandwich!' 'Then go to the 'king bakery!') But the Cone dug in and fought its corner with admirable tenacity, using Lyons Maid's tactical advantage of cinema distribution. With the usherettes' trays of the Odeons and ABCs commandeered, resistance against the Unilever axis was bravely upheld, although as a result very few people have ever eaten a King Cone in broad daylight.

Blurring the boundary between junior and senior ices, along with a few other things, was booze. The child's tipple of choice was enshrined in lolly form by Wall's when they teamed up with Bulmers to wrap a few fluid ounces of the latter's Woodpecker cider round

**Opposite:** Wall's sophisticated choc ice range (1976).

a stick to create the Cider Gold lolly in 1970. Three years later came the same firm's Shandy Man, complete with 'Oyoy!'-gurning pint mug on the wrapper, followed in 1979 by the double delights of the Cider Barrel and Shandy Barrel, all promising grown-up fun with a fraction of the alcoholic content. It took until 1984 for this inoffensive trend to garner the inevitable headlines, when Lyons Maid's Cocktail range of lollies came under the scrutiny of the PTA. In Pina Colada, Tequila Sunrise and Brandy Alexander varieties, these 35p wonders enabled the teenage sucker to imagine themselves lounging at the bar of the local Stroller's nightclub. While acknowledging that the range had minimal booze content, the PTA complained, 'It is obviously going to encourage children to think about alcohol.' Oh for a world where such encouragement was required. Lyons Maid played the common sense card, mumbling about it being 'just a bit of fun' and musing, 'They'll be banning wine gums next!' until the non-story melted away. The market for sophisticated lollies was also evaporating. In 1982 Wall's switched their attention to desserts, starting with that immortal re-creation of an Italian waiter's shirt front in ice cream form, the Vienetta. This was the first entry in their swanky Sweet Trolley canon, followed by the Sonata, Carissima and, less successfully, the weird octagonal Royale. In finest corporate 'we'll have some o' that' style, Lyons Maid launched the strikingly similar Encore in 1984, and got an injunction from Wall's for their trouble. They made up for that boob with the success of the Chipwich, a slab of vanilla sandwiched between two chocolate chip cookies, imported from New York. And then they lost it again, with the dubious trifle-on-a-stick delights of the Polar Pudding Pantry.

In 1987 the Cornetto returned, bigger, creamier – and yes, pricier – as the Magnifico, the main player in Wall's 'a truly adult affair' line, along with the Sorbetto, the Bonanza and the less exotically named Chunky Choc Ice. The adverts established a precedent that lasts to this day, with their entry-level sauciness of disembodied lipsticked mouth biting off a chunk while a honeyed Frostruppian voice coos a randy paean to the tenacious paste of solid milk on display. In fact, you can't move in the freezer cabinet these days for breathy paeans and tarty gobs. Phew! It's getting a bit hot in here, isn't it? Anyone fancy a Mini Milk?

**'"It is obviously going to encourage children to think about alcohol." Oh for a world where such encouragement was required.'**

## GIVE THEM SOME STICK

In January 1973 Lyons Maid replaced all its existing signage with a new, cheery illustration of three children dancing. Drawn in the classic, storybook style, the 'Good Time Sign' as it became known, was an attempt to create a new 'fun food' image for the brand, though why the kids in the picture had to look quite so Dutch remained a mystery.

Getting boys and girls enthused about frozen water is quite possibly the summit of food marketing achievement, but there are severely limited means at your disposal. Once you've run the gamut of loony shapes and exotic centres, there's only one place left to go: the ever-popular domain of the cheap free gift.

First, and most straightforward, was the cardboard freebie. Picture cards were tucked under Lyons Maid's lolly wrappers from 1962 onwards, covering topics from the impossibly exciting (Space Age Britain!) to the deadly dull (Birds and Their Eggs). Lavishly illustrated though they were, these were just a straight translation of the old bubble gum/sweet cigarette card (to say nothing of the endless series of collectables in boxes of Lyons tea). The race to provide innovative stimulation of the brain cells as well as the taste buds began in 1972, when Lyons Maid jazzed up their top-selling Cola Rola delicacy with an animal-based 'Who's Zoo?' quiz on the back. Following suit a year later, the sturdy toffee and fudge aristo-lolly Lord Toffingham, aimed by Wall's at 'those ever-hungry, fun-loving children', carried 'Wizard Wheezes' on its reverse, providing stock brainteasers of the 'how to walk through a postcard' variety. From then on, from Wall's *Incredible Hulk* to *Space: 1999*, no themed lolly

**Below:** We certainly enjoyed these so-called 'iced lollies.'

was complete without a little serialised story or numbered Fact File on the back of the wrapper.

Ice cream firms began the 1980s with trepidation, after three duff summers in a row. Gimmicks were needed, and fast. Wall's pushed the soggy paper envelope by cladding their Magic Monster ice lollies in wrappers adorned with one of twelve ghostly images (skull, claw, bride of Frankenstein and the like) which only became visible when the lolly was removed from the freezer, turning an intervening panel of red thermochromic ink transparent. Two years in development, the Magic Monster wrappers were the first to offer a life beyond that of their contents – pop them back in the freezer and the ghoulish image vanished once more, and you could repeat the process forever, or at least until it induced a bout of Edgar Allen Poe-like delirium.

Sturdier yet than a thermochromic wrapper was the lolly's supporting stick. While the traditional wood variety was all well and good, lolly firms looked towards moulded plastic for a way to put the novelty inside the ice. The first, crude attempt came in 1972 from the sub-zero division of Midland Counties Dairies, who stuck their range of otherwise unremarkable Wild West lollies on the ends of latticed strips of plastic which, should the hungry child manage to amass enough of them, could snap together to construct what Midland claimed was a 'Wild West fort', though on closer inspection it bore an uncanny resemblance to an NCP car park. Wall's provided an ingenious variation on the theme with their 1975 Super Spy lolly, in which the sticks doubled as stencils carrying secret code messages. Lyons Maid's Goal, a soccer-themed lolly endorsed by the mighty Kevin Keegan, brought art to the lolly stick in 1978, with a range of miniature representations of star players on the ends – a mass-produced version of those McWhirter-troubling microscopic matchstick carvings.

It was from good old wood, though, that the greatest piece of lolly-flogging ephemera was hewn. Once again, its existence was all down to the Great British Weather. Autumn 1974, and the mood at Wall's was sombre. The combination of a truly crap summer and increasingly nimble manoeuvres by their arch-rival Lyons Maid gave their sales a sharp kick in the goolies. Something had to be done to make Wall's products stand out, it had to be done by next spring, and most importantly it had to be dirt cheap. From such dire predicaments are works of genius born, and this particular one was crucial in giving Wall's a leg-up in the public's estimation, bringing them nearer to the status of National Ice Cream Maker, just as Cadbury was becoming National Chocolatier and Walkers would later assume the mantle of National Crisp Fryer. Never underestimate the power and influence of the joke on the stick.

Stamping the funnies on the sticks themselves captured the imagination in a way that wrappers didn't. Punters fell in love with the concept from the moment in the spring of '75 that Wall's unveiled 'your favourite lollies: now with a riddle-up-the-middle!'. The content, admittedly, was nothing

**Opposite:** The T-Rex song that never was. Lyons Maid's Lolly Gobble Choc Bomb (1974). As sucked by Smiley's people – Wall's Super Spy (1975).

**Below:** Cryogenic Keggy Keegle Capers. Lyons Maid Goal (1978). Children's TV animation stalwarts FilmFair plug Wall's Mini Milk (1975).

special: the usual range of nervous wrecks, custard-infesting sharks and ducks flying upside down that was fast becoming the Old Testament of children's humour, with a few additions of Wall's own that were hardly classics, and occasionally made no sense as gags at all. ('What has two legs and flies over Russia? Peter Pansky!')

But as any comedian will tell you, delivery is half the art, and a crap gag delivered on either side of six ounces of strawberry Mivvy often finds a more receptive audience than one spun from the lips of *Crackerjack*'s Peter Glaze. By 1978, Wall's even began crowdsourcing new gags with a national competition. Here the beautiful simplicity of the form was laid bare: a maximum of seventy-six characters, thirty-eight for both feedline and punchline, including punctuation and spaces. Twitter is a rambling bore by comparison.

Wall's phased the gags out in 1988, possibly mindful of their corny reputation among a new generation of *Blackadder*-quoting playground sophisticates, but have been promising their return sporadically ever since. In 2008 they even enlisted James Corden to write some – a project that came to nothing, Corden deciding to star in *Lesbian Vampire Killers* instead. No sign yet of any Mini-Milk tie-in picture cards for that one.

## * FAB

Lyons Maid, always ahead of the game, jumped on board the starship Telly Tie-In long before man even set foot on the moon. A hook-up with Gerry Anderson's puppet series *Fireball XL5* in 1963 led to the launch of Zoom, a three-stage fruity rocket aimed at viewers catching the space bug. The following year's Sea Jet (available in strawberry, vanilla, lemon or orange flavours) quenched the *Stingray* fans'